And Then There Was Reasonable Doubt

The State of Ohio v.
Charles "Keith" Wampler

JACK BARNHART

PAGE PUBLISHING, INC.
New York, NY

First originally published by Page Publishing, Inc. 2017

ISBN 978-1-68409-953-5 (Paperback)
ISBN 978-1-68409-954-2 (Digital)

Printed in the United States of America

Contents

Preface

An injustice anywhere is a threat to justice everywhere.
—Dr. Martin Luther King Jr.

The month of February is normally cold in Ohio. February 1982 was frigid in Moraine, Ohio, because on or about February 6, 1982, one life would tragically end and another one would be changed forever. On February 6, 1982, at approximately 3:50 p.m., the body of Robert David Rowell (known as David) was discovered in a vacant field along Krietzer Road in Moraine, Ohio. On the surface, this appears to be similar to many crimes committed in the United States every day. However, when one looks past the surface, one finds a broken criminal justice system. One finds a criminal justice system that is more concerned with egos and reputations than seeking the truth and justice. On February 6, 1982, the wheels of the criminal justice system in Montgomery County, Ohio, would begin to grind and break down a sixteen-year-old boy, and by the end of the year, Charles "Keith" Wampler (known as Keith) will be forced to become a man behind the bars of the Ohio prison system, after having been convicted of a crime that he did not commit.

This book chronicles the events leading up to and surrounding *State of Ohio v. Charles "Keith" Wampler (82-CR-764)*. This book will review the original investigation conducted by the Moraine, Ohio, Division of Police, examine the autopsy conducted by the

Montgomery County Coroner's Office and the conduct of the attorneys involved in this case, and study the original trial transcripts. Then the book will focus on the 2015 investigation of this crime and discuss evidence uncovered. Unlike the 1982 investigation, the 2015 investigation sought the truth. The 2015 investigation into this case was conducted *pro bono* by an impartial third party. This permitted the case to be investigated in an unbiased way. This allowed the only driving force in the investigation was the desire to seek the truth. The goal was to gather facts and make a determination as to whether or not sufficient evidence exists regarding Charles "Keith" Wampler being Robert "David" Rowell's killer or does reasonable doubt exist, which may suggest someone else killed David Rowell.

One of the focuses of this book will be on how the "professionals" handled this case. The first group of professionals examined is the Moraine Division of Police, primarily Detective William Mullins. Did the Moraine Police properly follow established police procedure when investigating David Rowell's murder? Did the Moraine Police conduct a thorough, complete, and impartial investigation into David Rowell's death? Did the Moraine Police use every tool at their disposal to find the killer of a thirteen-year-old boy? Why did the Moraine Police (a small department with limited resources and experience in homicide investigation) not seek help from the Dayton Police, the Ohio Bureau of Criminal Investigation (BCI), or the Federal Bureau of Investigation (FBI)? Did the Miami Valley Regional Crime Laboratory use every tool at their disposal in examining the evidence collected?

The second group of professionals this book examines is in the Montgomery County Prosecutor's Office, namely Assistant Prosecutor Dennis Langer and Assistant Prosecutor Robert Head. This book looks into the conflicts between the police reports and trial testimony, which raises serious questions about the ethics of the Montgomery County Prosecutor in this case. Those conflicts were confirmed, and the questions regarding the integrity of the Montgomery County Prosecutor's Office were reinforced in the 2015 investigation of the murder of David Rowell, namely Robert Head's checkered past as an attorney in the State of Ohio.

Another group of professionals that this book examines is the defense team, Wayne Stephan and Robert Bostick. This book questions whether or not the defense team did everything they could in developing a proper defense for Keith Wampler. Wayne Stephan and Robert Bostick were court-appointed attorneys in this case and were appointed several months after Keith Wampler was charged. This book brings into question the defense team's ethics in this case. This book will reveal that these two attorneys did not even begin to conduct an investigation into this case. In fact, the question here is whether or not the defense team even approached the bare minimum required by the Canons of Ethics.

A final professional this book examines is Judge John W. Kessler. A judge is supposed to be impartial. The judge is supposed to ensure that the defendant receives a fair trial. But was that done in this case? Did this trial meet that very basic principle of fairness? Or was the trial managed because the primary focus of Judge Kessler was being able to leave for his vacation on schedule?

In order to obtain a conviction in a criminal trial, the due process clause of the Fifth Amendment of the United States Constitution requires juries to reach their decision "beyond a reasonable doubt." What is reasonable doubt? Reasonable doubt is the standard of proof that the prosecution must meet in order to convict a criminal defendant. To better explain this, one should visualize the scales of justice. Now place the evidence that the prosecution has on one side and the evidence and/or explanation that the defense has on the other side. The evidence on the prosecution's side must considerably, not slightly, tip in favor of the prosecution. If that considerable tip is there, then the jury or judge must find the defendant guilty. If that considerable tip is not there, then the jury or judge, in bench trials, must find the defendant not guilty. This Constitutional safeguard protects the citizenry from being indiscriminately charged and convicted of crimes by the government. You will see when the evidence in this case is placed on the scales, the scales will hardly move. Therefore, a great deal of reasonable doubt exists. Additionally, much of the prosecution's "evidence" should never have been admitted or at least called into question by the defense team.

In juvenile court, the burden of proof is by preponderance of the evidence. This means when all the evidence presented is placed on the scales, the scales slightly tip one way. In 1970, the United States Supreme Court ruled, in *In re Winship 397 U.S. 358 (1970)*, that when a juvenile is charged with an act that would be a crime if committed by an adult, then every element of the crime must be proven beyond reasonable doubt, not preponderance of the evidence, which is the standard used in juvenile court. This decision is significant in this case because Charles "Keith" Wampler was charged as an adult with aggravated murder[1], rape[2], abuse of a corpse[3] and abduction.[4] Keith Wampler's was tried in Montgomery County Common Pleas Court, not Montgomery County Juvenile Court. This book examines and questions which standard of proof was used in this case. It is also important to discuss this because another defendant, Michael Johnson, was tried and convicted of the charged for the same crime. Johnson's case was heard in Montgomery County Juvenile Court. The question arises, how could the State of Ohio, namely the Montgomery County Prosecutor's Office, try two different defendants, with two different theories of the crime, in two dif-

---

[1]   Ohio Revised Code, Section 2903.01.
[2]   Ohio Revised Code, Section 2907.02.
[3]   Ohio Revised Code, Section 2927.01.
[4]   Ohio Revised Code, Section 2905.02.

ferent courts? If both of these boys committed the crime, then why not try them together? Why was only one tried as an adult?

This book will focus on the initial investigation into the murder of David Rowell, as well as the reinvestigation of this case in 2015. A comparison of the original investigation to the reinvestigation will reveal serious discrepancies. This book will question the integrity of the prosecution's case. Major issues will be revealed regarding the witnesses in this case, calling the veracity of their testimony into question. Evidence will be revealed that some of the witnesses told bold-faced lies to the court and were encouraged to do so by the prosecutors who were willing to do whatever was necessary to obtain a conviction.

This book will review the criminal justice system, most specifically the inability to correct an injustice that has taken the entire adult life of a man. The integrity of the Ohio Department of Rehabilitation and Corrections, as well as the Office of the Governor and the Ohio Attorney General, will come into question. In particular, this book will examine the Ohio Parole Board's constant violation of an inmate's Fifth Amendment right against self-incrimination.

Finally, this book will recommend changes to the system. These changes will require public involvement and oversight. These changes will hold everyone involved in a wrongful conviction case accountable for their decisions and actions. While Article III of the United States Constitution, which established the judicial branch, may have been an afterthought, it still requires the same public oversight and scrutiny as the other two branches. Judges and lawyers are not above the law and must be held accountable because they apply their trade in facilities that are built by, funded by, and maintained by the people.

This book will not only bring attention to an injustice that is presently occurring in the State of Ohio but bring to light problems within the criminal justice system. The reader should approach reading this book with a question in the back of his or her mind, "If they can do this to an innocent sixteen-year-old boy, then what is to stop them from doing it to me?"

CHAPTER 1

The Actors

A nation's culture resides in the hearts and in the soul of its people.
—Mahatma Gandhi

In order to understand this case, one has to look at the people involved, the actors. It is important to comprehend their backgrounds. It is important to see where they were in 1982 and where they were in 2015. It is also important to get a feel for the city of Moraine and the Miami Valley.

Moraine, Ohio

Moraine, Ohio, is a working-class suburb of Dayton, Ohio, in Montgomery County, which is located in Southwestern Ohio. The area is referred to as the Miami Valley because of the Great Miami River flows through the region from Russells Point, Ohio, in Logan County to the north and the Ohio River to the south. According to the United States Census Bureau, the population of Moraine in 1980 was 5,325, compared to today where the population is 6,307.

Statistics, provided by the United States Census Bureau, indicate that a steady 9.6 percent of Moraine's population lived, or lives, below the poverty line. In 1982, many of Moraine's residents worked at various factories located within the city, with the main factory being a General Motors plant, which produced the Chevrolet S-10 Blazer. Some of the city's residents worked at nearby Wright-Paterson Air Force Base. The city rolled with the ebbs and flows that are associated with being a manufacturing town. If the economy is good and the products that the factories produce are selling, then the city, and its residents, thrived. If the economy is bad, then the city, and its residents, struggled.

Interstate 75 (I-75), a major interstate that runs from Sault Sainte Marie, Michigan, to Miami, Florida, transits the City of Moraine. With the interstate transiting the city, various hotels and restaurants, designed to cater to the travelers, were located in Moraine. In 1982, and again today, the neighborhoods immediately adjacent to I-75 can be described as blue-collar. One neighborhood, located at the intersection of Dryden Road and Kreitzer Road, contained two trailer parks, Gem City Estates Trailer Park and Gordon's Trailer Park. In 1982, Gem City Estates had nearly 100 percent occupancy rate. A vacant field was located adjacent to the trailer park's western border and acted as a buffer between Gem City Estates Trailer Park and I-75. The field contained patches of thornbushes, grass, and was home to various animals, such as rabbits. The residents of the trailer used the field to walk dogs and dump garbage. Some residents trapped rabbits in this field. Today, the field is home to a light industrial facility. I-75 is located only a few hundred feet away from the field. The growling of the truck traffic can clearly be heard.

The Moraine Civic Center is located at the end of Kreitzer Road with the traffic of I-75 a few feet away. In 1982, before video cassette recorders were popular, the civic center showed movies for the children on Friday evenings. The neighborhood south of the civic center is nicknamed Dog Patch, named after the town in the comic strip written by Al Capp. The description of the Dog Patch's population is similar to the residents residing along Kreitzer Road and in the Gem City Estates Trailer Park, largely blue-collar residents. In 1982, many of these residents worked at the Chevrolet S-10 assembly plant in Moraine. Dog Patch is also home to Moraine Meadows Elementary School. A sidewalk connected the two neighborhoods and was often used by residents, especially the children, to go from one neighborhood to another.

Charles "Keith" Wampler

Charles "Keith" Wampler, who went by the name Keith, was a normal sixteen-year-old boy. However, he did not come from a normal caring-and-loving family. At sixteen, Keith found himself being used as a pawn in a battle between his mother and father. Keith lived with his family in Waynesville, Ohio, which is in Warren County, Ohio. When his parents separated, Keith moved with his father, Charles "Cecil" Wampler, to Kettering, Ohio. In the summer of 1981, Cecil Wampler spent four thousand dollars on a single-wide trailer at 2753 Cozy Lane in the Gem City Estates Trailer Park in Moraine, Ohio. Cecil and Keith moved into the trailer and called it their home.

Charles "Cecil" Wampler retired from the United States Air Force and maintained his access to the base store at Wright-Patterson Air Force Base, near Dayton, Ohio. Cecil Wampler was not much on providing guidance or discipline to his son. When the pair moved to Moraine, Cecil Wampler did not enroll Keith into Moraine public schools, thus allowing Keith to drop out of school. When Cecil Wampler would shop at the base store, he would purchase Old Milwaukee Light Beer and cigarettes for his son. Free access to beer and cigarettes made Keith popular with some of the other teens in the neighborhood. These teens, who themselves were unencumbered to close parental supervision, knew they could go to Keith's trailer to smoke and drink. In addition to drinking beer and smoking cigarettes, Keith, like so many teenagers, used marijuana. His marijuana use caught the attention of the authorities in Warren County, who issued a warrant for his arrest for failure to appear in juvenile court to answer to a marijuana-related charge. Keith was, as defined by the Ohio Revised Code, a juvenile delinquent[5] at the time he took residence in Moraine, Ohio.

Keith spent his days hanging out at his trailer and his nights hanging out with his father or John McGarvey, the next-door neighbor. McGarvey would spend time with Keith and teach him how to do things, such as repair a car or trap rabbits. Though Keith had some friends in the neighborhood, he was still an outsider. He was born in Oklahoma while his father served at Tinker Air Force Base and, as earlier stated, was new to the neighborhood.

Robert "David" Rowell

Robert "David" Rowell, who went by the name David, in many ways was a typical thirteen-year-old boy, yet in other ways he was not. David was small for his age, standing four-and-a-half-feet tall and weighing only sixty-five pounds.[6] He was described as being a prankster or a troublemaker. David had a history of getting into trouble not only at school but with the police. In December 1981, David served a thirty-day suspension from riding the school bus because he had caused problems on the bus. According to Moraine Police, David was a suspect in a criminal damaging investigation—that is, he was believed to have broken the windows of a nearby business.

---

5   Ohio Revised Code, Section 2152.02.
6   Montgomery County Coroner's Report AC-81-82 dated 02/08/1982.

Though never charged, David was questioned by police. Many people have described David as having a foul mouth.

When David was not getting into trouble or hanging out with his friends, he often could be found following his older brother, Michael Patrick Rowell. David was two years younger than Michael and looked up to Michael. Both boys were known to smoke cigarettes and drink. At times, Michael viewed David as being a pest. David was known to try the patience of his family, especially his father, Robert "Bobby" D. Rowell. David lived with his family at 2970 Kreitzer Road in Moraine, directly across Kreitzer Road from Gem City Estates Trailer Park.

Michael Patrick Rowell

Michael Patrick Rowell was David's older brother. It is more accurate to say that he was David's older half-brother. Michael and David shared the same mother, Myrtle Rowell; they did not share the same father. After Bobby married Myrtle, he adopted Michael. Michael was a fifteen-year-old teenager that attended Moraine public schools. After Keith Wampler moved into the neighborhood, Michael befriended him. The two boys often hung out together, commonly smoking cigarettes and drinking.

Robert "Bobby" D. Rowell

Robert "Bobby" D. Rowell was David's biological father. Robert Rowell was commonly known as Bobby. In 1982, Bobby Rowell was an unemployed forty-six-year-old father of three—at least that is what he claimed in his trial testimony. Bobby Rowell was an electrician who moved his family to the Dayton area around 1979 to find work. Bobby did work as an electrician in a nearby factory until he was laid off. At first, the family settled in New Carlisle, Ohio, but later moved to Moraine. The reason for the move is not clear. Some say that the family moved to Moraine because they alerted the police to some drug activity in the New Carlisle area. Bobby Rowell denies this.

Many people described Bobby Rowell as being a strict disciplinarian. Several people, and he confirmed this, reported that Bobby Rowell once locked David and Michael in a closet after he caught them smoking. He gave them cigarettes and forced the boys to smoke them. Bobby hoped the boys would get sick and give up smoking. However, the opposite happened, and the boys continued to smoke.

As with Keith Wampler, the Rowell family is not originally from Ohio. Bobby Rowell is originally from the Mobile, Alabama, area. Prior to coming to Ohio, the family resided for a time in Florida.

Myrtle Rowell

Myrtle Rowell, David's mother, was described as being a religious woman. Many witnesses said that she was a devout Pentecostal woman who attended church every Sunday. Myrtle wore her hair in a tight bun and wore long dresses. According to witnesses, Myrtle did not socialize with many of her neighbors.

The Rowell family was often described as being weird or strange. During the course of the Moraine Police investigation into David's murder, the police received an anonymous tip that the family were Satan worshipers.[7] Though there is no evidence to prove or disprove this claim, the caller also stated that Myrtle was overheard asking Michael if he had killed David. The police did not identify the caller.

---

[7]   Moraine Police report dated 02/10/1982 (anonymous tip), case number 82-184.

Michael Johnson

Michael Johnson was a fifteen-year-old teenager who befriended Keith Wampler when Keith moved into the Gem City Estates Trailer Park. Johnson's family was poor. In his own words, Johnson described that he had only one pair of shoes, and those were hiking boots. Johnson was living in an abandoned, later condemned, house in the Gordon Trailer Park. When forced to leave the condemned house, Mike Johnson and his family moved to West Carrollton, Ohio. However, Johnson would frequently visit his cousin, Judy Tabor, who lived in a trailer in the Gem City Estates Trailer Park.

During the course of the investigation in 2015, the words *mean* and *vicious* were often used to describe Johnson. Johnson, and he also can be described as a juvenile delinquent. Mike Johnson was convicted in Montgomery County Juvenile Court for his alleged role in the murder of David Rowell. When interviewed in 2015, he claimed he was "railroaded." However, Mike Johnson's refuses to sign a release that would allow access to his juvenile, including trial, transcripts. Juvenile court transcripts are sealed in Ohio unless a release is signed by the defendant.

Wayne P. Stephan

Wayne P. Stephan was one of Keith's court-appointed attorneys. Mr. Stephan has practiced law in Ohio for forty-one years. In 1982, Mr. Stephan had eight years of practice under his belt. Mr. Stephan was awarded a bachelor of science degree from the University of Dayton in 1971 and a juris doctorate degree from Ohio Northern School of Law in 1974. Mr. Stephan was admitted to the Ohio bar in 1974 and the United States Court for the Southern District of Ohio in 1975. The areas of law that Mr. Stephan practices are criminal defense, personal injury, and divorce. Mr. Stephan's record would not be considered unblemished since in 2006 the Ohio State Supreme Court suspended his license for two years for failure to adequately represent a client.[8]

Robert Bostick

Robert Bostick was another one of Keith's court-appointed attorneys. Bostick has practiced law in the state of Ohio for fifty-eight years, and in 1982, Bostick was the more senior member of Keith's defense team. Bostick received a bachelor of arts degree from Bowling Green State University in 1954 and obtained a law degree from Baldwin Wallace University School of Law in 1957. He was admitted to the Ohio bar in 1958 and the United States Court for the Southern District of Ohio in 1959. Bostick's areas of expertise are criminal defense, civil law, personal injury law, family law, probate law, commercial law, and traffic law. Since 1982, Bostick has served as adjunct professor of law at the University of Dayton, School of Law. Bostick has worked as both an assistant Montgomery County prosecutor and a city attorney with the city of Dayton. Bostick has a history of serving on various panels and boards in the Dayton area. According to AVVO.com, Bostick was reprimanded by the state licensing agency for an ethics violation.

Robert D. Head

Robert D. Head was one of the assistant Montgomery County prosecutors who tried Keith Wampler in Montgomery County Common

---

[8]   *Dayton Bar Assn. v Stephan*, 108 Ohio St. 3d. 327, 2006-Ohio-1063.

Pleas Court. Head has practiced law in Ohio since 1978. Head received a bachelor of science degree from the Ohio State University and a juris doctorate degree from Northern Kentucky University. According to the Ohio State Supreme Court, Head received an indefinite suspension of his license on September 12, 1984. His license was reinstated by the Ohio State Supreme Court on August 24, 1988. According to AVVO.com, potential clients are advised to use caution when retaining Robert Head.

Dennis J. Langer

Dennis J. Langer was the lead prosecutor who tried Keith Wampler in Montgomery County Common Pleas Court. Langer was admitted to the Ohio bar in 1976. He received a bachelor of arts degree from John Carroll University in 1973 and a juris doctorate from Boston University School of Law in 1976. From 1976 to 1995, Langer was an assistant Montgomery County prosecutor. In 1983, he was promoted to first assistant Montgomery County prosecutor. In 1995, Langer was elected to the Montgomery County Common Pleas Court, where he is currently serving as a judge. Langer has served on many panels and committees within the Dayton legal community and is an adjunct professor of law at the University of Dayton School of Law.

Judge John W. Kessler

Judge John W. Kessler was the presiding judge over Keith Wampler's trial. Judge Kessler was admitted to the Ohio bar in 1968. Judge Kessler received a bachelor of arts degree from Miami University in Oxford, Ohio, in 1965 and a juris doctorate degree from the University of

Toledo in 1968. Judge Kessler served on the Montgomery County Common Pleas Court from 1981 to 2007. Prior to serving as judge for the Montgomery County Common Pleas Court, Judge Kessler served as assistant Montgomery County prosecutor, executive director of the Montgomery County Public Defender's Office, and was a partner at the law firm of Hunt, Dodge, Little & Kessler in Dayton. Judge Kessler is an adjunct professor of law at the University of Dayton School of Law.

Detective William Mullins

Detective William Mullins was a veteran Moraine Police officer. He was the lead investigator on this case. Detective Mullins was the investigating officer and was mentioned in malicious prosecution case that was heard by the Ohio State Supreme Court in 1990.[9] The street reputation of Detective Mullins was not good. According to various witnesses that were interviewed in the 2015 investigation, Detective Mullins was described as being a punk and a bully. Several persons opined that Detective Mullins would do anything to win a case, including planting and fabrication of evidence.

Officer Dennis Adkins

Officer Dennis Adkins was a Moraine police officer in 1982. He served as the evidence technician for the Moraine Police and was the officer who processed the crime scene in this case. Adkins received a bachelor of science degree from the University of Dayton in 1982 and a juris doctorate from Northern Kentucky University in 1986.

---

[9]   *Trussell v. General Motors*, 53 Ohio St. 3d (1990).

After resigning from the Moraine Police in 1986, Adkins had a private law practice until 2011, where he handled criminal and civil law. While maintaining his practice, Adkins served as acting judge with Kettering Municipal Court. In 2011, Adkins was appointed to the Montgomery County Common Pleas Court.

CHAPTER 2

The Crime

Friday, February 5, 1982, was a typical Ohio winter day. A cold front was moving through the Miami Valley area of Ohio. The temperatures started out in the 20s and would steadily fall into the single digits before the sun rose on February 6. At 5:00 p.m., a light snow began to fall in the Moraine. It would continue to snow until about 10:00 p.m., but only 0.2 inches of snow would accumulate.[10] With the temperatures falling, wind chill was becoming a factor. By 10:00 p.m., the wind chill in Moraine was 13 degrees with the actual temperature being 22 degrees.

The citizens of Moraine, Ohio, were going about their day. The historical assembly plant was busy producing Chevrolet S-10 Blazers. The plant had reopened in 1981 after being closed for two years due to retooling. From 1951 to 1979, the plant produced refrigerators for Frigidaire, which was a division of General Motors. In 1979, General Motors sold Frigidaire but kept this plant and retooled it to make sport utility vehicles. By midafternoon, Moraine public schools released the students for the week. Many of the children were looking forward to attending the movie at the Moraine Civic Center that

---

[10]   Moraine Police Report dated 02/08/1982, case number 82-184.

evening. The Moraine Civic Center was hosting a showing of *Benji*. This was an era prior to video cassette recorders being popular.

For Charles "Keith" Wampler, he maintained his typical routine of hanging out at his trailer at 2753 Cozy Lane in the Gem City Estates Trailer Park. The trailer afforded Keith some privacy because, unlike other trailers in the cul-de-sac, the front door of his trailer faced west, toward a vacant field that ran along Kreitzer Road. Keith did not have much to do but prepare for his sixteenth birthday party, which was on Saturday, February 6, 1982. Keith was looking forward to turning sixteen because he would gain some freedom by obtaining his Ohio driver's license.

Since dropping out of school, Keith did not have that much to do but smoke cigarettes or marijuana and drink beer. He would often do odd jobs for his neighbor, John McGarvey, who treated Keith like a little brother. McGarvey taught Keith how to fix things, woodworking, and trapping rabbits in the vacant field along Kreitzer Road. McGarvey resided in a trailer adjacent to Keith's, so it common to see Keith hanging out at McGarvey's trailer. As a matter of fact, McGarvey's fiancé was planning the birthday party for Keith.

Sometime in the morning of February 5, 1982, Charles "Cecil" Wampler left for work. Keith and Cecil were the only occupants of 2753 Cozy Lane. Cecil Wampler would work until late afternoon or early evening and then return home, where it was only Keith and him. Cecil Wampler would have dinner, drink beer with Keith, watch television, then go to bed. Once in a while, Cecil Wampler would come home and pick up Keith, whereupon the two of them would go to Waynesville, Ohio, to visit relatives. There were nights when Cecil Wampler would go alone to visit relatives in Waynesville. Cecile would then tell Keith, who would often then hang out at John McGarvey's trailer until it was bedtime.

When Cecil Wampler left for work on February 5, 1982, Keith was expecting him home later that day because Cecil had a big role in planning Keith's sixteenth birthday party. Unbeknownst to Keith, Cecil Wampler went to Waynesville after work. Because he drank several beers and the roads were slippery, due to the freshly fallen snow, Cecil decided to spend the night at his brother's house in Waynesville. Cecil Wampler would not return to Moraine until the morning of February 6.

About 3:30 p.m. on February 5, Keith saw his friend, John McGarvey, and his fiancé loading up McGarvey's truck. John McGarvey was going to take his fiancé to his future in-laws' residence in Vandalia, Ohio, which is in northern Montgomery County, where they would do laundry and have dinner. Keith fixed the fiancé a drink and took it to her while she was sitting in the truck. In the process of getting into the truck, Keith moved some wood, and he got a splinter stuck in his hand. While talking to McGarvey's fiancé, Keith removed the splinter and rubbed his hands on his jeans. McGarvey told Keith after they did the laundry and had dinner, the two of them were planning to return home and plan Keith's birthday party. Unbeknownst to Keith, McGarvey and his fiancé decided to spend the night in Vandalia due to the slick road conditions in the Miami Valley. Keith returned to his trailer and was looking forward to both his father's and McGarvey's return because a big birthday celebration was planned for February 6.

At 4:00 p.m. on February 5, Michael Patrick Rowell visited Keith Wampler at 2753 Cozy Lane. Michael came into Keith's residence, and Keith fixed Michael a drink of vodka and grapefruit juice. The two sat in the living room, drinking, smoking, and watching television. At 5:00 p.m., Keith heard a knock on the door. When Keith answered the door, he found Robert "David" Rowell on the front steps and let him into the trailer. David walked to Michael, his older brother, and took the drink from his hand and took a sip. At which point, Michael retrieved the drink from David. David took a seat in the living room on top of a blanket that Keith often had in his bedroom.

The three were watching television until about 5:30 p.m., when Keith excused himself to go to the bathroom. Upon exiting the bathroom, Keith noticed Michael gone and David was still sitting in the living room. Wondering why Michael was abruptly leaving, Keith exited the trailer chasing Michael. Keith suspected Michael stole cigarettes and had suspected him of doing this for some time. Michael, knowing Keith was following him, doubled his pace. Michael was walking south on Cozy Lane, toward Kreitzer Road. Keith just cleared his cul-de-sac when he decided to return home. It was cold, and he was without a shirt. As he walked to his trailer, Keith saw David at the Shipman trailer, 2754 Cozy Lane, which is located in a cul-de-sac opposite Keith's trailer. Shortly after returning home, Keith Wampler wrapped himself in his blanket and took a nap.

While at the Shipmans' trailer, David talked to James Shipman Jr., and in the course of the conversation, David asked for a cigarette. According to Joey Shipman, James Jr.'s seven-year-old brother, David, said he was planning on "getting drunk."[11] David left the Shipman trailer. In his trial testimony, Joey said that he saw David returning to Keith's trailer.

At 6:00 p.m., Robert "Bobby" D. Rowell returned home from Huber Heights, Ohio. According to Bobby Rowell, the only person home was Myrtle Rowell.[12] Bobby Rowell also said that Michael came home around 7:00 p.m. without David. Michael claimed that he was at Lisa Collins's trailer, which was located in the southern part of the Gem City Estates Trailer Park, from the time he left Keith's

---

[11]   Joey Shipman's trial testimony, *State of Ohio v. Charles "Keith" Wampler* (82-CR-764).

[12]   Robert D. Rowell's trial testimony, *State of Ohio v. Charles "Keith" Wampler* (82-CR-764).

trailer until he came home.[13] Again, according to his testimony, Bobby Rowell sent Michael out looking for David.

Meanwhile, at approximately 7:00 p.m., Lori and David Johnson dropped off their brother, Michael, and sister, Alice, at Judy Tabor's trailer, which was located in Gordon's Trailer Park. Judy Tabor is a cousin to the Johnsons. In their statement to the Moraine Police, Lori and David claimed they saw David Rowell with Ted Ritchie and that, upon exiting their vehicle, Michael Johnson joined the two. This claim was not substantiated by the Moraine Police investigation. However, the statement is documented in the Moraine Police case file, case number 82-184.

At approximately the same time, James Shipman Jr. and his brother, Joey, walked to Tabor's trailer. According to James Jr., he saw Michael Johnson, Judy Tabor, and Ted Ritchie at Tabor's trailer.[14] James Jr. said Joey and he stayed for about fifteen minutes before they left to go to Darrell Doan's trailer.

At 7:30 p.m., the Moraine Civic Center began showing the movie *Benji* for Moraine's children. The civic center frequently showed free children's movies for the residents of Moraine. In his trial testimony, David Miller, manager of the Moraine Civic Center, said that the movie started at 7:30 p.m. and ran until approximately 9:00 p.m. Miller told the court that once the movie starts, the doors to the center are locked so that the manager and staff could monitor who entered and exited. According to Miller, he knew David Rowell but did not see him on the night of February 5, 1982. Miller said he received a couple of calls where the caller inquired about David's whereabouts and did see Michael Rowell a couple of times while the movie was playing. It is worth noting that the Shipman brothers were

---

13   Michael Patrick Rowell's trial testimony, *State of Ohio v. Charles "Keith" Wampler* (82-CR-764).

14   James Shipman Jr.'s trial testimony, *State of Ohio v. Charles "Keith" Wampler* (82-CR-764).

present for the first few minutes of the movie but left to return to Doan's trailer. According to James Shipman Jr's trial testimony, Mike Johnson and Ted Ritchie were at Doan's trailer.

At 7:00 p.m., Michael Rowell returned to Keith Wampler's trailer. According to Michael, he was looking for David,[15] but according to Keith, Michael never asked about David. In his testimony, Keith stated that Michael Rowell made some small talk and asked to borrow a cigarette. Michael Rowell said he left Keith's trailer to continue the search for David. Michael said he went to the Moraine Civic Center and Moraine Meadows Elementary School in his search.

Bobby Rowell said sometime between 7:30 p.m. and 8:30 p.m., Michael Rowell returned home. Bobby could not be exact on the time because, according to him, he was taking a bath. Bobby told the court Myrtle Rowell was already looking for David and he sent Michael back out to look for his brother.

According to James Shipman Jr, between 8:30 p.m. and 9:00 p.m., Mike Johnson, Ted Ritchie, Joey, and he left Darrell Doan's trailer to go to Keith's trailer.[16] However, it must be noted that there is a discrepancy regarding which trailer the group left. James Jr. claimed it was Doan's trailer, yet in their trial testimony, Ted Ritchie and Judy Tabor said it was Tabor's trailer. The one thing that is not in dispute is the fact that Mike Johnson, Ted Ritchie, and James Shipman Jr. were under the influence of alcohol and marijuana at this time. In their open court testimony, they stated two or three marijuana cigarettes (joints) were shared among the group. Seven-year-old Joey Shipman hung out with the others but was the only one not using marijuana or alcohol.

---

[15] Michael Patrick Rowell's trial testimony, *State of Ohio v. Charles "Keith" Wampler* (82-CR-764).

[16] James Shipman Jr.'s trial testimony, *State of Ohio v. Charles "Keith" Wampler* (82-CR-764).

While the group of inebriated teens worked their way to Keith's trailer, Bobby Rowell began his search, on foot, for David.[17] Bobby Rowell said that he searched near I-75, the Moraine Civic Center, the field along Kreitzer Road, and the Gem City Estates Trailer Park. However, even though he stated he searched diligently for David, Bobby Rowell also stated that he did not knock on any doors or inquire with any neighbors regarding David's whereabouts. The question is begged, "Why, with a wind chill close to zero degrees, would the father think his son would not be inside somewhere?"

At approximately 9:00 p.m., the group, containing Joey Shipman, James Shipman Jr., Ted Ritchie, and Michael Johnson, arrive at Keith's trailer. Upon entry into Keith's trailer, the group, with the exception of Joey Shipman, continued their night of drinking. While at Keith's trailer, the group consumed many cans of Old Milwaukee Light Beer and listened to music or watched television. Sometime during this party, Ted Ritchie needed to relieve himself and went to the only bathroom in the trailer, which was located between Keith's bedroom and his father's bedroom. During the festivities, an inebriated James Shipman Jr. attempted to show the group how macho he was by tearing an aluminum beer can in half. In doing so, James Jr. cut his hand. It was at that point when he felt the need to lay down. He was shown to Keith's room, where he rested upon Keith's bed, while his little brother, Joey, stood in the doorway. James Jr. said he was in Keith's room for approximately twenty minutes.[18] Then, according to James Jr., he heard a loud scream while he was laying in Keith's room. At that point, James Jr. got out of bed, gathered his brother, and left Keith's trailer. Upon exiting the trailer, the

---

17 Robert D. Rowell's trial testimony, *State of Ohio v. Charles "Keith" Wampler* (82-CR-764).

18 James Shipman Jr.'s trial testimony, *State of Ohio v. Charles "Keith" Wampler* (82-CR-764).

Shipman brothers passed Michael Johnson, Ted Ritchie, and Keith, who were in Keith's living room drinking beer.[19]

This party continued until approximately 11:00 p.m., which is when Michael Johnson and Ted Ritchie departed Keith's trailer. The two would walk through the field along Kreitzer Road, cross Kreitzer Road, take the sidewalk that runs from the Moraine Civic Center to Moraine Meadows Elementary School, and then down Holman Street to Andrew Choate's house in Dog Patch.

Brian "Cappy" Canterbury, a friend of David Rowell, was leaving the Moraine Civic Center after watching *Benji*. It was about 9:15 p.m. As Brian was walking, he heard someone, from the area of the barbeque pit, shout, "Hi, Cappy." Brian recognized that voice as being that of David Rowell. Brian returned the salutation by saying, "Hi, David."[20] Brian did not stop and talk because he had to return to his grandparents' trailer, which was located on the north end of Gem City Estates Trailer Park. Brian had a curfew of 9:30 p.m.

Gwen Hudson lived in a trailer on the south end of Gem City Trailer Park. Her residence would be between Keith Wampler's trailer and David Rowell's house. Gwen was a single mother who lived with her daughter, Amy. According to Gwen's statement to the Moraine Police, Amy and she went to bed shortly before 9:30 p.m. At approximately 10:00 p.m., Amy was wakened by a scream that came from the neighborhood. Amy was disturbed so much by the scream that she woke her mother.

At 10:00 p.m., Michael Rowell returned home after searching for his little brother, David. In his testimony, Michael said he searched for David and could not find him. According to Michael, Randall Hendricks, a friend of David, assisted him in looking for David.

---

[19]   Moraine Police Report dated 02/06/1982 (Shipman's statement), case 82-184.

[20]   Moraine Police Report dated 02/06/1982, case number 82-184.

Michael said he went to bed after returning home.[21] It needs to be noted, and will be discussed in detail later, that Randall Hendricks did not search for David Rowell on the night of February 5, 1982, as Michael claimed.

According to Bobby Rowell, at 10:30 p.m., he began another search for David. This search, as with the previous one, was conducted on foot. He claimed he searched the field along Kreitzer Road and the area around the Moraine Civic Center. He was unable to find David.

At 11:00 p.m., Myrtle Rowell called the Moraine Police to report David Rowell missing. The Moraine Police dispatched Officer Arnold to the Rowell residence at 2970 Kreitzer Road. Officer Arnold had prior encounters with David Rowell. On a previous call, David was reported missing, and Officer Arnold found David near the Moraine Civic Center. After interviewing Myrtle, Officer Arnold began a search for David Rowell. As a part of the search, he drove his patrol car through the Gem City Estates Trailer Park. Officer Arnold reported not finding anything out of the ordinary or suspicious.

Meanwhile, as Myrtle was reporting David missing, Keith Wampler picked up the empty beer cans that his guests left in the living room. He gathered his blanket from the couch, unplugged the portable television, and retired to his father's room for the night. Keith had expected his father to return that evening but then came to the conclusion that his father must be spending the night in Waynesville. So Keith decided to take advantage of his father's absence and use his room because it was warmer than Keith's room and also it had enough room for the portable television. Keith covered himself with his blanket and began watching television.

While Myrtle was reporting David missing to Moraine Police, Bobby Rowell decided to search the house. The Rowells were renting

---

21   Michael Patrick Rowell's trial testimony, *State of Ohio v. Charles "Keith" Wampler* (82-CR-764).

the house at 2970 Kreitzer Road. This house was built in 1949 and is 1,312 square feet with two bedrooms and two bathrooms. The house has a cellar, which cannot be accessed directly from the house's interior. If someone wanted to go to the cellar, they would have to exit the house and use the exterior cellar doors. While Bobby Rowell searched the house and after Myrtle filed the missing person's report with Moraine Police, Myrtle and Michael began a search, by vehicle, of the area.

When the search of the house did not yield results, Bobby Rowell decided to take his van and conduct a wider search of the area. In his statement to the Moraine Police on February 10, 1982, Bobby said he drove along Dryden Road, where he drove through the parking lot of the Holiday Inn and looked around Stone's Sunoco and T.J. Restaurant. When that yielded no results, he then drove to the Dayton Mall. That is when he ended his search and assisted a motorist along Stroop Road.[22]

At 11:30 p.m., Michael Johnson and Ted Ritchie left Andrew Choate's residence on Holman Street in Dog Patch. The two teens were returning to Judy Tabor's trailer at Gordon's Trailer Park. The half-mile walk would not take long. The path the teens took would run them past the vacant field on Kreitzer Road. It was during this time that Bobby Rowell was searching that field for David.[23] Neither teen mentioned that if they saw Bobby Rowell in that field. It is also important to note that Bobby Rowell contradicts himself regarding his activity during this time.

Keith Wampler said he finished watching television and turned out the lights at about 12:40 a.m. on February 6, 1982. However, Adrian West, a neighbor who resided in a trailer near Keith's, tes-

---

[22]   Robert D. Rowell's trial testimony, *State of Ohio v. Charles "Keith" Wampler* (82-CR-764).

[23]   Ibid.

tified that it was closer to 1:30 a.m. on February 6, 1982.[24] It is during this time frame that Bobby Rowell claims to have conducted another search of the Gem City Estates Trailer Park.[25] Again, there is no report of him knocking on anyone's door looking for David. Between 2:00 a.m. and 2:30 a.m., Myrtle and Michael Rowell were conducting their own search for David. As with Bobby's search, this search yielded no results.

On February 6, 1982, at approximately 7:00 a.m., Bobby Rowell took the family dog into the vacant field on Kreitzer Road. The field is diagonally located northwest from Bobby Rowell's house on Kreitzer Road. Bobby Rowell, like most of the people in this neighborhood, walked his dog in the field. He reported no signs of David in the field. After walking the dog, Bobby Rowell decided to take another drive around the area to look for David. According his statement, this lasted until 9:15 a.m.[26] At that time, Bobby Rowell returned home. He was home for a short time before he left to go to a friend's television repair shop in Huber Heights. Bobby would be in Huber Heights until approximately 1:00 p.m.

At 10:00 a.m. on February 6, 1982, Michael Rowell visited Keith's trailer, where he encountered Charles "Cecil" Wampler. In his trial testimony, Michael claimed he saw two tiny specks of blood on the trailer's screen door. After visiting Keith's trailer, Michael then went to Lisa Collins's trailer, located at 2754 Quail Lane in the Gem City Estates Trailer Park. Michael would remain at Collins's trailer until 12:30 p.m. After 12:30 p.m., Michael Rowell said he went to the house of a friend, Doug Perry.

24 Adrian West trial testimony, *State of Ohio v. Charles "Keith" Wampler* (82-CR-764).

25 Moraine Police Report dated 02/10/2982, case number 82-184.

26 Robert D. Rowell's trial testimony, *State of Ohio v. Charles "Keith" Wampler* (82-CR-764).

At 12:00 p.m., Myrtle Rowell left the Rowell home on Kreitzer Road to go to Kettering. This was an era before cellular telephones became popular, so this meant that there was nobody at the residence for the Moraine Police to contact or a telephone number they could call if they found David. The mother was in Kettering, the father was in Huber Heights, and Michael was at a friend's house.

Bobby Rowell returned home around 1:00 p.m. According to his statement, nobody was home. So he made a pot of coffee. He poured himself a cup of coffee and decided to go to the cellar. Bobby Rowell stated that at about 3:30 p.m., he received a "vision of thornbushes." At that time, he exited the cellar and walked directly to the vacant field along Kreitzer Road, which is diagonally northwest of his home. Bobby Rowell stated that he walked 279 feet into the field directly to a patch of thornbushes. Within the patch of bushes, Bobby claimed he found the naked body of his son, David. A paper shopping bag was placed on the body's head, and the penis was amputated. The body was laying on top of 0.2 inches of snow, which had fallen the previous evening, and in the −7-degree wind chilled air.[27] At 3:50 p.m., Bobby Rowell called the Moraine Police to report finding his son's body.[28]

Several minutes after Bobby Rowell called the Moraine Police, Officer Brun arrived on the scene. Bobby showed the officer where David's body was located. In the meantime, several other patrol cars from the Moraine Police arrived at the scene. Aside from Officer Brun, Officer Dennis Adkins and Officer Robert Schmidt were present. In his report, Officer Brun stated the body had bruising around the mouth. He also reported a set of footprints coming from 2753 Cozy Lane to the body. His report also stated there was a second paper shopping bag, located approximately 20 feet northeast

---

[27] According to the National Weather Service, the air temperature was nine degrees with approximate ten miles per hour breeze.

[28] Moraine Police Report dated 02/06/1982, case number 82-184.

of the body that contained clothing and David Rowell's Moraine Civic Center membership card. Officer Robert Schmidt was asked to secure the footprints. Officer Adkins, who served as the Moraine Police evidence technician, began looking for additional evidence in the field.

Officer Robert Schmidt, Moraine Police Division, conducted an initial examination of the area. In his report, Officer Schmidt stated Officer J. Brun and Robert D. Rowell were present when he arrived. Officer Schmidt stated in his report he was lead to an area in the field that contained the body of a white male juvenile lying on his back. Officer Schmidt reported the body was nude and had a brown paper shopping bag on top of it. According to the report, Officer Schmidt saw a yellow towel beneath the body and the towel had bloodstains. Officer Schmidt further reported that Bobby Rowell was advised to return to his residence and stand by for questioning.[29]

The report documented items that were found at the scene. Officer Schmidt stated in his report that after the scene was photographed, he removed the bag from the victim's body and recovered the penis from the bag and placed it in a plastic evidence bag. Officer Schmidt observed dark marks around the victim's neck, indicating possible strangulation. Officer Schmidt also inventoried the shopping bag that was found twenty feet from the victim's body. According to his report, Officer Schmidt found the following items in the bag: one pair of boy's blue Levi jeans, brown velvet long-sleeved shirt, maroon-and-silver nylon jacket, a pair of Western-style boots, a pair of white tube socks with red-and-blue trim, black leather belt inside the loop of the jeans, a book of matches from Golden Dawn dairy, and a City of Moraine Parks and Recreation Activity card in the

---

[29]   Moraine Police Report dated 02/06/1982 filed by Officer Schmidt, case number 82-184.

name of David Rowell.[30] According to Officer Schmidt, the items were bagged and tagged to be send to the Miami Valley Regional Crime Lab in Dayton, Ohio, for analysis.

At approximately 4:18 p.m., Investigator J. C. Joyce, Montgomery County Coroner's Office, arrived on the scene.[31] In his report, Investigator Joyce reported finding the body lying on its left side in a fetal position with his head pointing toward the west and the legs pointing northeast. Investigator Joyce documented finding a shopping bag on the body's head and that the bag contained a penis. The report continues to state there was some blood in the body's right nostril and that the body was nude. According to Investigator Joyce, a yellow towel was directly beneath the body.

Investigator Joyce stated he found a brown-paper Kroger shopping bag approximately seven feet east of the body. However, the Moraine Police reported the bag was twenty feet northeast of the body. Investigator Joyce documented that the bag contained a pair of blue Levi jeans with belt, a pair of white socks with red-and-blue bands on the top, and a light-blue long-sleeved button-up shirt.

A visual examination of the body, as reported by Investigator Joyce, revealed the penis was amputated from the body with portions of the scrotum intact, and the amputation occurred postmortem due to the fact that very little blood was found around the wound. Investigator Joyce stated the cause of death appeared to be manual strangulation due to the bruising about the neck. Investigator Joyce reported finding bruising on the back and legs of the body. The report also documented scratches on the body, which appeared to have occurred postmortem and possibly from the body being placed amongst the thornbushes.

---

[30]   Moraine Police Report dated 02/06/1982 filed by Officer Robert Schmidt, case number 82-184.

[31]   Montgomery County Coroner's Report of Investigator Joyce dated 02/08/1982.

Investigator Joyce also documented his interview of Bobby Rowell. According to Investigator Joyce, Bobby told him the last time he saw David was at 5:30 p.m. on February 5, 1982.[32] It should be noted the statement Bobby Rowell gave Investigator Joyce contradicts the statement he provided to the Moraine Police and his trial testimony at Keith Wampler's trial. In his statements to the police, Bobby Rowell said that he did not see David at all on the afternoon of February 5, 1982. This point will be addressed in great detail later, but it is worth noting now.

After the initial investigation was complete, the body of thirteen-year-old Robert David Rowell was placed in a body bag, put in an ambulance, and transported to the Montgomery County Coroner's Office, where a complete autopsy would be conducted. The work of the Moraine Police on this case would fall on the shoulders of Detective William Mullins. Meanwhile, the people of the Miami Valley would be bombarded with news reports of this crime. Due to the age of the victim and the condition of the body, the various news outlets in Dayton would be busy reporting on this case for many weeks and months ahead.

---

[32] Montgomery County Coroner's Report of Investigator Joyce dated 02/08/1982.

CHAPTER 3

The Investigation

The Initial Field Investigation

While the Moraine Police and Montgomery County Coroner were conducting the initial investigation into the death of Robert "David" Rowell, his older half-brother was standing on the patio of Charles "Keith" Wampler's trailer watching the activity in the field seventy-seven feet away. For some reason, Michael was not home with his mother and father. According to Michael, he was on the patio for about one hour before Keith came out to inquire about what was happening.[33] Michael claimed Keith said, "Man, that's gross. How can anyone do that?"

One of Keith's neighbors, James Combs, came to Keith's trailer to inquire about what was occurring along Kreitzer Road and in the field. Combs just returned from attending a family function when he saw the police cars and flashing lights. In his trial testimony, Combs claimed Keith told him that someone strangled David Rowell.[34]

---

[33] Michael Patrick Rowell's trial testimony, *State of Ohio v. Charles "Keith" Wampler* (82-184).

[34] James Comb's trial testimony, *State of Ohio v. Charles "Keith" Wampler* (82-CR-742).

Once he was completed with the inventory of items discovered near David's body, Officer Robert Schmidt began to canvass the neighborhood in a search for witnesses. Officer Schmidt was the first officer to make contact with Keith Wampler at 2753 Cozy Lane. The subsequent interviews were conducted by Chief of Police Glenn Carmichael and Detective Williams Mullins, both from the Moraine Police Division.

Officer Schmidt conducted an initial interview with Adrian West, 2765 Cozy Lane, whose trailer was located two trailers to the south of Keith's trailer. West told Officer Schmidt that he heard yelling during the evening of February 5, 1982, and believed it came from the direction of Keith's trailer. West did not give a specific time on when this yelling occurred. West confirmed, for Officer Schmidt, that teenagers often visited Keith's trailer, and one of those teens was Michael Johnson, who resided at 2971 Kreitzer Road.[35] A formal interview of Adrian West would occur on February 11, 1982, at 7:45 p.m., conducted by Sergeant Joseph Wynne and Officer Dennis Atkins. In this interview, West claimed he was home with his wife and daughter on the evening of February 5. According to West, he observed Keith checking his mailbox and Keith was not wearing a shirt. West further stated he did not see anything out of the ordinary until 10:50 p.m. West said that is when he saw James Shipman Jr. and his brother, Joey, leave Keith's trailer. West further stated he heard some hollering coming from the direction of Keith's trailer around 11:00 p.m. West went on to say that at 11:30 p.m., he saw Bobby Rowell walking through the trailer park.[36]

Officer Schmidt interviewed Brian "Cappy" Canterbury at his grandparents' trailer, 2779 Cozy Lane. Canterbury stated he was at

---

[35]   Moraine Police Report dated 02/06/1982 filed by Officer Robert Schmidt, case number 82-184.

[36]   Moraine Police Report dated 02/12/1982 filed by Sergeant Wynne, case number 82-184.

the movie on February 5 and he saw David Rowell at the Moraine Civic Center. Canterbury told Officer Schmidt he did not recall seeing David inside the civic center. Canterbury said David was wearing a silver-and-dark-colored jacket. Brian "Cappy" Canterbury provided a written voluntary statement to Sergeant Alexander and Lieutenant Atchison of the Moraine Police Division. In that statement, Brian repeated he left the Moraine Civic Center around 9:15 p.m. when he saw a boy he believed to be David Rowell near the circle beside the civic center. In his statement, Brian said he recognized the coat the boy was wearing as being one similar to a coat that David owned. Brian said the boy had on a silver-and-dark-colored jacket. Brian further stated the boy yelled "Hello, Cappy" to him and he returned the salutation by saying "Hello, David."[37]

Gwen Hudson, 2969 Schoolhouse Lane, was another person interviewed by Officer Schmidt. In her statement, Ms. Hudson said that her daughter, Amy, heard a scream sometime during the evening. Ms. Hudson said Amy woke her to tell her about the scream.

Officer Schmidt's report indicates he interviewed the staff at the Moraine Civic Center, specifically Becky Martin, Peggy Bond, and Dave Miller. They told Officer Schmidt they were familiar with David Rowell and that David associated with Roy Elam. All three staff members told Officer Schmidt they did not see David Rowell that evening, but they did see his brother, Michael.

The last paragraph of Officer Robert Schmidt's report documents his interview with Michael Rowell. According to the report, Michael said David had enemies, though he did not provide any detailed information. The report continues to state that Michael said David and he had a rough home life. Michael told Officer Schmidt he got along with his brother, though they sometimes argued. This

---

[37] Canterbury's written voluntary statement dated 02/06/1982 at 6:30 p.m.

interview was conducted near the scene where David's body was discovered.

As stated earlier, Detective William Mullins was the lead investigator in this case. It was his job to question witnesses and gather evidence in order to bring the killer to justice. It is clear by the police reports that Detective Mullins became fixated with the footprints that lead from 2753 Cozy Lane, going in a southwest direction, to the body. These footprints led to Detective Mullins focusing on the occupants of 2753 Cozy Lane.

Sometime after 3:50 p.m. on February 6, 1982, Detective Mullins interviewed Charles "Keith" Wampler at 2753 Cozy Lane.[38] In his report, Detective Mullins noted Keith was residing with his father, Charles "Cecil" Wampler, at 2753 Cozy Lane, and Keith's mother was residing in Waynesville, Ohio. Keith told Detective Mullins the last time he saw David Rowell was in the late afternoon of February 5, 1982. In his statement, Keith said he was coming out of the bathroom in his trailer when he noticed Michael Rowell left and David was sitting on the couch. Keith said he ran after Michael to see why he was leaving but never caught up with him. Keith further stated when he was returning to his trailer, he noticed David Rowell at the Shipman trailer. Detective Mullins's report reflects that Keith told him that was the last time he had seen David Rowell. At 5:33 p.m., Keith provided a written statement to the Moraine Police in support of his verbal statement.

On February 6, 1982, at approximately 5:38 p.m., Detective Mullins interviewed James Shipman Jr. (James Jr.) at 2754 Cozy Lane.[39] This address is in the cul-de-sac opposite the cul-de-sac that contained Keith's trailer. In his statement to Detective Mullins, James

---

[38] Moraine Police Report dated 02/06/1982 (Wampler interview), case number 82-184.

[39] Moraine Police Report dated 02/06/1982 (Shipman Interview), case number 82-184.

Jr. claimed to have known David Rowell for six months and was friends with Michael Rowell. James Jr. stated that he attended Van Buren Middle School with Michael. James Jr. told Detective Mullins on February 5, 1982, at 5:00 p.m. was the last time he saw David Rowell alive. James Jr. said David had visited the Shipman trailer for a short time. According to Shipman, David said he was "going to get fucked up tonight." In addition, James Jr. claimed he saw Myrtle Rowell, David's mother, sometime during the evening of February 5. James Jr. said Mrs. Rowell told him that she was looking for David and claimed David had run away from home.

James Shipman Jr. confirmed that his brother, Joey, and he went to the Moraine Civic Center to watch the movie. In his statement to Detective Mullins, he claimed that he stayed for the entire movie. However, in his trial testimony, he said he stayed for only a few minutes and then left to go to Darrell Doan's trailer. In his statement to Detective Mullins, James Jr. confirmed Joey and he went to Keith's trailer, where he saw Michael Johnson and Ted Ritchie. James Jr. said he drank some beer, became ill, and then laid down on Keith's bed. James Jr. told Detective Mullins at some point he heard a scream. At that point, he collected his brother, Joey, and left Keith's trailer to return to his home. James Jr. said that he had to pass through Keith's living room in order to exit the trailer and in doing so passed Michael Johnson, Ted Ritchie, and Keith, who were still in the living room.

While the field interviews were occurring, Officer Dennis Adkins was conducting a search of the vacant field.[40] Officer Adkins mentioned the body, some towels, Old Milwaukee Light beer cans along a path between the field and the trailer park, the bag containing the clothing, and footprints in the snow. Those were the *only* items mentioned by Officer Adkins. There is no report indicating the

---

[40]   Officer Dennis J. Adkins trial testimony, *State of Ohio v. Charles "Keith" Wampler* (82-CR-742).

exact date and time he examined these items in his role as evidence technician.

A review of the Moraine Police reports indicated there is no record of any other interviews conducted by any member of the Moraine Police Division on February 6, 1982. Shortly after David Rowell's body was removed from the vacant field along Kreitzer Road, the Moraine Police departed the area.

The Interview

Sometime before 11:00 p.m. on February 6, 1982, Detective Mullins conducted a check of the Ohio Law Enforcement Automated Data System (LEADS). As standard police procedure would dictate, he was checking the criminal history of the people he encountered while at the field where David's body was recovered. When he ran a computer check of Keith Wampler, he learned of a warrant out of Warren County for Wampler's arrest for failure to appear on a drug abuse charge. At 11:00 p.m., Sergeant Joseph Wynne and Detective Mullins returned to 2753 Cozy Lane to execute the arrest warrant from Warren County.[41] The report does not reflect that Keith was advised of the *Miranda* warning.[42] Keith was transported to Moraine Police Headquarters for questioning.

Keith was placed in an interview room at 11:19 p.m. At that point, Sergeant Wynne and Detective Mullins began to question Keith.[43] While the transcribed report documents the presence of

---

[41] Moraine Police Report dated 02/06/1982 documenting Wampler's arrest, case 82-184.

[42] *Miranda v. Arizona 384 US 486* (1966).

[43] Transcription of the taped interview of Charles "Keith" Wampler, case 82-184, being play at Keith's trial, *State of Ohio v. Charles "Keith" Wampler* (82-CR-742).

Sergeant Wynne, Detective Mullins, and Charles "Keith" Wampler, it does not mention anything about Keith's legal guardian, Charles "Cecil" Wampler, being present. Though Keith was only a teenager, having just turned sixteen on February 6, his legal guardian was not permitted in the interview room.

The first several questions asked by Detective Mullins were to obtain background and biographical information about Keith, such as birthday and address. After the preliminary questions were out of the way, Detective Mullins began to question Keith about his activities on February 5. It must be stressed that Keith had not yet been advised of the *Miranda* warning, even though he was clearly in custody and being questioned with respect to a crime (the murder of David Rowell) that had nothing to do with the arrest warrant out of Warren County, Ohio, that the officers maintained was their authority to make the arrest. Keith told Detective Mullins that he was home on February 5 and that his trailer was close to the field on the western boundary of the Gem City Estates Trailer Park, in other words, the vacant field along Kreitzer Road where David Rowell's body was discovered. Sergeant Wynne asked Keith what time he went to bed. Keith stated he did take a nap around 5:30 p.m. on February 5, after Michael and David Rowell left his trailer. Keith then told the police officers later that evening Michael Rowell returned to his trailer. Keith said Michael came in and asked for a cigarette. At that point, Detective Mullins asked about the earlier visit of Michael Rowell. Keith said Michael came to his trailer around 3:00 p.m. or 4:00 p.m.; he was not sure of the time. Keith continued to state that about forty-five minutes later, David came to his trailer while Michael was still there. Keith described David as being "kind of small." Keith said the two Rowells and he were watching television. At that point, Detective Mullins asked if Keith attended school. Keith said, "I quit today," and explained his father had been taking him to Waynesville to attend school.

Detective Mullins then inquired about the time David and Michael Rowell left Keith's trailer. Keith stated that it was around 5:00 p.m. When asked where the Rowells went, Keith stated David went to "Jim's house." Keith stated he did not know Jim's last name, just that he lived in a trailer across the street from his. Keith said he did not know where Michael went but believed that it was some girl's house. Detective Mullins asked Keith if Jim's last name was Shipman, and Keith stated it could be. Keith further stated Jim's mother worked at Save Mart. At that point, Detective Mullins asked Keith how he knew David Rowell went to the Shipmans' trailer. Keith told him that he saw David on the front porch of the trailer. It was then 11:25 p.m., and Sergeant Wynne stopped the tape recorder.

The taped interview resumed with Detective Mullins asking clarification of whether Keith was coming or going when he last saw David Rowell. Keith stated he was returning to his trailer after chasing Michael Rowell. Keith said it was cold and he was not wearing a shirt. Keith repeated he went home and went to bed. Later that evening, according to Keith, several people—Michael Johnson, James Shipman Jr. and his brother, Joey, and some guy named Ted—came to his trailer. Keith said they were drunk, and James Jr. was so drunk that he needed to lay down. Keith stated the Shipmans were the first to leave his trailer followed by Michael Johnson and Ted Ritchie. Then, according to Keith, he laid down because he had a headache. Keith stated he was watching *Family Feud* for a while. At that point, according to Keith, he took the television back to his father's room and watched it in there.

At that point, Detective Mullins went back to asking Keith why he followed Michael Rowell from the trailer at 5:30 p.m. Detective Mullins wanted to know if Michael seemed upset. According to Keith, Michael Rowell was not upset. Keith then repeated he never caught up with Michael and he saw Michael's brother, David, at James Shipman Jr.'s front porch. According to the transcripts, it appeared as if Detective Mullins continued to badger Keith regarding these events. Sergeant Wynne then asked about the time Michael Rowell returned to Keith's trailer and if Keith asked Michael for a reason why he left. Keith told Sergeant Wynne that he never brought it up and that Michael came to borrow a cigarette. Keith told the police officers that Michael Rowell came back before the group of youths came.

The police officers wanted to know how long Keith knew the Rowells. Keith explained he was better acquainted with Michael and that Michael had visited his trailer four or five times. Then Keith said David came to his trailer three or four times, sometimes with Michael and sometimes without. Keith told the police officers the Rowells knew James Combs, but they would not have gone to Combs's trailer because Combs's was grounded.

Sergeant Wynne wanted to know how long Keith resided in Moraine. Keith said he lived at his current address for five or six months. Keith told the police officers about his family situation. Keith said he lived with his father and they used to live in Waynesville. Keith also told the law enforcement officers his grandmother recently passed away. Keith said his father might have known Michael Johnson, but he was not sure. Keith indicated he could not understand how someone could murder David Rowell and repeated the Rowell brothers were often together.

At that point, Detective Mullins apologized for keeping Keith up so late. Keith responded by stated he was going to stay up late anyway to celebrate his sixteenth birthday. Then Keith went back to telling how Michael Rowell would come over to his trailer and, soon after his arrival, David would appear. Keith indicated David Rowell often followed Michael around. Detective Mullins then asked if Michael Rowell was capable of doing something like this. Keith said he was not sure and began to tell of a time when Michael came over and soonafter David appeared. In this incident, Michael hid in the bathroom because he did not want to be around David. Keith reiterated that he was not sure if Michael was capable of murdering David. Keith then told the police officers of how he used to hide from his sisters because he did not want to be bothered by them.

Keith mentioned rumors about guys around the trailer park. According to Keith, there were rumors that one of the residents of the trailer park was homosexual.[44] Keith described this guy as being in his forties. Detective Mullins asked Keith to provide additional information about this man. Keith said he heard from other neighbors that this guy was weird. Keith continued to say he met several people since moving to Moraine, and he named Michael Johnson as one of them. Keith told the police officers the police knew Michael Johnson, but he did not elaborate. Keith said he knew James Combs and thought Combs was on probation. Sergeant Wynne then asked why was Combs on probation. Keith stated he did not know but thought Combs was a good kid. Keith then speculated Combs may have been involved in a theft. Keith then described how he met some other people in the trailer park.

Detective Mullins asked if Keith knew if David Rowell had any enemies. Keith stated he did not have any information regarding that. Keith then described David as being a good kid with a smart mouth. According to Keith, David would go around and threaten other kids with telling his dad on them. Keith said David was capable of saying something smart to the wrong person, but he could not imagine someone killing him. Sergeant Wynne wanted to know if Bobby Rowell was mean, and Keith stated he did not know and he never met Bobby Rowell.

At that point, Sergeant Wynne went back to Keith's education situation and asked him about school. Keith repeated he used to attend Waynesville schools but dropped out. Keith further described

---

[44]   The name is being withheld because there is no evidence this person is associated with this case.

his attendance in Waynesville schools as being off and on. Keith said he did attend school in Las Vegas, Nevada, for a while. Keith described how he got into trouble at one of his schools for snapping a girl with his comb after she did the same to him. Keith said he had to serve a week detention for that. Keith said he was sent to the office once to receive corporal punishment. According to Keith, that is when he walked out of school and told his mother. Keith said this occurred while he lived in Waynesville. At that point, Keith rambled about his experiences in school and his decision to drop out of school.

By this time, it was 11:42 p.m. Detective Mullins decided to take a break in the interview, and he stopped the tape. It was then he decided Keith was a suspect.[45] The taped interview resumed at 12:53 a.m. on February 7, 1982. Still there was no indication that Keith was advised of the *Miranda* warning, nor was his father, Cecil, permitted into the interview room. It also appears the police asked Keith questions regarding a knife. Those questions were asked prior to Detective Mullins restarting the tape recorder. The question regarding a knife is evident because Keith said he obtained the knife from someone in Kettering, Ohio. The answer was recorded.

Also, sometime while the tape recorder was turned off, Detective Mullins asked Keith about the towels. This is known because Detective Mullins said, "Let's go back to the towels." Prior to the tape being stopped, there was no question regarding the towels. Keith apparently told the police that he did not remember the towels. Keith was questioned again about his knowledge of the towels. His answer remained the same—he did not remember the towels. At that point, Detective Mullins began asking about the knife. Again, Keith said he obtained it from some kid in Kettering. Keith described the knife as being big with a brown wooden handle. With

---

[45] Detective William Mullins trial testimony, *State of Ohio v. Charles "Keith" Wampler* (82-CR-742).

a little prodding from Sergeant Wynne, Keith estimated the length of the blade to be two and a half to three inches. Detective Mullins suggested that Keith was talking about a buck knife, but while Keith was attempting to answer, Mullins interrupted. Detective Mullins described a buck knife to Keith. Detective Mullins wanted to know how Keith carried his knife. Keith stated he carried his knife in his pocket. When asked about the whereabouts of the knife, Keith said he either gave it to his father or traded it to Michael Johnson. Keith stated he could not remember. Keith indicated his father may have disposed of the knife because he did not want Keith to have one.

In an attempt to learn more about the towels, Detective Mullins asked Keith when he last took a shower. Keith stated two or three days earlier and could not remember what kind of towels he used to dry himself.

After a couple questions regarding Keith's coats, Detective Mullins began to question about the events surrounding 5:00 p.m. on February 5. Keith repeated the same story he said earlier in the interview. Keith stated he went to the bathroom, and when he came out, Michael Rowell was leaving his trailer and David Rowell was sitting on the couch. Keith said he followed Michael in order to see why he was leaving. Keith stated he was not wearing a shirt and confirmed that he was wearing his boots. As he stated earlier in the interview, Keith said when he began to go back to his trailer, he saw David at the Shipman trailer. Keith stated he saw David Rowell talking to James Shipman Jr. but could not remember if he saw James's little brother, Joey.

Keith repeated the story about later in the evening of February 5 when James Shipman Jr., Joey Shipman, Michael Johnson, and Ted Ritchie visited his trailer. He stated everyone, except Joey, had some beer to drink. Keith also told Detective Mullins everyone, except Joey, was high. Keith repeated the story about James Jr. being so intoxicated that he needed to lay down on Keith's bed. Keith denied that a disturbance occurred in his trailer that evening.

Then Detective Mullins asked if Keith would know of any reason somebody would kill David Rowell. Keith said it could be possible that David said something smart to the wrong person and then described David as being a nice person. After being asked by Detective Mullins, Keith said David Rowell never said anything to him that would cause him to be upset with David.

Detective Mullins asked Keith about when Michael Rowell returned to Keith's trailer later that night. Keith stated he did not ask Michael about why he left his trailer. Keith repeated Michael Rowell asked for a cigarette. Then Detective Mullins inquired about why, earlier in the day, Keith, without a shirt, would chase Michael. Keith said he only went as far as a little distance past Shipman's trailer, then he started back to his residence. Detective Mullins wanted to know why Keith went to all the trouble to follow Michael then later that evening Keith did not ask Michael about the abrupt departure earlier in the day. Keith said he simply forgot about it. Keith repeated when he returned to his trailer, he took a nap. Detective Mullins then badgered Keith about possibly offending or upsetting Michael Rowell. Keith denied doing either. Keith said Michael may have wanted to leave suddenly to visit a girl.

Detective Mullins continued to badger Keith regarding Michael Rowell's sudden departure from Keith's trailer. Keith repeated he did not know why Michael left but did not think anything of it later that evening. Keith confirmed Michael and he had been drinking vodka prior to Michael suddenly leaving. Then Detective Mullins, and it is best described as harping, repeated his questions regarding why Keith did not ask Michael as to why Michael suddenly departed. Again, Keith repeated he did not ask about it, and it did not concern him when Michael returned.

In switching subjects, Detective Mullins asked again about the knife. Keith repeated his earlier answer in that he either gave it to Michael Johnson or his father, Cecil. In a rapid-fire succession, Detective Mullins asked several questions about when Keith gave the knife to Cecil. Keith finally asked Detective Mullins to stop so he could answer the questions. Keith said he was trying to remember if he gave it to his father or to Michael Johnson. At that point, Detective Mullins wanted to change the subject. Keith then asked for some coffee. It was 1:05 a.m. on February 7, 1982. The tape was stopped.

At 1:23 a.m., Detective Mullins restarted the tape recorder. Again, there is no evidence that Keith was advised of the *Miranda* warning. It is also worth noting that he was in custody because the Moraine Police executed the arrest warrant out of Warren County on an unrelated charge. Detective Mullins began this portion of the interview by asking about the towels.

Detective Mullins claimed Cecil Wampler believed the towels were from Cecil's trailer. At that point, Keith said someone could have taken the towels because he does not pay attention to the towels in the trailer. Keith continued his response by saying that he takes a shower, dries off, and throws the towel in the hamper. Keith was not given the opportunity to finish his answer because Detective Mullins interrupted to ask about grocery shopping.

Keith said every once in a while, he would go grocery shopping with his father, and sometimes they would use the base store on Wright-Patterson Air Force Base. Again, Keith was interrupted by Detective Mullins before he could finish his answer. Mullins wanted to know if Keith ever went to Imperial Food Town in Centerville, Ohio. Keith responded by telling Mullins his father and he would shop there from time to time. He also said they shopped the IGA in Springboro, Ohio, as well. Keith confirmed his father, Cecil Wampler, and he would bring home their groceries in a shopping bag, and the IGA gave you a choice between paper or plastic. Keith said his father would often get the groceries in plastic bags but sometimes in paper bags.

Detective Mullins switched the topic back to the knife. He asked Keith about the knife's whereabouts, at which point Sergeant Wynne suggested it was in Keith room. Keith said it was not in his room. Again, Detective Mullins asked about the knife's whereabouts. Again, Keith said he was not sure. Detective Mullins, beginning to refer to Keith as young man, suggested young men like to collect pocketknives. Then he asked Keith Wampler if Keith was satisfied with the coffee. At that point, he again asked whether or not Keith can recall the whereabouts of the knife. Keith again said he did not know.

The topic switched to Keith's clothing. Detective Mullins asked how long Keith had been wearing his pants. Keith said it could have been two or three days. Mullins then inquired about Keith's underwear. Keith gave the same response. Mullins wanted to know about the jacket, and Keith said the he normally wore the jacket that was with him in the interview room, which was a blue jacket. Sergeant Wynne asked if Keith had gone to school on February 5. Keith stated he did not.

The next line of questioning dealt with whether or not Keith worked on cars. Keith stated he did work on his father's car and on a neighbor's car. Then, out of the blue, Detective Mullins asked Keith about a fight at Keith's trailer. Keith stated he was not aware of one. Keith further stated Michael Johnson and he would wrestle, but not fight. Mullins then asked if Keith ever fought with David Rowell. Keith said he did not but said he wrestled with Michael Rowell, but no fighting.

Detective Mullins wanted to know if Keith was home all day on Friday, February 5. Keith said he was except for a small period of time, when he threw an old grill away in the patch of weeds near his trailer. Detective Mullins wanted to know if anyone was cut and bleeding at Keith's trailer. Keith stated the only person who was cut was James Shipman Jr., and that happened when James Jr. cut himself on a beer can. Keith said he was not sure how serious the cut was. Keith stated there was blood, but it was not spirting out. Detective Mullins asked if James Jr. got blood on Keith's trailer. Keith said he was not sure, but it could be possible. Detective Mullins then inquired about when Keith last changed the sheets on his bed. Keith believed it was about a month.

Sergeant Wynne wanted to know if Keith could think of anyone in the trailer park that was capable of murdering David Rowell. Keith said he did not know. Keith also stated he was not sure about Ted Ritchie. Keith claimed he never met Ted prior to February 5. Keith stated he did see Ted Ritchie with Michael Johnson one time at the Moraine Civic Center. Keith believed Ted Ritchie to be about seventeen years old. When asked, Keith told the police officers Ted wore a blue jacket on February 5.

The interview concluded at 1:31 a.m. on February 7, 1982. It is worth repeating that Keith, who was in police custody, was never advised of the *Miranda* warning anytime during this interview. Sometime after questioning, Keith was transported to the juvenile detention facility in Warren County, Ohio. Keith was not yet arrested for the murder of David Rowell. The Moraine Police had executed the warrant out of Warren County Juvenile Court.

The Searches

While Keith was being held at Moraine Police headquarters, at 3:50 a.m. on February 7, 1982, twelve hours after David Rowell's body was found, Officer Dennis Adkins searched 2753 Cozy Lane, Keith's residence, for evidence. It should be noted a third search would be conducted on February 9, 1982, at 3:30 p.m. Also, it should be noted at no time during this investigation was 2753 Cozy Lane treated as a crime scene, which meant it needed to be secured. Keith's trailer, 2753 Cozy Lane, was never secured by the Moraine Police.

Officer Dennis Adkins, who worked as the evidence technician for the Moraine Police Division, logged the following items into evidence: one pair of brown Acme cowboy boots, size ten and a half D, and one blue hat, with blue-and-white patch, from Gale Long & Sons Grain Company. Officer Adkins claimed these items were taken from Keith. However, in his report, Officer Adkins failed to state when he obtained the evidence.

In the same report that documented the property taken from Keith Wampler, Officer Adkins listed property that was seized from 2753 Cozy Lane, Wampler's residence. A leather strap, many Old Milwaukee Light beer cans, various steak and kitchen knives, yellow foam mattress, piece of vinyl flooring from the bathroom, one jar of Vaseline, a bag of trash from the porch, bag from a sweeper, a book of matches, and a Moraine Parks and Recreation Activity Card in the name of David Rowell. It needs to be noted that the activity card is the same card that the Montgomery County Coroner's Office and Officer Brun claimed was in the shopping bag containing the David's clothing, which was found approximately twenty feet from the body, not in the trailer at 2753 Cozy Lane. Officer Adkins's report indicates the activity card was found in the trailer, yet the coroner's investigator and another member of the Moraine Police said it was found in the bag with the clothing. Which is it? Again, Officer Adkins failed to document the time and date when he obtained this evidence.

The most disturbing search was conducted on February 12, 1982, six days after David Rowell's body was discovered. The search was conducted by Officer Dennis Adkins with the help of the United States Army Reserve. Officer Adkins led the search of the vacant field along Kreitzer Road. Officer Adkins previously stated he had searched this field on February 6, 1982, after David's body was discovered. This time, Officer Adkins, with the help of the United States Army Reserve, found a faded green toilet seat lid with possible bloodstains on it. This lid was fifty-nine feet north of where David's body was discovered. It needs to be noted that between the time David's body was removed from the field on February 6, 1982, to when this second search of the field was conducted on February 12, 1982, the field was not secured. Anyone could and did have access to this field. As a matter of fact, the news media and thrill seekers had access to the field. For days, this field sparked the interest of the public because it was a crime scene.

The Autopsy

On February 7, 1982, at 9:00 a.m., Dr. Donald E. Schaffer, MD, performed the autopsy on the body of David Rowell, with Lou Stange, CD Lett (photographer), Jerry Phipps (physician assistant), and Dr. James H. Davis (Montgomery County Coroner) being in attendance. The autopsy identified the cause of death being cerebral anoxia due to acute cardiorespiratory failure due to manual strangulation.[46] In layman's terms, someone placed enough pressure on David's respiratory system to cause the system to fail, thus cutting off oxygen to the brain. In his report, Dr. Schaffer placed the time of death at 1:00 a.m., plus or minus two hours, on February 6, 1982, and this conclusion was based on lividity and rigor mortis.

The gross anatomic summary of the autopsy report stated manual strangulation with hemorrhages in the right and left side of the neck were present. Petechial hemorrhages (breaking of blood capillaries that causes minor bleeding, indicative of strangulation) were

---

[46]   Montgomery County Coroner's Report, case AC-81-82, dated 02/08/1982.

present in the eyes, face, oral cavity, pleural surfaces of the lungs, and epicardial surfaces of the heart, larynx, and trachea. This section of the report documented various bruises on the body, along with postmortem scratches. Dr. Schaffer concluded the amputation of the penis was postmortem with numerous lacerations and the area of the amputation measuring five and a half inches by three inches. Because there was no blood around the amputation area, the amputation was postmortem. Dr. Schaffer found perianal tears and bilateral pulmonary edema. The autopsy found acute congestion of the lungs, and there was evidence David aspirated gastric contents into the trachea, bronchi, and bronchioles. Dr. Schaffer described the cerebral edema as being moderate. The report noted the body was in early stages of decomposition.

The autopsy report described David Rowell as a thirteen-year-old Caucasian male with fair complexion and light-brown hair, weighing sixty-five pounds, and fifty-three-and-a-half inches tall. The remainder of the autopsy report documented the examination of the various organs. The examination supported Dr. Schaffer's conclusion on the cause of death. According to the autopsy report, the stomach contained a "green food substance" and pink chewing gum. The food substance was never tested by the Montgomery County Coroner's Office.

The autopsy also revealed superficial tears in the anus. The tears are one-half inch along the anterior aspect of the anal opening and were premortem. Another tear was discovered along the posterior aspect of the anal opening and was three-eighths of an inch. The autopsy noted the appearance of blood near the tears.

The court summary of the autopsy is as follows: "This 13-year-old Caucasian male died as a result of acute cardiorespiratory failure due to manual strangulation. He likewise had terminal aspiration of gastric contents into the trachea, bronchi and bronchioles. He had numerous post mortem abrasions and scratches on the body, as well as post mortem bruises. He likewise had post mortem amputation of external genitals and premortem tears of anal region."

The toxicology analysis was conducted on February 7, 1982, at 3:30 p.m. The test was conducted only on David's blood. The test showed negative for any drugs. The blood alcohol (ethanol) level was 0.02 percent.

Forensic Reports

The other items seized during the course of this investigation were submitted to the Miami Valley Regional Crime Laboratory in Dayton, Ohio, for forensic analysis. On February 8, 1982, the Miami Valley Regional Crime Laboratory reported receiving the following items for fingerprint analysis: a Super Rite brown paper shopping bag, an Imperial Food Town brown paper shopping bag, a Stump's brown paper shopping bag, a cardboard Old Milwaukee Light Beer can container, four three-by-five latent print cards, and fingerprints and palm prints of Charles "Keith" Wampler. The fingerprints on the items listed were compared with the fingerprint cards. The report indicates that the prints found on the items could not be used for identification purposes. Therefore, they could not be compared to the print cards submitted. The findings were inconclusive.[47] On February 12, 1982, Officer Adkins received a report from the Miami Valley Regional Crime Laboratory regarding fingerprint analysis of three Old Milwaukee Light beer cans. Again, the report was inconclusive, and the prints could not be used for identification purposes.

On February 8, 1982, Larry Dehus, technical supervisor, Miami Valley Regional Crime Laboratory, filed the following report regarding hair analysis. Dehus stated he received the following items for

---

[47] Miami Valley Regional Crime Lab report, by Det. H. Baumgardner, dated 02/08/1982.

analysis and to be compared to hair samples obtained from Charles "Keith" Wampler and Charles "Cecil" Wampler: a yellow hand towel, a pink-and-white hand towel, a white towel, a pair of cowboy boots, a shopping bag containing David Rowell's clothing, a loose hair found on David's left calf and was recovered by the Montgomery County Coroner's Office, and four hairs from David's genital area recovered by the Montgomery County Coroner's Office. The report stated the hair found on the cowboy boots was human head hair, but it was not consistent with David Rowell's or Keith Wampler's hair. As for the other hairs that were analyzed, Dehus stated there were microscopic similarities, but they were not conclusive.[48] On March 2, 1982, Dehus filed a report regarding additional analysis of hair. The first section of the report discussed the analysis of hairs found on some moldy tissue in the bathroom of 2753 Cozy Lane. The analysis determined these hairs belonged to Charles "Cecil" Wampler. As a follow up to the February 8, 1982, report, the Moraine Police obtained additional hair samples from Charles "Keith" Wampler. Again, Dehus said that examination of these hair samples and compared other samples collected were inconclusive.

On April 1, 1982, the Miami Valley Regional Crime Laboratory filed the following report. In this report, the analysis of one lock blade knife indicated no visible stains for blood, but the blade did test positive for blood residue. It needs to be noted that this knife was not recovered at 2753 Cozy Lane but at John McGarvey's residence, next door to Keith Wampler's trailer. The other pieces of evidence analyzed in this report were the following: one leather strap, one orange Kawasaki T-shirt belonging to Michael Johnson, one red-and-blue flannel shirt belonging to Michael Johnson, one pair of Wrangler blue jeans belonging to Michael Johnson, one blue denim jacket belonging to Michael Johnson, one pair of brown hiking boots

---

[48]   Miami Valley Regional Crime Lab report, by Larry Dehus, dated 02/08/1982.

and two pairs of tube socks belonging to Michael Johnson, and one pair of cowboy boots belonging to Charles "Keith" Wampler. The report stated there were no bloodstains or traces of blood found on the items of clothing submitted. Also, several samples of vegetation were submitted to analysis. The vegetation was grass near and around 2753 Cozy Lane. Again, the test for bloodstains or traces of blood were negative.[49]

The final crime lab report was filed on June 9, 1982. In this report, Larry Dehus stated he examined the blood and hair samples obtained from Michael Johnson. According to Dehus, the blood samples indicated Michael Johnson has blood type O and he is a secretor. The report continued to identify Michael Johnson's enzyme subgroup. Regarding the hair samples, the report indicated that the samples did not match any samples obtained from 2753 Cozy Lane.[50]

In short, the various crime lab analysis report failed to identify a suspect, nor did they rule anyone out as being a suspect. Many of the reports were inconclusive.

More Field Investigation

With the autopsy of David Rowell complete and the Miami Valley Regional Crime Laboratory working on forensic analysis of the evidence submitted, Detective Mullins began to question other witnesses to this crime. Meanwhile, his prime suspect, Keith Wampler, was already in custody in Warren County. At this point, it appears as if Detective Mullins was trying to make the crime fit the suspect instead of the suspect fitting the crime.

---

[49]   Miami Valley Regional Crime Lab report, by Larry Dehus, dated 04/01/1982.
[50]   Miami Valley Regional Crime Lab report, by Larry Dehus, dated 06/08/1982.

On February 8, 1982, at 4:18 p.m., Detective Mullins and Officer Robert Schmidt interviewed Sharon Gilbert at 2628 Holman Street. Gilbert is Andrew Choate's mother, and the residence is located in Dog Patch. This is also the address where Ted Ritchie and Michael Johnson visited after they left Keith's trailer. Gilbert claimed in October 1981 she saw Keith with a knife when Keith came to her residence looking for Michael Johnson. According to Gilbert, Andrew claimed Keith was trying to sell the knife. Detective Mullins claimed Gilbert provided a written statement to police.

On February 9, 1982, at 12:30 a.m., Sergeant Coffey, Moraine Police, reported receiving information regarding the murder of David Rowell. In his report, Coffey stated Lori and David Johnson dropped their sister and brother, Michael Johnson, off at the Gordon Trailer Park, 2971 Kreitzer Road. According to the report, after Michael Johnson was dropped off, he was seen with Ted Ritchie and David Rowell. The three were reportedly seen walking along Kreitzer Road. The report goes on to speak about a subject, by the name of Keith, and two boys who were seen at a residence (does not make clear what residence). Supposedly, the subjects were drunk, and someone made a sexual advance toward Michael Johnson, who left the residence and went to Andrew Choate's home on Holman Street. Michael Johnson allegedly told his mother that he had been at a scene of a crime and Michael observed a white towel near the body, according to Sergeant Coffey. The report claims Michael Johnson said he saw the same white towel at Keith's residence. The report also stated the two other males at Keith's residence resided at Duke Bangert's former trailer.

It should be stressed that Sergeant Coffey failed to identify who provided him with this information for the report. It is not clear if Sergeant Coffey conducted a formal interview of a witness. No recordings or transcripts of any such formal interview were ever produced by the Moraine Police.

On February 9, 1982, at 9:00 a.m., someone with the Moraine Police interviewed John McGarvey at 2759 Cozy Lane. The purpose of the interview, according to the report, was to gather information on Keith Wampler. McGarvey stated he was friends with Keith, as was his fiancé. McGarvey told the police he never saw Keith with a knife. Also, McGarvey stated he did not believe Keith would hurt anyone.

McGarvey stated his fiancé and he left their trailer at 3:30 p.m. on February 5 and went to Vandalia, Ohio. McGarvey said they did not return home until 2:30 p.m. on February 6. After returning home, the police report stated that McGarvey left again, this time to play racquetball.

Whomever wrote this report claimed McGarvey said he saw Michael and David Rowell at Keith's trailer on several occasions. In one instance, according to the report, Michael used McGarvey's trailer to hide from David. Question, how can such a report be written and included in the case file without the officer being identified? This speaks volumes toward the unprofessionalism of the Moraine Police *and* the Montgomery County Prosecutor's Office that did not catch the omission. The report concluded with, "John could not provide any useful information."

On February 9, 1982, at 9:57 a.m., Detective Mullins stated Sergeant Joseph Wynne and Officer Dennis Adkins interviewed Ted Richie at the Moraine Police Division headquarters. According to Mullins, this interview was taped; however, he did not transcribe the interview for a report. According to Moraine Police, the tape was destroyed in 1997. Question, did they not include any information that did not support their case against Keith Wampler, as required by *Brady v. Maryland* (1963)?

On the same day at 3:00 p.m., Cecil Wampler was informed that his son, Keith, would be charged in the murder of David Rowell. Cecil gave permission for the Moraine Police to conduct another search of his residence, 2753 Cozy Lane. While the officers were searching the trailer, another group of officers went to the Warren County Juvenile Detention facility to arrest Keith Wampler for murder. Keith was transported to Dayton, Ohio, and placed in juvenile detention. Keith would remain in juvenile detention until April 19, 1982, when he would be transported and held at the Montgomery County Jail. On April 19, 1982, it was decided that sixteen-year-old Charles "Keith" Wampler would be tried as an adult.

Chief Glenn Carmichael and Sergeant Joseph Wynne questioned James Combs at 2941 Schoolhouse Lane, on February 9, 1982, at 7:00 p.m. Combs described David Rowell as being a "pest" and told the police that David and he did get into trouble for breaking windows in May 1981. Combs told the police officers Keith was well mannered and nice. Combs believed Keith could not harm anyone. The officers questioned Combs about Keith's sexuality, and Combs stated he did not believe Keith to be a homosexual.[51]

On February 10, 1982, at 10:30 a.m., an unidentified female caller called the Moraine Police Division. The caller stated the Rowell family was involved in Satan worshipping. According to the caller, the mother, Myrtle Rowell, asked the brother, Michael Rowell, if he (Michael) killed David. There is no evidence that Moraine Police investigated this tip. In fact, the Moraine Police never investigated the members of the Rowell family, never searched the house for clues, and only conducted a formal interview of the father *after* the family moved to Mobile, Alabama.

Finally, Detective Mullins interviewed Robert "Bobby" D. Rowell. The interview occurred on February 10, 1982, at 2:29 p.m. and was conducted by telephone. After David Rowell's body was released, Bobby Rowell moved the family back to their hometown, Mobile, Alabama. There is no indication that Detective Mullins

---

[51] Moraine Police Report dated 02/09/1982, (Combs interview), case number 82-184.

questioned any of the Rowell family on February 6, 1982, when David's body was discovered. There is no indication Myrtle Rowell, the mother, was ever interviewed by police.

According to Bobby Rowell, he did not see David Rowell on the afternoon of February 5, 1982, but claimed Myrtle did. Bobby Rowell stated David asked to go to the movie at the civic center and Myrtle told him no. Bobby Rowell said David stormed out of the house at approximately 5:00 p.m. Bobby Rowell told Detective Mullins he began searching for David around 10:30 p.m., claiming he searched, by foot, the area around Moraine Meadows Elementary School, Moraine Civic Center, the vacant field along Kreitzer Road, and the Gem City Estates Trailer Park. Then, according to Bobby Rowell, he got into his van and began to search for David by driving streets in the area. He claimed while he was driving around looking for David, he assisted a stranded motorist along Stroop Road. Bobby said he got home around 1:00 a.m. and began another foot search of the area. Bobby Rowell told Detective Mullins he was unable to find his son, David.[52] That was the only documented formal interview of anyone in the Rowell family.

At 3:00 p.m. on February 10, 1982, Detective Williams Mullins and Sergeant Shaneyfelt, of the Centerville Police, interviewed Lisa Collins at 2754 Quail Lane. According to the report filed by Detective Mullins, Collins said that on February 5, 1982, at 4:45 p.m., David Rowell visited her trailer looking for his brother, Michael. Collins also stated David wanted to know if Roy Elam was looking for him. In his report, Mullins claimed Collins said David went to school that day and got into trouble on the school bus, and the old man on the bus accused David of something, and David responded by saying, "Fuck you, old man."

---

[52] Moraine Police Report dated 02/10/1982, (Rowell interview), case number 82-184.

The report indicates Collins told Mullins that Michael Rowell came to her trailer at 5:30 p.m. on February 5, 1982. Collins claimed Michael Rowell was drunk and she put him to bed. In the report, Mullins wrote Michael Rowell became rowdy and that Mike John called her mother a bitch. Mullins stated Collins told him Michael returned to her trailer a short time later, when *Fantasy Island* was on television, and stayed for a while. Collins told Mullins on February 6, 1982, Michael Rowell came to her trailer at 10:30 a.m. and stayed until 12:30 p.m.

Detective Mullins stated Collins claimed David Rowell had access to drugs, such as Darvon, tranquilizers, Lillys, and valium. In the report, Mullins said in her statement, Collins said that she was close to David and that he would confide in her. Collins allegedly said David desperately wanted a girlfriend. Collins described Myrtle Rowell as a religious fanatic and Robert Rowell as being strict. In the report, Collins told Mullins Keith was weird and he only associated with young boys. She also provided a story about Keith, while in Kettering, was at the house of Brian Lewis. In this story, Keith pulled down the shades and wanted to have some fun.

In this interview, Collins stated Michael Rowell claimed he had to check on Keith Wampler because Keith was hurt. Collins apparently stated to Detective Mullins that Michael Rowell told her Keith grabbed Michael's balls and once burned Michael with a cigarette. Collins described Michael Rowell as a heavy drinker and stated he could drink a half gallon of booze and a twelve-pack of beer.

In this interview, Collins said on February 5, 1982, David Rowell wanted to attend the movie at the Moraine Civic Center, and he was told no by his parents. Collins claimed David came to her trailer. Collins continued by stating that David was supposed to meet Roy Elam, and later that evening, Roy Elam, Darrell Combs, and David Estes came to her trailer looking for David.

According to the police report, Detective Mullins wrote that Collins told him about Michael Rowell, telling her about a drug-and-booze party at the Travel Lodge and that Keith was hurt. Collins told Mullins that Michael Rowell never described how Keith was hurt. Collins claimed Michael went to Keith's trailer and he was gone.

Collins, allegedly, said James Shipman Jr. told her on February 5, 1982, that he wanted to kill something.

Collins, in this statement, changed one aspect of her previous declaration from David Rowell wanting a girlfriend to David having a girlfriend. Collins identified this girlfriend as a seventh-grade student named Tammy, and David may have told Tammy, "This is the last day you will see me. I am going to die."

Also, Collins claimed Michael Rowell, Roy Elam, and Ted Ritchie know more about the crime than what they are telling.

It needs to be noted the integrity of this entire report regarding Lisa Collins's statement to the Moraine Police is questionable at best, a complete fabrication by the police at worst. The questions regarding the integrity of this report will be addressed later in this book.

On February 15, 1982, Charles "Cecil" Wampler ended all cooperation with the investigation. Cecil believed his son, Keith, was being charged with something that Keith Wampler did not commit. Cecil stated towels were stolen from his trailer, and he accused Ted Ritchie of stealing them. It was at this point Cecil advised Keith, who was charged with David Rowell's murder and was facing an indictment, not to cooperate with the police or prosecutors.

In fact, Charles "Keith" Wampler was indicted by a Montgomery County Grand Jury for violating Ohio Revised Code 2903.01 (aggravated murder), Ohio Revised Code 2907.02 (rape), Ohio Revised Code 2905.02 (abduction), and Ohio Revised Code 2927.01 (abuse of a corpse). Pursuant to Ohio law, this indictment was handed down within fourteen days of Keith Wampler being initially charged with murder, which was February 9. Keith Wampler, a sixteen-year-old boy, would be tried in Montgomery County Common Pleas Court.

Almost a month after Keith was charged with and indicted for the murder of David Rowell, Detective Mullins conducted an interview of Michael Johnson. This interview was conducted on March 3, 1982, at 9:00 a.m. and would last until 3:15 p.m. The interview was conducted at the Centerville Police headquarters and included Sergeant Steve Walker, of the Centerville Police, who conducted a polygraph examination of Michael Johnson. Detective Mullins claimed Michael Johnson's mother gave permission for Michael to be interviewed and polygraphed by the police.

According to the report, the polygraph test was administered at 9:34 a.m. The report failed to indicate the results of the polygraph examination. However, this two-page report does indicate Michael Johnson was questioned after the polygraph exam. In the report, Detective Mullins claimed Michael Johnson gave him a verbal statement, which was recorded, and a written statement regarding the events of February 5, 1982. Detective Mullins claimed Michael Johnson told him Keith asked Michael if he wanted to kill David Rowell. According to Detective Mullins, Michael told Keith that he was nuts. The report claimed Keith told Michael Johnson to return later that night and Michael agreed to it.

At 3:15 p.m., Detective Mullins placed Michael Johnson under arrest for the murder of David Rowell. Prior to Keith Wampler's trial in Montgomery County Common Pleas Court, Michael Johnson was tried in Montgomery County Juvenile Court, where the burden of proof is much less rigorous for the prosecution.

On May 7, 1982, at 5:00 p.m., Detective Mullins and Officer Dennis Adkins, Moraine Police, filed another intriguing report. In this report, Detective Mullins documents scratches on Keith's lower arms, hands, and wrists. The report indicates that Officer Adkins noticed these scratches when Keith was processed. Keith was taken into custody on February 6, 1982, and there was no mention of the scratches then. He was taken to Warren County, where there is no report regarding scratches. This book will discuss the accuracy of this report later. Needless to say, the fact that ninety days transpired between the supposed observations of scratches on a suspect and the documentation calls into question many aspects of the case. First of all, the veracity of the observation and the officers comes into question. Second, the professionalism of the review process by the Moraine Police and the Montgomery County Prosecutor's Office, who was directing the investigation. Finally, the defense for not challenging the admission of such "evidence" conveniently remembered ninety days after the fact.

CHAPTER 4

The Trial

The *State of Ohio v. Charles "Keith" Wampler*, case number 82-CR-764, was scheduled to begin in Montgomery County Common Pleas Court in Dayton, Ohio, on July 20, 1982. The trial would last a week. Prior to this trial in Montgomery County Common Pleas Court, Michael Johnson was tried in Montgomery County Juvenile Court, where the burden of proof is much lower for the same crime, the rape and murder of David Rowell. Review of those trial records will require a court order or a waiver from Michael Johnson, who, to date, refuses to cooperate. This chapter is written from, and based on, the trial transcripts.

Judge John W. Kessler was assigned this case. Judge Kessler was one year into his first term as a Common Pleas Court Judge in the general division. Prior to this case, Judge Kessler had fourteen years of experience in practicing law. That experience was on both sides of the aisle, prosecution and defense. Judge Kessler let it be known prior to this trial that he had a vacation scheduled after this trial concluded, and he was not, under any circumstances, going to postpone that vacation.

In 1982, Dennis J. Langer was an assistant Montgomery County prosecutor and was assigned as lead prosecutor in this case. Langer had six years of experience, all in the Montgomery County Prosecutor's Office, under his belt when this case started. Robert Head would be the second chair in the prosecution of Keith Wampler. The year 1982 marked Robert Head's fourth year as assistant Montgomery County prosecutor. Review of records indicate that Head was responsible for preparing most of the witnesses in this prosecution.

Keith Wampler was declared indigent by the court. The Montgomery County Common Pleas Court appointed two attorneys to represent him, both of whom were in private practice. This defense team had a combined thirty-two years of legal experience compared to the prosecution's ten years. The more senior defense attorney on this team was Robert Bostick. Bostick had experience in both state and federal courts. He would be assisted by Wayne P. Stephan, another Dayton attorney, who practiced in both state and federal court.

On the surface, it appeared that Keith Wampler could expect a fair trial. All five attorneys in this case were highly educated and appeared to be ethical, honest, and diligent in carrying out their duties as officers of the court. In this case, appearances and reality are at two opposite ends of the spectrum. Prior to the start of Keith's trial, some activity was taking place that would bring into question the integrity and fairness of this trial. Most notably was Michael Johnson's trial in juvenile court.

The Pretrial

In a pretrial hearing in Judge Kessler's chambers, the prosecution and defense met to discuss the upcoming trial. Based on the transcripts of this hearing, there is no evidence that defense counsel filed any motions. The main focus of this hearing was whether or not Michael Johnson would be called to testify against Keith Wampler.

Dennis Langer, assistant Montgomery County prosecutor, informed Judge Kessler that he was told by Michael Johnson's attorney that if Michael was called, he would exercise his right against self-incrimination under the Fifth Amendment and therefore not testify. Robert Bostick, defense counsel, did push for a decision from the prosecution regarding whether or not they were going to call Michael Johnson. According to Langer, it would be doubtful. Bostick then requested if Michael Johnson is not called to the stand, then there should be no mention of him during the trial. Judge Kessler agreed to that. This ruling would be ignored during the prosecution's closing arguments, where, several times, they mentioned Michael Johnson as participating in this crime. There was not one objection from the defense nor one peep from Judge Kessler concerning the prosecution's violation of this pretrial agreement in closing arguments. This raises questions regarding why Robert Bostick and Wayne Stephan, defense team, did not seek a mistrial when the prosecution mentioned Michael Johnson in closing.

One has to ask if this pretrial agreement was not in place, would the defense team have called Michael Johnson as a witness? Because Michael Johnson was tried and found guilty of this crime by the juvenile court before Keith Wampler, double jeopardy was attached to his case. Therefore, anything he would say could not be viewed as self-incriminating. If the prosecution would not call him, there is no reason why the defense could not call him as a witness. The jury is out as to whether or not the defense team was men of integrity and simply honored the gentlemen's agreement or were totally incompetent. The jury is also out regarding if they had a strategy that included trying to win this case.

As stated earlier, Keith was charged with aggravated murder, rape, abuse of a corpse, and abduction. Langer moved to have the abduction charge dropped because he believed the prosecution could not prove the elements of that specific crime. Without objection from defense, Judge Kessler allowed the indictment to be modified to reflect that the abduction charge was dropped.

On July 20, 1982, one of the most astonishing events that occurred during this case happened during voir dire. In jury trials, voir dire occurs immediately prior to the start of the trial. This is when potential jurors take an oath to tell the truth and to truthfully answer questions asked of them by the attorneys and the judge. In short, voir dire is the selection of the jury.

It was during this phase of the case when a potential female juror was asked, by the prosecution, if she had prior knowledge of this case other than what was reported in local media. This potential juror answered in the affirmative and told the court Detective Mullins and she were patients of the same dentist in Moraine. According to this potential juror, she was at the dentist's office waiting for her appointment when Detective Mullins entered the waiting room. He too had an appointment with the dentist. The potential juror told the court while they were waiting for their appointments, Detective Mullins discussed the case and showed the other patients and the potential juror the crime scene photos. This potential juror was excused, but it should be noted the defense counsel, on July 8, 1982, did seek a change of venue. However, there is no evidence to indicate Robert Bostick or Wayne Stephan renewed their motion for change of venue due to Detective Mullins's activity, which poisoned the jury pool. It is clear the spirit of *Sheppard v. Maxwell* (1966) was ignored in this case.

In *Sheppard v. Maxwell* (1966), the United States Supreme Court, in an eight–one decision, stated the freedom of expression must not be so broad as to divert the court's true purpose: adjudicating criminal and civil matters in a calm, objective, and solemn setting. In *Sheppard*, the court found the pretrial publicity prohibited Dr. Sam Sheppard from receiving a fair trial in Cuyahoga County, Ohio. In the *State of Ohio v. Charles "Keith" Wampler*, not only was there pretrial publicity, but the Moraine Police conducted themselves in an unprofessional manner that did nothing less than poison the jury pool. The fact that a potential juror, who was under oath, stated that Detective William Mullins passed around the crime scene photos in a dentist's office coupled with the pretrial publicity made it practically impossible for Keith Wampler to receive a fair trial in Montgomery County, Ohio. This resulted in Keith Wampler's right regarding a fair trial, afforded to him by the Sixth Amendment of the United States Constitution, being violated.

Opening Arguments

In their opening arguments, the prosecution laid out the theory of the crime they were attempting to prove beyond reasonable doubt. Dennis Langer, assistant Montgomery County prosecutor, told the jury the prosecution believed David Rowell returned to Keith Wampler's trailer, 2753 Cozy Lane, at 5:30 p.m. on February 5, 1982. Langer said the prosecution would prove beyond reasonable doubt that Charles "Keith" Wampler held David Rowell against his will for hours while savagely beating and sexually assaulting him. It needs to be noted that Dennis Langer mentioned that David Rowell was being held against his will, which is the mere definition of abduction. Then, one has to ask, why did the prosecution drop the abduction charge?

David Rowell's small size, compared to Keith Wampler's size, was emphasized by Langer. Langer then said that after hours of torture and perversion, Keith Wampler strangled David Rowell to death. After Keith successfully killed David, Keith mutilated the dead boy's body by amputating his penis. In his opening arguments, Langer said Keith acted alone. Langer said that he would present evidence to support this theory, which conflicts with the prosecution's closing argument *and* the trial in juvenile court in which Michael Johnson was convicted.

In the vast majority of cases, defense counsel uses their opening arguments to show weaknesses in the prosecution's case. Often times, defense attorneys will discuss where the prosecution's case does not make sense. Good defense attorneys will use their opening arguments to plant the seeds of doubt in the jury's mind. Robert Bostick decided to take a different approach. He decided to use this important stage of the trial to lecture the jury about the king's cloak of innocence that every defendant has when they come into court. He went on to say this cloak comes from English Common Law and dates back to Olde England. It was at that point the prosecution objected to the defense's opening argument.

Coroner's Testimony

Dr. Donald Schaffer, chief deputy forensic pathologist for the Montgomery County Coroner's Office, was the first witnessed called for the prosecution. Dr. Schaffer performed the autopsy on David Rowell. Dr. Schaffer was questioned by Dennis Langer. After telling the jury his background and credentials, which included performing between 4,000 and 4,500 autopsies, Dr. Schaffer said he performed the autopsy on David Rowell on Sunday, February 7, 1982, at the Montgomery County Coroner's Office. Dr. Schaffer identified those who assisted him in the autopsy but could not name the officers from the Moraine Police because they came and went while the autopsy was being performed.

Dr. Schaffer described the appearance of David Rowell to be a Caucasian male, approximately thirteen years old, weighing sixty-five pounds and fifty-three and a half inches in length, with fair complexion, and with brown hair. Dr. Schaffer said David's eyes were blue, and examination of the eyes revealed petechial and pinpoint hemorrhages, especially in the right eye. The examination of the mouth revealed some petechial hemorrhage. The examination revealed a postmortem bruise on the bridge of David's nose. He found lividity, pooling of the blood after death, on the back and posterior part of the body, as well as the left side of the face and neck. Lividity was also found on the inner portion of the right leg and the outer portion of the left leg and thigh. Rigor mortis was still present in the body, but not much. Dr. Schaffer described the body as being cold to the touch, but not frozen.

Further examination of the body revealed the genitals were amputated postmortem, or after death, with the area of the amputation as being three and a half inches by three inches, with irregular lacerations. Dr. Schaffer stated a small portion of the scrotum, closest to the anus, was still intact. A plastic bag containing a four-and-a-half-inches-by-two-and-three-fourth-inches circumcised penis and testicles accompanied the body. In his testimony, Dr. Schaffer said no blood was present on either portion at the time of the examination, which indicated that the amputation occurred postmortem, or after death.

In his testimony, Dr. Schaffer described several postmortem scratches on the body, as well as postmortem bruising on the chest and jaw. After discussing several more postmortem scratches he found, Dr. Schaffer testified that there was a predeath bruise on right side of the face. He described it as a lateral bruise along the base line of the jaw. This bruise measured one-eighth of an inch by one-eighth of an inch. After discussing this bruise, Dr. Schaffer continued to tell the jury about other postmortem scratches and bruises about the body. Dr. Schaffer then discussed an area of postmortem pressure on David's left leg, as if something had been laying against him. This pressure indented the skin. He described the bruising on the right leg, toward the groin area. He stated this bruise was prior to death.

According to Dr. Schaffer, David Rowell's toenails and finger-nails were a purplish blue, which is called cyanotic, or peripheral cyanosis. Dr. Schaffer told the jury this occurs in fair-skinned people who at the time of death are in a cold environment. He found postmortem abrasions on both feet. On the front outer region of the right thigh, Dr. Schaffer discovered a bruise that occurred prior to death. Several more postmortem bruises and abrasions on the back and posterior portion of the body were described to the jury, including a pressure bruise on the left index finger and a two-inch by two-inch bruise on the left buttock. These bruises were prior to death. Another postmortem abrasion was discovered on the upper portion of David's left knee, on the back of the knee. Brown stickers, as if they came off of a plant, were discovered on the body. *Stickers* is a vernacular term for achene to a small dry fruit produced by flowers and weeds that can adhere to clothing or on the fur of animals to spread the seeds. *Stickers* is an ambiguous term that is not within the normal lexicon of scientific or medical communities.

Dr. Schaffer described, for the jury, the condition of David's anus. He stated it was open and dilated. He discovered a half-inch perineal tear at the opening and toward the testicles. This tear was prior to death. Superficial perineal tears were discovered in the anus. He further stated these were tear-type lacerations as opposed to cutting-type lacerations.

At that point, Dr. Schaffer was asked to continue his testimony with showing the jury slides that were taken of the autopsy. Dr. Schaffer took his place beside a movie screen and began to explain what each slide was depicting. The slides contained pictures of the bruises, tears, and other things that he discussed on the witness stand. In his discussion of the predeath bruises around the mouth, Dr. Schaffer stated, while pointing to the slide depicting these bruises, that the bruises were consistent with something being placed over the mouth and not someone punching the mouth because if David

Rowell had been punched, the coroner would have found swelling. Dr. Schaffer said he did not find any swelling.

Dr. Schaffer said lividity is a good tool that indicates whether a body had been moved. Lividity begins to set in about a half hour after death and becomes fixed within six hours. Lividity is fixed six to twelve hours, then after twelve hours, the pooled blood would become more fluid, thus lividity would become fluid. The posterior lividity is consistent with the position of the body at the time it was discovered. In Dr. Schaffer's opinion, the posterior lividity occurred shortly after death, indicating when the body was placed in this position. The lividity found on David's body was pinkish in color. Dr. Schaffer said lividity of a person who died in a closed environment, such as a home, would be dark blue—purplish in color, not pink. The pinkish color occurs when the cause of death is carbon monoxide poisoning or when the body is kept in a cold environment.

In the next phase of testimony, Langer showed the jury a slide of David on his stomach. This slide depicted the various scratches found on the body. Dr. Schaffer was asked about how the coroner was able to determine if the scratches were prior to death or postmortem. Dr. Schaffer gave a detailed answer and explained that the presence of blood and the color of the scratch were determining factors. Also in his explanation, Dr. Schaffer discussed the drying effect of blood on scratches.

Dr. Schaffer, using the slides, discussed the postmortem amputation of the penis. The lacerations were caused by a sawing motion instead of a cutting motion. David Rowell was on his back when his penis was amputated because only ten ccs of blood was lost. In his description, Dr. Schaffer said that the genital area has many blood vessels. If the victim were alive, he would have lost more blood. Also according to Dr. Schaffer, if the amputation would have occurred with the victim on his stomach after death, he would have lost more blood due to gravity.

Langer asked Dr. Schaffer to explain the differences in the discoloration of bruises found on the buttock. Dr. Schaffer stated the dark-purplish-blue color bruises are actually lividity and are postmortem. The brighter-reddish-colored bruises are before death. Then Dr. Schaffer discussed the tears found in the anus. In his opinion, the tears were caused by an object from the outside of the body as opposed to something from the inside. Dr. Schaffer emphasized that the tears were superficial, thus could not be caused by a sharp object, such as a knife.

The next part of Dr. Schaffer's testimony dealt with the examination of the head. His first area of discussion was the bruising found in the parietal area (the upper posterior wall) of the scalp. The bruise was caused by some sort of trauma to the area prior to death. Dr. Schaffer believed this trauma caused David to lose consciousness.

The next slide was graphic. It showed David's chest cavity with the organs removed. In this slide, Dr. Schaffer's testimony focused on the neck area, especially the soft tissue region of the neck. Dr. Schaffer pointed out the superficial hemorrhage found in the soft tissue.

The courtroom was shown a slide of the area where David Rowell's body was found, the vacant field along Kreitzer Road. The slide showed the body in the patch of thornbushes with snow underneath the body. Dr. Schaffer said he believed the thornbushes caused the postmortem scratches on the body. At that point, Dr. Schaffer, who was standing beside the movie screen, returned to the witness stand.

Dennis Langer, assistant Montgomery County prosecutor, asked the doctor what caused the death of David Rowell. Dr. Schaffer responded cerebral anoxia, the lack of oxygen circulating and entering the brain, due to acute cardiorespiratory failure due to manual strangulation. He concluded this because of mottled type bruising on the neck, the finding of bruising near the vocal cords and in front of the larynx, as well as presences of petechial hemorrhages in front of the larynx and in the tracheal area. There were bruises on the spine of the hyoid bone, and he described this bone as providing support for the airway. The hyoid bone and the cartilage around it was not fractured, which is not uncommon in over 50 percent of cases where manual strangulation was the cause of death.

Langer then shifted to the presence of alcohol in David's bloodstream. David's blood alcohol level was at 0.02 percent and further stated that the body does not metabolize alcohol after death. Therefore, at the time of death, David Rowell had this amount of alcohol in his system. Dr. Schaffer stated the size of an individual does not matter when metabolizing alcohol, but it does regarding the amount of concentration of alcohol in the bloodstream. Given David's size, if he drank one can of beer, six ounces of wine, or a shot of whiskey one hour prior to his death, the doctor would have expected to see the blood alcohol level close to 0.04 percent. Then Dr. Schaffer explained to the jury the accentuated effect of alcohol. Using the scale of 0.01 percent to 0.09 percent, the further up the scale you go, the more a person would lose inhibitions, feel light-headedness, but not too much in other activities. According to Dr. Schaffer, at 0.1 percent to 0.15 percent, a person can develop a feeling of being able to do more than they really can. At this level, one will lose some critical mental functions, such as thinking rationally. After 0.15 percent, an individual will become sleepy, experience slurred speech and lose the ability to handle themselves, such as being able to walk. Finally, at 0.4 perent, an individual can become comatose or even die. Dr. Schaffer then emphasized this scale discusses adults, not children, and in smaller individuals, such as children, less alcohol would be required to reach the higher concentrations of alcohol in the bloodstream.

The prosecution switched the topic to the amputation of the genitals. Dr. Schaffer stated he had seen cases in which the genitals were amputated, but not in Montgomery County. He saw these cases in Los Angeles County, California, and he continued to say that the Los Angeles County Coroner would receive such cases on a regular basis.

Dr. Schaffer said he estimated the time of death to be around 1:00 a.m., plus or minus two hours, on February 6, 1982. He took into consideration the environmental conditions. In his opinion, he believed the range for the time of death to be between 11:00 p.m. on February 5 to 3:00 a.m. on February 6. The body was in early stages of decomposition, which was caused by the body being rewarmed at the morgue and is common when a body is going from a cold environment to a warm environment. Decomposition is greatly affected by temperature. The body was found on top of recently fallen snow, and it stopped snowing at 10:30 p.m. on February 5.

After showing the doctor the various plastic evidence bags containing the items obtained during the course of the autopsy, Langer asked the doctor about the anal swabs. Dr. Schaffer said when he suspects anal or oral trauma, he will swab the area. He would take multiple swabs of the area and that some of the smears would stay with the coroner for further testing and the others would be sent to the crime lab. The smears, he would keep for the coroner; he would later examine for the presence of sperm. Langer then asked if this was inconsistent with anal rape. In his response, Dr. Schaffer said it was not inconsistent with anal rape. He went on to explain two points. The first point was if one did not ejaculate into the anal cavity, then sperm would not be present. The second point was sperm would not be present if someone superficially ejaculated into the victim, meaning the perpetrator superficially, or shallowly, entered the victim. The sperm would flow out of the victim. He examined, under a microscope, the anal swabs taken from David Rowell's body and did not find evidence of sperm. Dr. Schaffer further testified that any chemical test was supposed to have been performed by the Miami

Valley Regional Crime Lab. Dr. Schaffer further stated he conducted the autopsy on Sunday and the samples were not turned over to the crime lab until sometime early in the week. Dr. Schaffer was not clear when the crime lab picked up the samples but said it was more than twenty-four hours after the autopsy was performed. According to Dr. Schaffer, bacteria formed on the samples; therefore, they could not be tested. This mishandling of evidence, which made the evidence useless, seriously damaged the defense's case. Under the law, defense is permitted to have their experts analyze the evidence, which could assist the defense in raising reasonable doubt about the prosecution's case. The careless handling of this evidence by the Moraine Police, namely Officer Dennis Adkins (the evidence technician), made it impossible for the defense to challenge the evidence. The result was an unfair trial that convicted a sixteen-year-old boy.

The next portion of Dr. Schaffer's testimony dealt with the hair samples he collected from David's body. Langer showed him the various samples, and he testified as to which portion of the body they were extracted. Langer then asked Dr. Schaffer if he found a hair on David's left leg. Dr. Schaffer said that he did remove a long stray hair from David's left leg but could not recall exactly where on the leg the hair was located. Langer suggested the label on the vial would identify the area. At that point, Dr. Schaffer removed the vial from the evidence bag and testified that it came from the calf area. After a brief explanation that once he sealed the bags, Dr. Schaffer marked them and stored them in a locker prior to turning them over to the investigator to take to the crime lab.

Now it was defense attorney Robert Bostick's turn to conduct a cross-examination. Bostick started out by questioning Dr. Schaffer about who was present during the autopsy. Dr. Schaffer confirmed five people were present: Lou Stange, Dave Lett, Jerry Phipps, Doctor Davis, and himself. Dr. Schaffer said he was assisted by Stange, and Lett took the photographs. Dr. Schaffer told Bostick, and the court, he performed the autopsy. Bostick indicated that he wanted to be clear as to who performed what procedure during the autopsy because Dr. Schaffer kept referring to "I" and "we."

Bostick wanted to know if these abrasions and scratches followed any type of pattern. Dr. Schaffer stated the only pattern he could determine was the postmortem scratches were consistent with brush-type markings. Then the doctor discussed the bruises again. Dr. Schaffer repeated his earlier testimony but did not go into detail regarding the bruising about the neck. He repeated the hemorrhages found were not consistent with blows to the neck but were consistent with manual strangulation.

Bostick focused a question about the ankles and indication of any marks or bruising. Dr. Schaffer stated there were no ligature marks on the ankles. The bruising found on the legs were not consistent with ropes or other restraints being used prior to death.

Bostick finished his cross-examination, at which point, Langer, assistant Montgomery County prosecutor, conducted redirect examination. Langer asked about those in attendance at the autopsy and what they wore. Dr. Schaffer provided an answer to that question. Then Langer began to ask about the long hair found on the calf of David's left leg. At that point, Bostick objected because he did not cover that in his cross-examination. Judge Kessler upheld the object, and Dr. Schaffer's testimony was concluded.

Robert "Bobby" Rowell's Testimony

After Dr. Schaffer's lengthy and technical testimony, the prosecution called Robert "Bobby" D. Rowell, David's father, as the next witness. Robert Head, assistant Montgomery County prosecutor, conducted the direct examination of Bobby Rowell. Bobby told the jury he is married to Myrtle Rowell and that he had two other children, Michael and Krista. Bobby Rowell told the jury the family returned to Mobile, Alabama, after David's murder. However, prior to the move, in February 1982, his family and he resided at 2970 Kreitzer Road in Moraine, Ohio. Bobby Rowell said he was the one who found David's body in the vacant field along Kreitzer Road on February 6, 1982.

Bobby Rowell described David as a good boy, though he had behavior problems in school and on the school bus. Bobby Rowell gave the jury an example of David's behavioral problem by telling the story of David being kicked off the school bus in December 1981. Bobby Rowell could not remember the reason David was punished, but he was very displeased with David because he had to take David to and from school during that time because he said he was unemployed and was trying to find work. Bobby Rowell claimed taking David to and from school was disrupting his whole day. On February 5, 1982, David was kicked off the bus again. Bobby Rowell then stated he told David in December that if he got kicked off the bus again, he would be in a lot of trouble and "God help [him]." Also, February 5, 1982, David received his report card, and David was receiving bad grades.

According to Bobby Rowell, he came home on February 5 at 5:00 p.m., and only Myrtle was home. At 6:00 p.m., Michael came home, and David was not with him. Bobby claimed he asked Michael about David's whereabouts, and Michael told him David was at the trailer park at someone's trailer. Bobby said he gave Michael a "talking too" and told him to go find David. Bobby guessed the time to be about 7:00 p.m. In his testimony, Bobby said he went to take a bath and that, sometime between 7:30 p.m. and 8:30 p.m., Michael came home. According to Bobby, David was not with him. At that point, Bobby said Myrtle was out in a car looking for David between 7:30 p.m. and 9:00 p.m.

After 9:00 p.m., Bobby got dressed and began to search, by foot, for David. At first, Bobby Rowell searched the civic center and school yard. He said he was looking for footprints because it was snowing. He said he looked around the barbeque-pit area at the civic center then walked through the vacant field along Kreitzer Road looking for David. He claimed he walked through the field to about forty yards from I-75. At that point, he cut back through the trailer park looking for David. Bobby Rowell said he saw a couple trash bags near a trailer, so he picked them up and shook them. He said he returned home because his feet were getting cold.

His testimony continued by Bobby Rowell claiming that, when he came home, he witnessed Myrtle calling the hospital and a few other people looking for David. After Myrtle made those calls, she called the Moraine Police. It was 11:00 p.m. Bobby Rowell stated it was about that time he told Michael Rowell to go to Lisa Collins's trailer to see if David was there. Bobby Rowell claimed he followed about fifty yards behind Michael. Michael Rowell went to Lisa Collins's to inquire about David, but Collins's stated he was not there.

At that point, Bobby Rowell saw two cars, an old white one and a blue Mustang. Bobby Rowell said he searched those cars looking for David, but when he did not find him, he resumed his search of the vacant field along Kreitzer Road. Bobby Rowell stated he searched the field and then made another search of the civic center area. Bobby Rowell concluded this search at 11:30 p.m.

Bobby Rowell returned home and then again searched the house for David. He searched the basement, the attic, the garage, and the area near the garage. When those searches yielded no results, Bobby Rowell then drove to the Dayton Mall looking for David, again with negative results. Bobby Rowell claimed it was about 1:00 a.m. on February 6 when he started on his way back home, and at that point, he saw a lady stranded along the Stroup Road with a car that was overheating. The lady had come from Dayton International Airport, and Bobby Rowell gave her a lift home. In the conversation he had with the motorist, Bobby Rowell told her he was looking for David.

It was about 1:30 a.m. when he drove around the Plat (a.k.a. Dog Patch), along Holman, Gladstone, and Cadillac streets. Bobby claimed he returned home and made another search of the trailer park.

The next step of Bobby Rowell's testimony was to use a map of the area to show the jury all the places that Bobby had said that he searched. He showed the jury that when he first started looking for David, he exited his house through the backdoor and walked down the driveway to the front of the house. He indicated that he went to the civic center and said he saw people leaving the civic center. He claimed he did not see any children at the civic center, just adults. According to Bobby Rowell, he said he stood there for a while. He showed the jury how he searched the baseball field and the playground near the civic center. According to Bobby Rowell, he searched a dumpster near the civic center. This raises the following questions: Why would Bobby Rowell search a dumpster? Did David Rowell commonly play in the trash? Did Bobby Rowell suspect David dead?

Also, Bobby Rowell said he went to a hilly area where David was known to go to smoke cigarettes. After the search of the exterior of the Moraine Civic Center, Bobby Rowell showed the jury how he walked to the Moraine Meadow Elementary School and how he searched the area around the school. He told the jury that David was picked up once trying to enter the school, but he did not know why David did this. In his testimony, Bobby repeated the night was bright with the freshly fallen snow. He even claimed he saw some little footprints in the snow and followed them to a window at the school but did not see David.

On the map, Bobby Rowell showed the jury the barbeque pit at the civic center and said that he searched that area. Bobby Rowell said he caught David smoking there once. Using the map, Bobby

Rowell showed the jury how he crossed Kreitzer Road and went to the vacant field. He repeated his earlier testimony about searching the field. Bobby Rowell showed the jury the location where he found David's body on February 6 and how he walked past that particular bush during his search for David. Bobby Rowell said the first time was about 10:00 p.m. on February 5. Again, he stated the area was bright from the newly fallen snow. He told the jury that he passed the bush where David's body would be found at 11:30 p.m. According to Bobby, the next time he went to the field was 7:00 a.m. on February 6. Bobby Rowell said he searched the field again and still could not find David. He returned home at 8:45 a.m. and had some coffee. Bobby noticed some people at the civic center, so he drove his van there to discover the center was hosting a flea market. Bobby Rowell said he did not find David. He then drove down Kreitzer Road toward the trailer parks. Bobby claimed he drove through Gem City Estates Trailer Park and Gordon's Trailer Park and found nothing. From the trailer parks, Bobby Rowell drove to Holman Street and Cadillac Street looking for David. His next stop was Frisch's Big Boy at the corner of Central and Springboro. He showed the jury all the places he drove until 9:15 a.m. on February 6. Bobby Rowell said that is when to drove to Huber Heights to visit a friend who owns a television repair shop.

Head asked Bobby Rowell if the family had a dog. Bobby Rowell said the family did own a dog and that he walked that dog in the vacant field along Kreitzer Road at least twice a day.

Bobby Rowell testified that he talked to Myrtle on the phone around noon on February 6. Bobby Rowell said Myrtle told her David was not home and that she was going to Kettering. It was about 1:30 p.m. when Bobby said he returned home. Bobby Rowell told the jury he did not immediately search the field when he arrived home. Bobby Rowell made some coffee and went to the basement and just sat there until he received a vision of bushes. At that point, sometime after

3:00 p.m., according to Bobby, he went to the field and to a patch of bushes that he claimed he never searched. Bobby Rowell claimed he looked for some hole in the field, but as he approached this area, he saw something shiny. Bobby Rowell explained to the jury that things began to flash and "a vision of a doll" came to his mind. That is when he found David's body. Bobby Rowell described towels being everywhere, and he found a shopping bag that contained David's clothing. At that point, he returned home and called the police.

Robert Bostick conducted the cross-examination of Bobby Rowell. Bostick asked Bobby Rowell about David's history of running away. Bobby relayed a story about David running off in the summer of 1981. According to Bobby Rowell, David left the house around midnight and did not return until 9:00 a.m. the next morning. David was in the neighborhood. Then Bobby told of a time when David was about to receive a whipping, and he ran out of the house. In the story, Bobby Rowell said David was found two hours later at a local convenience store.

Bostick continued to question Bobby Rowell about the times David would run off from the house. Bobby claimed David never left the general area when this occurred. Bostick focused on the night of February 5 and asked Bobby why he searched areas outside of the neighborhood in the search for David. Bobby Rowell said David was allowed to take the bus to the Dayton Mall, so that is why he searched that area. Bostick pressed Bobby Rowell about not keeping track of his boys. Bobby told Bostick, and the jury, he kept a good track of David. According to Bobby Rowell, David would either be at the Plat or the trailer park, and he could not go to the mall without permission. Bostick asked Bobby if he whipped David for the times he ran away. Bobby claimed he did not and he did not know what to do with him. He did give David a talk about the dangers of being out at night. Bobby Rowell claimed David's comings and goings worried the family.

Bostick asked Bobby Rowell if he or his family received any threats about family members. Bobby said he did not, but Myrtle told him about a threat. He described the threat that Myrtle told him about, but he did not have firsthand knowledge because he worked at nights when it occurred. Bostick asked Bobby Rowell what actions he took after this conversation with his wife. Bobby said he installed a deadbolt lock on the door because he was concerned for his family's safety. He did not allow the children out after dark. Bostick asked how much time occurred between the threats to the family and the disappearance of David. According to Bobby Rowell, the family received the threats in November 1980, when he was working at the Chevrolet plant in Moraine. The threats continued until he got laid off from the plant. Bobby Rowell claimed someone would call his house and then hang up. Bobby Rowell thought these threats were kids playing pranks.

Michael Rowell's Testimony

Whereas Robert Head questioned Bobby Rowell, Dennis Langer, assistant Montgomery County prosecutor, questioned Michael Patrick Rowell, David's brother. Michael Rowell was the prosecution's next witness. Langer began his questioning by asking Michael Rowell his name and age, which he said he was fifteen years old. Then Michael was asked if he knew Charles "Keith" Wampler. Michael Rowell said he did and then pointed him out to the jury.

In his testimony, Michael Rowell first met Keith Wampler at Andrew Choate's house, located in the Plat (a.k.a. Dog Patch) in 1981, when Keith and James Shipman Jr. came to Choate's residence. Michael Rowell claimed Keith had some long sword with him at the time. Michael Rowell described the sword as being four feet long. Michael Rowell said after that first meeting, Keith and he became friends.

Michael Rowell told the jury he had been to Keith's trailer about eight times, where he would watch television or listen to music. Michael Rowell admitted to drinking at Keith's trailer but claimed he only did it once or twice. Of those eight times he visited Keith's trailer, Michael claimed David came with him four times. Michael Rowell claimed Keith and David did not get along and that Keith did not like David. Michael Rowell accused Keith of calling David a "smart-ass."

Michael Rowell talked about an incident that occurred approximately a week prior to David's murder. In this incident, David, Krista Rowell, Keith Petry, and Michael went to the vacant field along Kreitzer Road to look at some rabbit traps. According to Michael Rowell, they destroyed the traps. Michael then said the day after this incident, David and he were at Keith Wampler's trailer, and Keith had a whip, which he would later describe as being four feet long and made of leather. Michael Rowell claimed Keith was hitting them with the whip and accusing him of messing up John McGarvey's traps. In his testimony, Michael Rowell claimed Keith said John had a shotgun and Keith would use it on anyone he finds messing with the traps. Then Michael Rowell claimed Keith not only had the whip but a pair of nunchaku that he was swinging around with one hand. Michael claimed Keith hit David with the whip, and David started to cry. Michael Rowell told the jury Keith accused David of destroying the traps. According to Michael, that is when David and he left.

Michael Rowell said he arrived at Keith Wampler's trailer around 4:00 p.m. on February 5, 1982, and he was alone. Michael Rowell said Keith was talking about a party that was being planned at John's trailer for Keith's sixteenth birthday. Then Michael said Keith got out some vodka and the two of them began to drink. Michael Rowell claimed he had four or five grapefruit-juice-and-vodka cocktails while at Keith's trailer that day. Michael Rowell said Keith and he started watching television, then they began to wrestle. At 5:20 p.m., according to Michael, David knocked on Keith's door. Keith opened the door, and David entered the trailer. Then David came to Michael, took his glass, smelled it, and took a drink out of it. Michael Rowell claimed he took the glass away from David.

David took a seat, and then Keith and Michael started wrestling. Michael Rowell claimed Keith hit him in the groin. At that point, according to Michael Rowell, he left to go to Lisa Collins's trailer. Michael said Keith chased him out of the trailer and told him not to come back. Michael said that Keith Wampler was wearing pants and boots. Michael Rowell claimed the last time he saw David alive was at Keith's trailer and David was sitting in Keith's living room. Then Michael Rowell told the jury he went home after going to Lisa Collins's trailer and that he arrived at home around 7:00 p.m.

Michael Rowell testified that after arriving back home, he spoke with his father, Bobby Rowell, for about an hour. Then Myrtle Rowell asked him to look for David. Michael said he went to Keith Wampler's trailer between 7:30 p.m. or 8:00 p.m. Michael Rowell knocked on Keith's trailer door, and Keith answered. Michael Rowell claimed only the kitchen lights were on in the trailer. Michael said Keith was wearing a blue silk shirt, blue disco-like pants, and boots. Michael remembered Keith's hair being wet. Michael Rowell claimed he inquired about Keith's hair, and Keith told him that he washed it. Michael asked Keith whether David was there, and Keith said no. Michael said he left Keith's trailer after being there for about two minutes.

After leaving Keith Wampler's trailer, Michael Rowell walked through the vacant field along Kreitzer Road and went to the Moraine Civic Center, where he encountered Lansing McQuinn. He asked McQuinn about David, and McQuinn told him he had not seen David. After he left the civic center, Michael Rowell went to

Moraine Meadows Elementary School. There he claimed he encountered six people, one of them Randall Hendricks, a friend of David. Michael Rowell said all the six stated that they had not seen David. Michael Rowell then testified that Randall Hendricks and he went to the civic center to play in the snow before he returned home around 10:00 p.m.

When Michael Rowell arrived home, his parents asked him about David. He told them he did not find David. That is when Bobby Rowell left the house to look for David. Michael Rowell could not say how long his father was gone before returning home. Michael Rowell was in bed when his father returned, then around 11:00 p.m., Myrtle and Michael went looking for David. According to Michael Rowell, they drove around the Plat, the trailer park, and the Holiday Inn without finding David. Michael Rowell testified that they returned home, only to repeat searching the same areas at 2:00 a.m. on February 6 after again searching these areas. Myrtle and Michael returned home around 2:30 a.m.

Michael Rowell said once he returned home, he went back to bed and slept through the night. He arose around 9:30 a.m., and at 10:00 a.m., he went to Keith Wampler's trailer, where he spoke with Keith's father, Charles "Cecil" Wampler, and noticed blood spots on the front door. Michael Rowell testified that he asked Keith's father about the blood, and Keith's father claimed he was intending to asking Keith about it. Michael Rowell described the blood spots as being a foot from the door knob. Michael said Keith was at James Combs's trailer. Michael Rowell said he left Keith's trailer and walked through the vacant field along Kreitzer Road to go to the civic center, where he met some of his friends, one of whom was Kenneth White. In his testimony, Michael Rowell said that Kenneth White and he went to Lisa Collins's trailer, where they stayed for forty-five minutes.

After leaving Collins's trailer, Michael Rowell said that he went to Doug Perry's house, where he stayed for a few minutes, before returning home. Michael claimed his father, Bobby Rowell, was on the phone with the police when he arrived, and at the time, his sister, Krista Rowell, told him that David was dead. Michael Rowell said that he left the house for the vacant field but was stopped by police officers from entering the field. Michael then went to Keith Wampler's trailer, where he stood on the patio to watch the police recover his brother's body from the vacant field.

Michael Rowell testified that he was on the patio for about one hour before Keith came out of the trailer to inquire about what was going on in the field. Michael Rowell claimed that he told Keith that David was in the field. Michael claimed Keith said, "Man, that's gross." Michael Rowell testified that Kenneth White was with him at the time.

Dennis Langer, assistant Montgomery County prosecutor, inquired about the harassing telephone calls the family received prior to David's murder. Michael Rowell confirmed the harassing telephone calls, but then he stated that they stopped eight months to a year prior to David's death. The threats were against Myrtle Rowell, his mother.

Robert Bostick, a member of the defense team, did the cross-examination of Michael Rowell. Bostick asked where Michael was living, and Michael told him that he was residing with his family in Mobile, Alabama. Then Bostick turned the questioning to the harassing telephone calls. Michael Rowell told the court that the calls happened when he was living in New Carlisle, Ohio. Bostick inquired about Michael's neighbors in New Carlisle, referring to them as "hippies." Michael Rowell said he did not know those neighbors because they kept to themselves. Michael also claimed he never lived beside hippies. Michael Rowell was asked about a time that the neighbors called the police. Michael said the neighbors did call the police and the neighbors gave his mother's name to the police. When quizzed about why was the police called, Michael Rowell claimed that he did not know because his mother did not tell him. Michael said the harassing calls started, and he thought someone was watching his mother. According to Michael Rowell, soon after the calls started, the family moved to Moraine, and that is when the calls stopped. Then Michael Rowell relayed a story about a red car following the family on a trip to Springfield, Ohio.

Bostick reminded Michael Rowell that on a previous occasion, Michael referred to David as being a pest. After further inquiry by Bostick, Michael Rowell said David was a pest for fighting over the television and aggravating him. Then Bostick asked Michael about returning to Keith's trailer on February 5. Michael Rowell said it was about 7:00 p.m. Bostick pointed out that Michael did not tell anyone about returning to Keith's trailer. Michael claimed he forgot and he remembered while he was talking to the police. Bostick reminded Michael Rowell that he first told the police that he did not return to Keith's trailer. In continuing to inquire about Michael's statement to the Moraine Police, Bostick reminded Michael that he told the police he went to Lisa Collins's trailer twice but did not return to Keith's trailer. According to the court transcript, Michael Rowell began shaking his head and then answered he does not remember giving those statements to the police. Then Bostick began to question Michael's honesty.

Bostick reminded Michael Rowell that he characterized Keith Wampler as being nice when Michael was questioned by the police. With further questioning, Bostick got Michael to admit that he thought Keith Wampler was nice and Keith minded his own business. Then Michael Rowell began to state he did not remember what he told the police about Keith.

Bostick began to inquire about Michael Rowell's relationship with David. Michael described David as being hyperactive and that David hung around Michael all the time. Bostick wanted to know if this bothered Michael, and Michael Rowell's response was, "I didn't care." Michael said David went with him to Keith's trailer three or four times.

Bostick asked Michael Rowell if he wrestled with his other friends like he told the court he wrestled with Keith. Michael said he did. In his questioning, Bostick wanted to know about Michael's statement regarding Keith striking him in the groin. Michael Rowell admitted he told the police Keith struck him in the kidneys because he claimed he was embarrassed to admit that Keith struck him in the groin.

"Are you telling us now, Michael, that when you originally told the police officers that you positively did not go back to Keith's trailer, that you were not telling the truth?" asked Bostick. Michael Rowell replied by stating he did not remember. After some prodding by Bostick, Michael Rowell maintained he did not remember and did not know if he told the police the truth. Bostick reminded Michael that he remembered everything else with clarity, but he could not remember if his statement to the police was the truth. Bostick then went point by point discussing all the details that Michael Rowell gave the court regarding the events surrounding David's murder, yet Michael still couldn't remember what he told the police regarding the wrestling match.

Bostick asked Michael Rowell if his parents got upset when David did not come home when he was told to come home. Michael confirmed it did upset his parents. Bostick pointed out to Michael that his father, Bobby Rowell, on February 5, made the statement that David was always doing this, and Michael confirmed that his father said that. Bostick then mentioned the time during the summer of 1981 when David stayed out all night.[53] Michael Rowell claimed David was only gone for an hour during that incident. Then Michael

---

[53]   In Robert "Bobby" Rowell's testimony, he told the court about a time when David stayed out all night.

changed his statement to indicate he did not know if David stayed out all night or not.

Dennis Langer, assistant Montgomery County prosecutor, conducted the redirect examination with questioning Michael Rowell about his statement regarding Keith being nice. Langer said Michael told the police that Keith Wampler was nice, but sometimes he was in a bad mood. Michael Rowell said that was what he told the police. Michael was asked to describe Keith's bad mood, and Michael Rowell responded that when Keith was in a bad mood, he liked to push people around. Langer reminded Michael Rowell that Michael told the police Keith's father, Charles "Cecil" Wampler, was not strict with him. Michael was asked to explain his observation, and Michael Rowell said it was because Keith's father allowed him to drink and smoke.

Robert Bostick, defense attorney, was allowed to re-cross-examine Michael Rowell. Bostick began to question Michael's recollection of changing his story in the interview that Michael had with the police. Bostick told Michael Rowell that he was readily agreeing with the prosecution, and Michael agreed that he was. Bostick then read from the transcript of the interview between Michael Rowell and the Moraine Police. According to the transcript, Michael told Detective Mullins that he cannot remember if he returned to Keith Wampler's trailer. At that point, according to the transcript, Sergeant Wynne suggested they take a break in the interview. Michael Rowell told Bostick, and the jury, he remembered this encounter. Bostick reminded Michael Rowell the interview, which was recorded, occurred on February 8, 1982. Bostick then stated that the interview began around 10:30 a.m. on February 8 and the break occurred at around 11:15 a.m. Bostick indicated since the tape was stopped, Michael Rowell was permitted to talk to his parents and get something to eat. The interview restarted at 4:09 p.m. Michael indicated he remembered that.

James Shipman Jr.'s Testimony

After the bailiff swore in James Shipman Jr., Robert Head, assistant Montgomery County prosecutor, began the direct examination. Head asked some preliminary questions, such as where James Jr. is living and where he did live, plus his age. James Jr. told the court that he was living in Piqua, Ohio, but prior to that, he lived in Gem City Estates Trailer Park in Moraine and was living in Moraine in February 1982. James Jr. said he was sixteen years old.

James Shipman Jr. told the court Keith Wampler was one of his neighbors, and he saw Keith at 5:30 p.m. on February 5. Keith was running home and was not wearing a shirt. James Jr. claimed he asked Keith what he was doing, but Keith did not respond. Keith kept going to his trailer.

James Jr. said he knew David Rowell. David was on James Jr.'s front porch when James saw Keith. According to James Jr., David bummed a cigarette and said that he was going to get drunk that night. David then left, and he saw him walking toward Cozy Lane but did not know what direction he went because James Jr. went into his trailer. Joey, James Jr.'s seven-year-old brother, was present.

Later that evening, James Jr. and Joey went to Judy Tabor's trailer at the Gordon Trailer Park. He saw Darrell Doan, Michael Johnson, Ted Ritchie, and Judy Tabor there. James Shipman Jr. described Darrell and Judy as being in their twenties. He drank a couple of beers while there and then followed everyone else to Darrell Doan's trailer. James Jr. admitted to drinking more beer at Darrell's trailer but denied smoking any marijuana. In his testimony, James Jr. said that Joey did not smoke or drink. According to James Jr., Michael Johnson, Joey, and he left Darrell's trailer to go to the Moraine Civic Center to watch the movie, but they only stayed for a few minutes and then returned to Darrell's trailer. James Jr. thought it was about

8:30 p.m. Upon arriving at Darrell's trailer, James Jr. drank another beer.

It was while James Jr. was drinking a beer that Michael Johnson suggested going to Keith's trailer. James Shipman Jr. said that after he finished his beer, Mike Johnson, Ted Ritchie, Joey, and he walked to Keith Wampler's trailer. They arrived at Keith's at around 9:00 p.m. According to James Jr., Keith was the only one at the trailer when his group arrived. James Jr. said Michael Johnson, Ted Ritchie, Keith, and he were all drinking beer. James Jr. cut his hand on a beer can while at Keith's trailer, as a result of tearing it apart. James Jr. described the cut as not being bad, but he was bleeding.

James Shipman Jr. described getting drowsy and sleepy after he cut his hand, so he went to lay down in Keith's bedroom. He had been to Keith's trailer before and knew that his room was the first room on the left down the hallway. While he was laying down, some of the other people in the party were standing in the doorway to the bedroom talking. According to James Jr., he laid down for about twenty minutes and then got up because it was getting late and he believed his parents might be looking for Joey and him. James Jr. and Joey left Keith's trailer at 11:00 p.m. to go home, and upon arriving at home, he received a telephone call from Ellen Purvis, a friend of his mother. After talking to Mrs. Purvis, Joey and he went to bed. It needs to be noted that according to Detective Mullins, James Jr. told the police that he heard a scream while at Keith's trailer. However, in his trial testimony, he does not mention anything about hearing a scream.

James Shipman Jr. admitted he first told Detective Mullins that Joey and he watched the entire movie, which was *Benji*, at the Moraine Civic Center on February 5, but he later changed his story. He lied to the police because he did not want his parents to learn about his drinking that night.

James Jr. said he had seen Keith with knives. Head showed James Shipman Jr. a knife, and James Jr. identified it as being the knife Keith had. James Jr. said Keith had the knife for a month or two.

Wayne Stephan, a member of the defense team, conducted the cross-examination of James Shipman Jr. After a few preliminary questions about James Jr.'s age and his relationship with his brother, Stephan began to ask about James Jr.'s parents and what they were doing on February 5, 1982. James Shipman Jr. said his parents managed two SOHIO gas stations, one in Sydney, Ohio, and the other in Piqua, Ohio, and normally worked days. They were usually home between 6:30 p.m. and 7:00 p.m. every night. However, when his parents were not home by 7:30 p.m., James Jr. decided to go to Judy Tabor's trailer. He did not know where his parents were that night because nobody called.

Then Stephan discussed the events of around 5:30 p.m. on February 5. James Shipman Jr. repeated he saw Keith returning home. He noticed this while talking to David Rowell, who was bumming a cigarette from him. James Jr. was standing in his doorway when he was talking to David.

The next focus of the cross-examination was the topic of the conversation between James Jr. and David. James Shipman Jr. confirmed that David said he was going to get drunk that night. Then Stephan asked about other topics the two boys discussed. James Jr. said David admitted to being banned from the bus again. According the James Jr., David was worried about being in trouble with his father regarding being banned from the bus. When asked about David's parents, James Jr. claimed he knew nothing about them and never met them.

Stephan inquired about the statements James Jr. made to Detective Mullins regarding the activities at Judy Tabor's and Darrell Doan's trailers. Stephan reminded James Shipman Jr. that he testified earlier that everyone was drinking beer, but he told the police that some people were smoking marijuana. James Jr. responded by saying that he did not know if anyone was smoking marijuana and he was only drinking beer. James Jr. claimed he cannot remember what he told Detective Mullins on February 6.

The rest of the cross-examination dealt with rehashing some of the same information that James Shipman Jr. already provided to the court. The interesting exchange was regarding the bedroom of Keith Wampler's father, Charles "Cecil" Wampler. Stephan asked if the door was open. James Jr. could not remember, but it may have been. Another point that came out of the cross-examination is James Jr. told the court he used his injured hand to open the door to leave Keith's trailer. James Jr. said it was the hand he cut when he ripped apart a beer can. After a few more questions, Stephan was finished cross-examining James Shipman Jr. He was excused from the stand.

Joey Shipman's Testimony

The prosecution then called Joey Shipman to the stand. Joey is James Shipman Jr.'s seven-year-old brother. Robert Head, assistant Montgomery County prosecutor, conducted the direct examination of Joey Shipman.

Head asked Joey about the last time he saw David Rowell. Joey said he saw David at 2:30 p.m. on February 5, 1982, when David bummed a cigarette from his brother, James Jr. Joey claimed David told James that he was going to Keith's trailer to get drunk. Joey said he saw David go to Keith Wampler's trailer. Joey was inside his trailer when this happened. Head, who was leading Joey through this testimony, asked if he saw this through a window. and Joey said yes.

Joey testified James Shipman Jr. and he did go to the Moraine Civic Center to watch *Benji*, but they did not stay for the entire movie. Joey claimed James Jr. and he went directly to Keith Wampler's trailer after they left the Moraine Civic Center. Joey then stated he remembered meeting Michael Johnson and someone named Ted, and they all went to Keith's trailer together. Head then asked what happened when Keith answered the door. Bostick objected because Head asked the question in a leading manner, in which Judge Kessler sustained the objection. Head rephrased the question about what occurred when Joey arrived at Keith's trailer. Joey said Keith thought the police were knocking at the door. Michael Johnson, Ted Ritchie, James Shipman Jr., and he entered the trailer, where they sat and watched television. James Jr. cut his hand while drinking beer and needed to lay down on Keith's bed. Joey said he noticed the door to the other bedroom was open about two inches. After James Jr. laid down for a while, the two boys left Keith's trailer and went home. Joey said that they both went to bed upon arriving at home.

Wayne Stephan did the cross-examination. Stephan started off by asking if Joey went to school that day. Joey said he did and that he attended first-grade classes at Moraine Meadows Elementary School. On February 5, 1982, at 2:30 p.m., he was released for the day, and he walked home. Joey repeated the story about David bumming a cigarette from James Jr. Joey was inside the trailer while James was on the front porch talking to David. Then Stephan asked if Joey saw David Rowell on February 5, and Joey said he did, but this time he said he saw David at 2:00 p.m. Joey would see David around the trailer court a couple of times per week. At that point, no further questions were asked, and Joey was dismissed from the witness stand.

There are a couple issues regarding Joey Shipman's testimony. One of those issues will be addressed later, but one needs to be addressed at this point. Joey Shipman said he saw David Rowell at 2:00 p.m., but then stated, in cross-examination, that he was not released from Moraine Meadows Elementary School until 2:30 p.m. The explanation could be that a seven-year-old boy has a limited grasp of time. However, it does not explain why the defense team did not exploit this testimony in order to raise reasonable doubt. Joey Shipman's testimony is three hours off the time that he actually saw David Rowell, which was closer to 5:30 p.m. A good defense attorney would have used this discrepancy in order to raise reasonable doubt.

Ted Ritchie's Testimony

The next witness was Ted Ritchie. Robert Head, assistant Montgomery County prosecutor, conducted the direct examination of Ted. Ted opened his testimony by telling the court in February 1982, he was living in Moraine, Ohio, but actually he resided in Orlando, Florida. Ted came to Moraine in January 1982 to attend the funeral of his brother. He was not living with his family at the time and was staying with some family friends in Orlando. Ted's family resided in Gordon's Trailer Park in February 1982. Ted did not know David Rowell but did remember the day that David's body was discovered in the vacant field along Kreitzer Road.

Ted knew Judy Tabor, and on February 5, he was at Tabor's trailer a few times. He said the first time was around 8:00 p.m., when three others were in the trailer. Those three were Alice Johnson, Michael Johnson, and Judy. Everyone was drinking beer and smoking marijuana. Soon, James Shipman Jr. and his brother, Joey, arrived. After a while, everyone walked to Darrell Doan's trailer, where they drank more beer. Michael Johnson, James Shipman Jr., Joey Shipman, and he went to Keith Wampler's trailer, but they stopped at Judy's trailer to tell Alice Johnson where they were going. The four boys arrived at Keith's trailer around 9:00 p.m. on February 5. They listened to the stereo and watched television. Keith offered the teens some beer. Michael Johnson asked Keith if he had any liquor or marijuana. Ted said Keith replied about having a fifth of vodka and claimed he heard

Keith tell Michael that David and he had a drink from it. Ted was interviewed by the police on February 6. February 5 was the first time he met Keith Wampler.

Head, in a leading manner, asked Ted about overhearing Michael and Keith talking about roughing up someone. At that point, Wayne Stephan, defense counsel, objected, citing hearsay. Judge Kessler overruled the objection but told Head to refrain from asking his questions in a leading manner. Judge Kessler then let the question stand. Ted told the court Michael Johnson and Keith were sitting at the far end of the sofa when Michael called Keith a queer. Ted overheard Keith and Michael talking about roughing someone up for one hundred dollars regarding something to do with pit bull dogs, but Ted only listened to portions of the conversation.

Ted Ritchie remembered James Shipman Jr. cutting his hand. He did not remember what James Jr. did after cutting his hand but did remember that James Jr. and Joey left Keith's trailer around 10:45 p.m. Ted and Michael Johnson stayed at Keith's for about fifteen minutes after the Shipman brothers left. Then Michael and he left Keith's trailer and walked to Andrew Choate's house. Ted identified the beer that he was drinking at Keith's trailer as being Old Milwaukee Light.

Michael Johnson and he walked through the vacant field along Kreitzer Road, then crossed Kreitzer Road near the Moraine Civic Center, and walked between the civic center and the school to go to Andrew Choate's house, which is located in Dog Patch. This was the first time he met Andrew, who was about fourteen years old. Michael Johnson and he stayed at Andrew's house for about one hour. After that, Michael and he returned to Judy Tabor's trailer, where Judy told him that his mother was looking for him.

The remaining direct examination dealt with Ted's activity during the rest of the night. Ted stated that his mother and he went to Frisch's Big Boy to get something to eat and did some shopping at 7-Eleven before returning home around 1:15 a.m. When he got home, he went to Judy Tabor's trailer, where he saw Michael Johnson sleeping on the floor. He was at Tabor's for about fifteen minutes before returning home. Ted said his mother went to bed at 2:00 a.m. on February 6, and that is when he left her residence and returned to Judy's trailer, where he stayed until 3:30 a.m. At that time, Darrell Doan, Michael Johnson, and he went to Darrell's trailer, where Michael would spend the rest of the night. Ted went home.

Robert Bostick handled the cross-examination of Ted Ritchie. Bostick inquired about Ted's activities during the two months in early 1982 that Ted resided in Moraine. Ted said that he did not attend school or work. Ted stated he hung around his mother's trailer.

Ted repeated his claim that February 5 was the only time he met Keith Wampler. Bostick pushed Ted to find out how much beer Ted consumed prior to arriving at Keith's trailer. Ted said he had three beers. Ted said Michael Johnson went to Keith's to look for more alcohol and some marijuana.

Bostick then read Ted's statement to the Moraine Police, where Ted stated Michael Johnson and he were walking around the trailer park because all the beer was gone and they were bored. In his statement to the police, Ted said Michael Johnson suggested going to Keith Wampler's trailer. Bostick asked if it would be fair to state Keith did not know that Michael or he would be visiting. Ted stated that would be a fair statement. Bostick pushed further, again reading from the police report, by reminding Ted that he told the police Keith was expecting his father home any minute. Ted stated Keith thought Michael and Ted were his father when they knocked on his door.

Ted knew Michael Johnson for only a month and the Shipman brothers for about three weeks. Ted hung out with Michael and James from time to time. Ted repeated the time that James and Joey left Keith's trailer as being around 10:45 p.m. Ted also repeated Michael

Johnson and he left Keith's trailer at 11:00 p.m. because the news was coming on television.

Judy Tabor's Testimony

The next witness for the prosecution was Judy Tabor. Her direct testimony was handled by Robert Head, assistant Montgomery County prosecutor. Judy confirmed she resided 2971 Kreitzer Road in Moraine, Ohio, which is the address of Gordon Trailer Park. She lived in a trailer inside the trailer park.

Judy told the jury that Michael Johnson is her cousin. Michael Johnson was at her trailer on the evening of February 5, 1982, and it was around 9:00 p.m. when he arrived with Ted Ritchie. Michael Johnson, Alice Johnson, Ted Ritchie, and she were at the trailer at 9:00 p.m. Judy denied anyone had beer at her trailer and could not remember if anyone smoked marijuana. At some point, Michael Johnson and Ted Ritchie left her trailer. She did not know where they went after leaving her trailer. They did not return to her trailer until around midnight, at which point Ted Ritchie went home after Judy told him his mother was looking for him.

Judy discussed how Ted Ritchie left her trailer then about an hour later he returned and stayed for a short time. Ted came to her trailer for a third time, and it was around 3:00 a.m. on February 6. Darrell Doan, Michael Johnson, Alice Johnson, and Michelle, Judy's daughter, were there when Ted Ritchie returned.

That was the extent of Judy Tabor's direct examination by Robert Head. Now it was defense counsel's turn to cross-examine the witness, which was conducted by Wayne Stephan.

Judy confirmed for the court that she was a twenty-four-year-old single mother with a four-year-old daughter, named Michelle, living with her at the time. Also, she had a boyfriend who lived with her most of the time. She described her relationship with Darrell Doan as being a good friend. Stephan repeated Judy's claim that nobody drank beer at her trailer on the night of February 5, and she stated that was true but could not disagree when confronted with Ted Ritchie's testimony about having a beer at her trailer. Judy admitted she was smoking marijuana that evening but claimed Michael Johnson and Ted Ritchie did not. Stephan pointed out that Ted Ritchie testified he smoked a joint at Judy's trailer, at which Judy disagreed.

Judy said Michael Johnson would come to her trailer and spend the weekend because he was bored at his new home in New Carrollton, Ohio. Michael Johnson was fourteen years old, and sometimes he would come and stay at her trailer, and other times he would go with his friends.

Adrian West's Testimony

Adrian West resided at 2765 Cozy Lane, which was two trailers from Keith Wampler's trailer. John McGarvey's trailer sat between West's and Wampler's. West was a prosecution witness, and Robert Head, assistant Montgomery County prosecutor, conducted the direct examination. Head asked some preliminary questions, such as the distance between West's trailer and Wampler's trailer. West estimated it was about sixty feet. West claimed he could see Keith's trailer from his kitchen window or the side window of his trailer. West confirmed he resided in the Gem City Estates Trailer Park in February 1982.

West was home all day and all night on February 5, 1982. He was unemployed at the time and claimed he spent most of his days sleeping and most of his nights sitting up watching television. Before 11:00 p.m. on February 5, West saw two boys leave Keith's trailer, and they were boys that lived in a trailer across the street.

He was sitting in his trailer, in the kitchen, with the lights off until 2:00 a.m. on February 6. He could still see lights on at Keith's trailer, and the lights went off at 1:30 a.m. on February 6. He first noticed the kitchen light was on for a while. He then noticed the lights going on and off in the trailer, as if someone was walking from the kitchen to the back bedroom. This happened shortly after the two boys left the trailer. West testified that the back bedroom light was on until 1:30 a.m.

At 11:00 p.m. on February 6, West saw Charles "Cecil" Wampler and John McGarvey at McGarvey's trailer. The two men then went to Keith Wampler's trailer, and McGarvey had something under his coat when McGarvey returned to his trailer. Head ended the direct examination of Adrian West.

Robert Bostick, defense counsel, handled cross-examination. Bostick took West back to February 1982 and asked West how he spent most of his time. West said he watched the neighbors' trailers. Bostick inquired if West was part of any neighborhood watch group, and West said he was not.

Bostick then inquired how West watched television, with the light on or off. West stated most of the time he watched his television with the lights off. Bostick asked West about his relationship with the neighbors, namely John McGarvey. West did not get along with the neighbors since "they tried to give [him] a hard way to go." Then Bostick turned West's attention to Keith Wampler. West did not have any issues with Keith. Bostick asked West about an incident where John McGarvey's fiancé backed into some bricks and West caused ruckus over it. West confirmed he had a heated encounter with John McGarvey and his fiancé, Gail, over the bricks. Bostick reminded West about threatening McGarvey's fiancé; at that point, West denied threatening her. According to West, he was only trying to scare her. Bostick asked West if he is feuding with McGarvey. West confirmed some hard feelings still existed. Bostick stated he is discussing this incident because it was Keith who had words with West about threatening McGarvey's fiancé. West denied it ever happened.

Bostick wanted to know how many times West spoke with the police regarding this case. West said February was the only time he spoke with Moraine Police regarding this case. West met with the prosecutors and the detectives on Sunday prior to his testimony. West admitted never mentioning his problems with the McGarveys to the police or prosecutor prior to his testimony.

Head was allowed to redirect. He asked West if he could tell the court if he saw a light from a television in Keith's back bedroom. At that point, Bostick objected, and Judge Kessler overruled. Judge Kessler told Bostick that he can deal with it on recross. West claimed he did not see any light from a television in the back bedroom of Keith's trailer.

In recross, Bostick asked West if anyone could see the lights of his television set if they looked into his trailer. West said they could not directly see the television, but they could see the light of it. West was then asked if he could see the television set in Keith's trailer. West said he could not. Bostick asked how West could tell if the television was turned on or off if he could not see it. West stated he was in his trailer and could tell if Keith had the television on or off because he was at an angle when he looked at Keith's trailer. Bostick pointed out that the McGarvey trailer was between West's trailer and Keith's trailer, therefore it was impossible for West to see any light from a television. Robert Head was allowed to ask another question to West. Head wanted to know if West could see all of Keith's trailer. West claimed that he could not see the back of the trailer.

Officer John G. Brun's Testimony

The next witness for the prosecution was Officer John G. Brun of the Moraine Police Division. Officer Brun was one of the first police officers responding to the vacant field along Kreitzer Road on February 6, 1982. Dennis Langer, assistant Montgomery County prosecutor, conducted the direct examination of this witness.

Officer Brun was dispatched to a field in the 2900 block of Kreitzer Road in Moraine at 3:50 p.m. on February 6, 1982, and was the first officer on the scene. He saw Robert "Bobby" Rowell standing along the road waiting for someone to arrive. The field was adjacent to the Gem City Estates Trailer Park. Officer Brun said Bobby Rowell showed him to David's body, which was laying in the field. Officer Brun secured the immediate area around the body and contacted the dispatcher to advise communications of the situation. Another officer arrived simultaneously to his arrival, and that officer assisted in securing the area. Additional officers arrived within two minutes. Officer Brun was on the scene for forty-five minutes before another officer, who was stationed in the trailer park, pointed out a set of footprints in the snow going from a trailer to the body.

Cross-examination was conducted by Wayne Stephan. The crux of the cross-examination was where were all the police officers who responded to the call. Stephan wanted to know which officer first located the footprints that ran between Keith's trailer and the body. Officer Brun identified Officer Robert Schmidt as first noticing the footprints. Also Stephan inquired about who got close to the body. According to Officer Brun, Officer Adkins, who was a Moraine Police evidence technician, and the coroner's investigator were the only people who got close to David Rowell's body. That concluded Officer Brun's testimony, and he was excused.

Officer Dennis J. Adkins's Testimony

The prosecution presented Officer Dennis J. Adkins, Moraine Police Division, as their next witness. Officer Adkins was the evidence technician who processed the crime scene in this investigation. Dennis Langer conducted the direct examination for the prosecution. Adkins opened his testimony by telling the jury he had been a police officer for nine years and an evidence technician for three and a half years. Adkins received his evidence technician training at the Miami Valley Regional Crime Laboratory in Dayton, Ohio. Adkins estimated in his three and a half years as an evidence technician, he handled seven or eight homicides and other types of death investigations for the city of Moraine.

Officer Adkins arrived at the 2900 block of Kreitzer Road at 3:58 p.m. on February 6, 1982. He was assisting with the investigation of a body that was found in the vacant field along Kreitzer Road. He was responsible for conducting various searches in this investigation. Officer Adkins showed the jury the field where he conducted a search for evidence after David Rowell's body was discovered. The next search was at 3:25 p.m. on February 7, 1982, and it was at Keith Wampler's trailer, 2753 Cozy Lane. The third search, conducted by Officer Adkins, was at 3:50 p.m. on February 8, 1982, and again, it was at Keith's trailer. The fourth search he conducted in this case was on February 12, 1982, at 3:45 p.m. and it was of the field where David's body was discovered on February 6. Finally, another search of Keith's trailer was conducted on February 13, 1982, at 7:00 p.m. It needs to be noted that Officer Adkins testified about five separate searches. With the exception of the short period of time in which the field was secured while the police and coroner's office were recovering David Rowell's body, none of the places searched were ever secured by the police or treated as a crime scene.

Langer took Officer Adkins back to the first search of the field, which occurred on February 6. Upon arriving at the 2900 block of Kreitzer Road, Officer Brun briefed Adkins on the situation. Several other Moraine Police Officers were used to secure the field so it would not be disturbed by the public. Officer Adkins claimed he processed the field for evidence. Langer then presented Officer Adkins crime scene drawings as evidence. In one of the drawings presented to the court, Langer asked Adkins about a set of footprints shown in a photograph that was attached to the drawing. Officer Adkins claimed, under oath, the footprints came from 2753 Cozy Lane and back. The footprints were broken due to the presents of high cornstalks and weeds that were in the field. Officer Adkins was shown several more photographs of the footprints, and he told the court that they came from the patio at 2753 Cozy Lane.

Langer showed Adkins several more photographs of footprints. Adkins testified they were taken on February 6, and they were shoe prints. Several more photographs of the footprints were presented to the jury. Each photograph was from a different angle. Langer asked Adkins if he could estimate the size of the shoe that made the print. Adkins said it was very difficult to estimate the shoe size, but Langer pressed the question. Adkins believed the shoe size was a 10 or 11 and were made by a shoe with slick soles.

On February 6, Adkins noticed bags of trash and a shovel on the patio of 2753 Cozy Lane and the field was used by local residents to dump trash. For example, he found an old barbeque grill in the field near 2753 Cozy Lane. Langer focused a couple questions on the barbeque grill. Adkins said he believed the grill was in the field for a while due to the fact it had rust on it.

The next line of questioning dealt with the shopping bags recovered in the investigation. Adkins told the jury he placed the bags into evidence bags then secured the evidence bags in the property room locker at Moraine Police Headquarters. Adkins was the only one with the key to the locker. Adkins was responsible for taking the evidence to the Miami Valley Regional Crime Laboratory on February 8, 1982. The Miami Valley Regional Crime Laboratory used ninhydrin to look for fingerprints on the shopping bags. The tests revealed no identifiable fingerprints on the bags.

Langer asked about the towels Adkins recovered from the area around the body. Adkins identified one of the towels as being recovered from under David's body. The towel had reddish spots on it, and he then explained the holes in the towel came from the crime lab cutting out sections in order to test for blood. Adkins was shown two other towels, and he identified them as being found about twenty-two feet away from the victim in an easterly direction toward 2753 Cozy Lane.

State's Exhibit Number 18 was the next focus of discussion. This exhibit was an evidence bag containing beer cans that were recovered from the field near David's body. Adkins walked to a diagram to show the jury where he found these beer cans. No fingerprints were recovered from the beer cans. The cans were Old Milwaukee Light Beer cans. In the course of the investigation, fourteen Old Milwaukee Light Beer cans were recovered, some empty and some full.

State's Exhibit Number 20 and State's Exhibit 21 were next. State's exhibit 20 was the shopping bag containing David's penis and was recovered from David Rowell's head when his body was discovered on February 6. The shopping bag had Super Rite Grocery Store markings. The crime lab failed to obtain any fingerprints from the bag. Langer turned Adkins's attention to State's Exhibit 21, which were Imperial Food Town and Super Rite Grocery Store shopping bags recovered from Keith's trailer. Langer presented another bag, which Adkins said he obtained from Springboro IGA. Adkins did not recover any Springboro IGA or Super Rite Grocery Store bags from Keith's trailer.

Now the focus was on the Imperial Food Town shopping bag that contained David's clothing and the Moraine Parks and Recreation Card in the name of David Rowell. Langer presented it as State's Exhibit 24. This bag was found approximately twenty feet from David's body. Langer held up State's Exhibit 25, which Adkins identified as an Imperial Food Town shopping bag he recovered from Keith's trailer. Adkins recovered this bag on February 7, 1982.

Adkins was shown another Old Milwaukee Light Beer can, and this one had reddish stains on it. Adkins stated he recovered that can from Keith's trash on February 7, along with a pair of Keith's blue jeans that were in the hamper at 2753 Cozy Lane. The blue jeans had a reddish stain on them.

Now the questions were about the bedding and other items seized at Keith's trailer. Adkins identified each item for the jury and stated there was a small reddish-brown stain on one of the curtains in Keith's room. All these items were submitted to the Miami Valley Regional Crime Laboratory for analysis.

After a brief discussion about an orange ashtray found in Keith's trailer, which contained cigarette butts and a possible residue from a marijuana joint, the questions centered around some bloodstains found on the end table in the living room. Adkins stated the stains were small and recent because they were on top of dust that was already on the table. He found these blood spots on February 9. Larry Dehus, a chemist with the Miami Valley Regional Crime Laboratory, collected the stains. On February 7, Adkins found a red leather strap on the floor between the couch and the wall in Keith's trailer. Adkins collected the less-than-a-quarter-of-an-inch suspected bloodstains found on the storm door of Keith's trailer and sent those to the Miami Valley Regional Crime Laboratory for analysis.

The next several questions involved the collection of various hair and blood samples, both from evidence and as comparison. Adkins identified which sample was evidence and which sample came from someone to be used for comparisons. Blood samples and saliva samples were taken from Charles "Keith" Wampler, Charles "Cecil" Wampler, Robert Rowell, Ted Ritchie, Michael Johnson, Michael Rowell, James Shipman Jr., and Joey Shipman.

Langer shifted gears in his questioning and asked about Adkins's first encounter with Keith Wampler. Adkins first saw Keith on February 6 when the police were recovering David's body from the field. Adkins said Keith was standing on his patio with some people. The next time he saw Keith was on February 7 at 5:00 a.m. Adkins examined Keith's genitals and claimed he noticed scratches on his hands. In his testimony, Adkins claimed Detective William Mullins asked Keith about the scratches, and Keith stated he did not know anything about them. It needs to be noted that Officer Adkins and Detective Mullins claim Keith Wampler had scratches, yet there is no documentation of these scratches dated on or around February 7. The first report documenting the scratches was written in May 1982. Ohio Revised Code, Section 2151.313, does permit such documentation and further allows juveniles charged with adult felonies to be photographed without a court order.

Langer then inquired about when Adkins seized and examined Keith's boots. Adkins seized the boots on February 7 and took them to Moraine Police Headquarters, where he, not the Miami Valley Regional Crime Laboratory, examined them. He found a piece of grass in a crease on the boot. Adkins was then shown envelopes of grass samples that he said he collected from the vacant field along Kreitzer Road where David's body was discovered.

Now the focus switched to a knife. Sergeant Joseph Wynne and Adkins took the knife from John McGarvey on March 9, 1982. Adkins seized a green toilet seat lid from the field and that the lid was fifty-nine feet north of where David's body was discovered. The toilet seat lid was found on February 12, 1982. The purpose of the February 12 search of the field was to find a knife. Adkins did not see the toilet seat lid on February 6 because it was getting dark and he was getting cold. In his questioning of Adkins, Langer was able to establish that the toilet seat lid was missing from the toilet because Adkins said he did not see the toilet seat lid on February 7, when he conducted a search of Keith's trailer. Then Dennis Langer, assistant Montgomery County prosecutor, admitted the colors of the toilet seat lid and the toilet were off, and he blamed that on the film the police used to photograph these items.

Wayne Stephan, defense counsel, handled cross-examination. In his first question, Stephan asked Adkins when was the first time he entered Keith's trailer. Adkins said it was 3:25 a.m. on February 7, 1982, and he was accompanied by Detective William Mullins, Sergeant Wynne, and Officer Hanks. Adkins admitted Cecil Wampler was not home when the officers entered his residence. Cecil was at police headquarters. Adkins did not know who had the key to the trailer. Adkins described this search as a consent search. Adkins then provided a description of the trailer as being clean, but it appeared that the trailer was not vacuumed that day. It needs to be noted that the prosecution did not enter a signed consent form into evidence that indicated Charles "Cecil" Wampler ever allowed the police to search his residence. It also needs to be emphasized that the Wampler trailer was never secured as a crime scene.

Stephan wanted to know if Adkins, or the other officers, conducted any tests to determine if cleaning agents were used. They did not. Stephan pressed Adkins on collecting the bed linens from Cecil's room and Keith's room. The linens were described as not being freshly laundered. Adkins gave detail of how extensive the officers and he searched Keith's trailer. The officers searched every inch of the trailer. Stephan turned Adkins's attention to the diagram that Adkins made on February 13 of the trailer, the field, and various items. Stephan pointed out that Adkins documented the presence of a white Opal vehicle and wanted to know the significance of this car. Adkins did not answer.

Stephan asked Adkins to describe what was in the field. The field had cornstalks, thornbushes, rabbit traps, garden area, and discarded cans. Adkins admitted that is where he saw the grill. Stephan reminded Adkins that on direct examination, he stated the grill was rusty. Stephan wanted to know if there were any other items near the grill. There was a discarded tricycle, plastic dishpan, and rubbish. Stephan wanted to know what role the grill played in this case. Adkins stated it was because Keith brought the grill up during questioning.

Cross-examination then turned to the February 12, 1982, search of the vacant field along Kreitzer Road that was conducted by the United States Army. The search team consisted of four army personnel and one police officer, and that is when the toilet seat lid was discovered. Stephan asked Adkins if the Moraine Police or any other law enforcement agency secured the field between February 6 and February 12. The field was not secure, and anyone could have access to it during that time. Wayne Stephan began on the right track in questioning the evidence from the field and getting Adkins to admit the field was never secured. It needs to be known that prior to the trial, there is no evidence that Wayne Stephan or Robert Bostick ever filed a motion to suppress the evidence recovered from the field on February 12, 1982.

Stephan questioned Adkins about the drawing that depicted the footprints. Adkins said there were footprints from the trailer to the body and from the body to the bag containing the clothes. However, there were no footprints from the bag to the trailer. Adkins did not take photographs of the footprints or any measurements. There were no signs of footprints from the trailer to the toilet seat lid or from the body to the toilet seat lid. When asked how the toilet seat lid was found, Adkins said Detective Mullins and he found the lid.

Stephan pursued the footprints. Adkins claimed that the prints lead from the trailer to the body but then, after being pushed by Stephan, admitted that the footprints could have continued past the body because it was hard to tell due to the terrain. Also there were two sets of footprints, a smaller print inside a larger print. Adkins could not tell what kind of shoe or boot made the footprints. Adkins did not see any other footprints in the field. Again, when pressed, Adkins said there were other footprints along the path and in the yard area of the trailer park. According to Adkins, some of those footprints went into the field. When asked if Adkins took any impressions of Robert "Bobby" Rowell's shoes for comparison, Adkins said he did not. According to Adkins, getting an impression of Bobby Rowell's shoes were not important because it was determined he was not around Keith's trailer. It needs to be noted that common police procedure would be to obtain an impression of Bobby Rowell's shoes because he was the person who found the body. The impression would be used as evidence or to eliminate Bobby Rowell as a suspect.

The next series of questions dealt with whether or not the photographs taken by Adkins were accurate depiction of the various pieces of evidence he seized or obtained. Adkins answered in the affirmative for each photograph. When the photographs got to the one depicting the shopping bag found under David's body, Stephan inquired about Adkins's expertise in fingerprint science. Adkins said he was trained in lifting prints, but not analyzing them. Adkins admitted the Federal Bureau of Investigation (FBI) had more sophisticated equipment in lifting fingerprints from the shopping bag than the Miami Valley Regional Crime Laboratory. Adkins never used the FBI or saw a need to use them in this case. It was common knowledge that the FBI would conduct further testing of evidence in order to obtain fingerprints, but he felt it was not necessary in this case. Stephan asked about the results of the fingerprint analysis on the evidence submitted to the Miami Valley Regional Crime Laboratory.

The crime lab reported no useable prints were discovered on any of the evidence. Again, Stephan asked if Adkins submitted any evidence to the FBI for further analysis. Adkins did not.

Stephan next discussed the Red White & Blue Beer can that was found in the field. Adkins stated it came from Darrell Doan's trailer and all the other beer cans were Old Milwaukee Light. As for the Red White & Blue Beer can, according to Adkins, it was used by one of the individuals who was at Keith's trailer. Adkins said he interviewed Darrell Doan and believes the can was used by either James Shipman Jr. or Ted Ritchie.

The grocery stores were the next topic of questions because of the shopping bags. Adkins admitted that there were seven Imperial Food Town stores in the area and he knew where the Springboro IGA was located. Imperial Food Town was a popular grocery store in the area, and many people shopped there.

The analysis of the Moraine Parks and Recreation identity card in the name of David Rowell was the next subject. Adkins analyzed this card, and it was not submitted to the Miami Valley Regional Crime Laboratory or the FBI for analysis.

The rest of the cross-examination dealt with the samples of hair and saliva that Adkins collected in this investigation. Adkins confirmed he did collect the samples and identified from whom they came. With only a few questions in redirect and recross completed, and those questions dealt with clarification on minor points of his testimony, Officer Adkins was dismissed from the witness stand.

What is astonishing about the defense's handling of Officer Dennis Akins is that they did not attack the evidence. The defense team did not file any motions to suppress. A motion to suppress would have been appropriate regarding the toilet seat lid, which was found six days after the David Rowell's body was discovered in the field and after the field was released by the police. There was not one attempt to make the prosecution prove they had consent to conduct some of these searches. Nor did the defense team attack the probable cause that supported the search warrants that the police did obtain. On top of that, Officer Adkins testified that more sophisticated evidence examination techniques were available, yet the Moraine Police did not use them. A below-average law student at a third-rate law school who stayed awake during the rules of evidence class would have attacked this evidence, thus creating reasonable doubt. Yet the self-proclaimed "best attorneys in Dayton" did not.

Detective William Mullins's Testimony

On July 24, 1982, the prosecution called Detective William Mullins to the witness stand. Mullins told the court he was a Detective with the Moraine Police Division. Robert Head, assistant Montgomery County prosecutor, conducted the direct examination of Detective Mullins.

Mullins arrived at the vacant field along Kreitzer Road at 4:15 p.m. on February 6, 1982. He was summoned to the field due to the discovery of a body. Mullins got within ten feet of the body before he stopped. Mullins could not tell the cause of death from his observations, but he did notice a set of footprints from the body to a trailer, which later was identified as Keith's trailer.

Mullins later went to the trailer, where he encountered Keith Wampler, Cecil Wampler, Michael Rowell, and some man with a young daughter. He had a brief conversation with Keith inside the trailer then later in his police car. Keith told the story about Michael and David Rowell coming to his trailer on February 5 and how Michael suddenly left and he (Keith) left the trailer to find out why Michael was leaving. Keith told Mullins the last time he saw David Rowell was when he was returning to his trailer and David was at the Shipmans' trailer. Keith showed him where the Shipmans lived.

According to Mullins, after Keith showed him where the Shipmans lived, he told Mullins about Michael Johnson, Ted Ritchie, and the Shipman brothers coming to his trailer looking for alcohol and drugs. Keith told Mullins it was sometime during the evening on February 5. Keith asked the detective not to say anything about the information he provided to the police. Keith did provide a written statement about those events.

Mullins gave various officers their assignments, and he interviewed John McGarvey. McGarvey told Mullins he was not home during the evening of February 5 and was with his fiancé in Vandalia, Ohio. Mullins then stated that Cecil Wampler was in Waynesville, Ohio, during the same time.

Mullins went to the Shipman trailer, and from that trailer, he could see the front of the Wampler trailer, which was on the east side. Then Mullins stated he sat in Adrian West's trailer and could see a portion of Keith's trailer.

The next time Mullins encountered Keith Wampler was at 11:00 p.m. on February 5, when he took him down to the police station. Mullins took Keith to the station for further questioning. Mullins claimed he stopped the interview after forty-five minutes to speak with Sergeant Joseph Wynne in the hallway because they decided Keith was their suspect. Upon returning to the interview, Mullins claimed he advised Keith of the *Miranda* warning. At that point, Mullins contended he contacted Cecil Wampler and asked him to come to police headquarters. Mullins read from a waiver of rights form that he claimed Keith and Cecil signed. Mullins claimed Keith agreed to be interviewed.

The interview lasted from 11:30 p.m. on February 6 to 1:30 a.m. on February 7, when Keith requested an attorney. Mullins claimed he stopped the interview. Mullins prepared a warrant for Keith's arrest. He also prepared a search warrant for Keith's trailer. The search warrant was authorized at 4:00 a.m. on February 7. This was the first time Mullins searched Keith's trailer. Mullins confirmed everything that Adkins stated to the court. Mullins also admitted he was in the courtroom for the entire trial, up to this point.

The next thing Mullins claimed he did in the case was go to the Montgomery County Coroner's Office to observe the autopsy, which occurred at 9:00 a.m. on February 7. The next several questions asked by Head dealt with the initial findings in the autopsy. This was when Mullins learned the cause of death was manual strangulation.

When asked about his 5:00 a.m. on February 7 encounter with Keith, Mullins claimed he noticed scratches on Keith's arms and hands. For the court, Mullins described the scratches as having just broke the skin. Mullins did not photograph the scratches because of law against photographing juveniles without a warrant from the juvenile court. Mullins photographed the scratches on February 9, and the scratches appeared to be different because the scratches appeared to be healing.

Wayne Stephan handled the cross-examination of Detective William Mullins. Stephan started his questioning by bringing up the towels found near the body. Mullins could not recall if he mentioned the towels to Keith during the interview at police headquarters. Stephan then read from the transcript of the recorded interview between Mullins and Keith, in which Mullins asked Keith about the towels and Keith said he thought they came from someplace in Kettering. Then Mullins remembered discussing the towels after he advised Keith of his rights.

Stephan pointed out to Mullins that Mullins spoke to Keith about a knife when the tape recorder was turned off. Mullins confirmed that but explained that he was trying to turn the recorder on so he could capture what Keith was saying. Then Stephan asked Mullins if Keith was considered a suspect or a witness. Mullins considered Keith a witness. Stephan wanted to know why he had Keith remove his boots if the police considered him a witness. Mullins made the claim that he collected the boots when Keith became a suspect.

Stephan changed subjects and asked Mullins about his first encounter with Keith, which was on the afternoon of February 6. After a brief back-and-forth on why Keith did not want anyone to know about the statement he gave the police, Stephan asked Mullins if Michael Rowell, David's brother, was at Keith's trailer. Michael Rowell was at Keith's trailer, and he did not appear to be upset. Michael Rowell knew the police were recovering his brother's body, and Michael was not at home with the rest of the Rowell family. Mullins was alone when he first encountered Keith at Keith's trailer.

In his cross-examination, Stephan was able to get Mullins to admit that Mullins considered Keith a suspect in a matter of fifteen minutes during a break in the interview at Moraine Police Headquarters, and the break occurred approximately forty-five minutes into the interview.

Mullins was then asked about the footprints in the snow. After some back-and-forth about the procedures in securing the footprints, Mullins admitted that Adkins told him it appeared that two different shoes made the prints. Mullins said this was in reference to the footprints that lead from 2753 Cozy Lane to David's body. Stephan asked if the prints were made from two different shoes, and Mullins avoided answering the question, then Robert Head objected, claiming hearsay. Judge Kessler sustained the objection.

Mullins was then asked about what occurred at the police station on February 6 at 11:42 p.m. Mullins claimed he advised Keith of the *Miranda* warning, but this was not done in the presence of Keith's father. Mullins admitted that he kept Cecil Wampler, Keith's father, away from Keith during the interview. Mullins then admitted that at 1:31 a.m. on February 7, Keith requested an attorney. Keith was held at the interview from 1:31 a.m. to 4:00 a.m., and he was not allowed to leave. Then Mullins lectured Stephan about the interview occurring in a conference room, not an interview room, and Mullins began to tell the court the difference. At that point, the testimony of Detective Mullins was concluded.

However, it should be noted that Stephan did not pursue any line of questioning regarding Cecil Wampler, Keith's father, not being permitted into the interview room. Nor did the defense team ask Detective Mullins about the primary crime scene or the place the actual murder occurred. Also, Stephan did not ask Detective Mullins about the various sets of footprints in the field on February 6, 1982, and if the police could account for each set of footprints. Finally, Stephan needed to ask why Detective Mullins did not take an imprint of Bobby Rowell's shoes. After all, Detective Mullins was the lead detective in this investigation.

James Combs's Testimony

The prosecution, then, called James Combs to the stand. The direct examination was conducted by Robert Head, assistant Montgomery County prosecutor. Combs was in the eighth grade and lived in the Gem City Estates Trailer Park. He was good friends with Keith Wampler and had known him for about a year.

Head asked about the evening of February 5. Combs was grocery shopping with his mother and was not allowed out because he was grounded by his parents. Combs he saw Keith sometime during midday on February 6, when Keith came to his trailer. Keith stayed for about five or ten minutes. Combs to attend a family function, so he could not talk long with Keith. He returned home around 6:00 p.m. on February 6 to find police in the area. Combs went to Keith's trailer to learn about what was happening. Combs claimed Keith told him that someone strangled David Rowell. Combs then told the court he did not mention this to the police when he was interviewed.

Head switched the subject to Combs's knowledge of Keith's footwear. Combs saw Keith wearing a pair of cowboy boots on February 6, which Keith obtained in December 1981. According to Combs, Keith's other shoes were a pair of gym shoes.

Cross-examination was handled by Wayne Stephan, a member of the defense team. Stephan wanted to know when Combs first told the authorities about what Keith said. Combs said the first time he told the authorities was when Robert Head told him about it at the prosecutor's office and that this occurred two weeks prior to his testimony. Then Stephan wanted to know if Combs talked to anyone about what Keith said prior to meeting with the prosecutor. Combs said that he told nobody, not even his mother, about what Keith might have said. Stephan asked Combs if he talked to anyone about it, even after the news coverage said David was strangled. Combs maintained he told nobody until he met with Robert Head at the Montgomery County Prosecutor's Office. That concluded James Combs's testimony, and he was excused.

Larry Dehus's Testimony

Larry Dehus, forensic scientist at the Miami Valley Regional Crime Laboratory, was the prosecution's next witness. Dennis Langer, assistant Montgomery County prosecutor, conducted the direct examination.

Langer asked Dehus about a tissue found in Keith's trailer. Dehus told the court the tissue contained semen and that the examination of the tissue and study of the semen determined the person who produced the semen was a nonsecretor; therefore, the person who produced this semen did not secrete their blood type through the semen. According to Dehus, only 20 percent of the population are nonsecretors, meaning that they do not secret their blood type through other body fluids.

Dehus discussed the various samples he tested and identified the blood type and if the person was a secretor or nonsecretor. Dehus said Ted Richie was type O secretor, Michael Johnson was type O secretor, James Shipman Jr. was type A secretor, Charles "Cecil" Wampler was type O secretor, Michael Rowell was type O secretor, and Charles "Keith" Wampler was type A nonsecretor.

Dehus was asked about the sheets and blankets that were seized from Cecil Wampler's bedroom. The sheets contained blood and semen stains. The semen stain came from a type A secretor, but he could not tell about the blood type due to the small quantity, but he could tell it was human blood.

At that point, Wayne Stephan requested to approach the bench. Stephan pointed out that the prosecution put a chart of blood types on the wall. Stephan expressed concern that the jury was looking at the chart while the witness is testifying and felt that the chart being displayed was inappropriate. Judge Kessler overruled the objection.

Dehus was asked about bloodstains on the curtains seized from Keith's trailer. The stains were small amounts of blood and could not be tested. Dehus was not present when the bloodstains were removed from the storm door in Keith's trailer. Those stains were human blood, but there were not enough to test for type of blood. Langer then showed Dehus a knife. Dehus tested the knife and found microscopic bloodstains but could not determine if it was animal or human blood.

Dehus's attention was drawn to the chart that the prosecution displayed in the courtroom and the defense objected to a few moments earlier. Dehus stated one column contained the various blood types and the other columns dealt with enzyme grouping. Then Langer showed Dehus various vials of blood, and Dehus identified the individual from whom the blood samples were obtained. Langer presented a torn beer can, and Dehus stated the can had bloodstains, which he examined. He only typed the bloodstains and found them to be type A. Dehus stated he did not conduct any further tests due to the fact David's blood type was O and he believed further testing would be irrelevant.

Dehus was shown some clothing taken from 2753 Cozy Lane. He found bloodstains on the clothing, and the blood was type A. He was then shown various blood specimen tubes that contained blood collected from various individuals in this investigation. One tube contained the blood of Robert "Bobby" Rowell, which he typed as O. Dehus discussed not only the blood type of each tube but the enzyme breakdown of the blood. One tube that was shown to Dehus was a tube of blood taken from David Rowell, which he identified as blood type O. In his testimony, Dehus said the blood of Ted Ritchie and the blood of David Rowell were not distinguishable.

Dehus told the court that the bloodstains recovered from the toilet seat lid were blood type O, as were the bloodstains found on the living room table at 2753 Cozy Lane. The bloodstains found on the towels were also blood type O, but he could not conduct any enzyme testing due to the small amount. Dehus was shown a pink-and-white towel that had bloodstains. The blood type of the stains on this towel was O. Langer showed Dehus the bag that contained David's penis when he was discovered. The bloodstains on the bag were identified as being type O.

Langer turned the jury's attention to the boots that were recovered. Dehus said the boots contained samples of grass and that the grass was similar to the grass found in the vacant field along Kreitzer Road, as well as the yard near 2753 Cozy Lane.

Dehus was shown various hair samples, and he subsequently identified the person who provided each sample. Each sample was read into record for the court. Then Dehus told the court how he compared the hair recovered from David's calf to each sample. He only did a microscopic analysis, and no chemical analysis was done. The hair was similar in microscopic characteristics to Keith's hair and was not forcibly extracted. It appeared to have naturally fallen from the owner's body. Then Langer turned Dehus's attention to hairs recovered from the towels. In his testimony, Dehus said the hairs from the towels had similar characteristics to Cecil Wampler's hair.

Langer questioned Dehus about the analysis of fibers found on David's boots and clothing. Dehus stated the fibers were similar to the fibers found on a blanket that was seized by the Moraine Police. The fibers could have come from that blanket or one similar to it.

Wayne Stephan, defense counsel, conducted the cross-examination of Larry Dehus. Stephan asked about the hair recovered from David's calf and Keith's hair. Dehus could not say for sure that the hair recovered from David's calf came from Keith because he only conducted a microscopic analysis and he did not conduct any chemical analysis, such as atomic absorption or neutron activation analysis. The Miami Valley Regional Crime Laboratory was capable of conducting atomic absorption analysis, but not neutron activation. Both tests do provide the tester with the same information. Dehus repeated he did not conduct any chemical analysis of the hair. Dehus did not document when each test was conducted, so Dehus was not sure what date he did the tests for this case. Stephan asked about the blanket that was seized. Dehus found nothing of significance on the blanket. Fibers do fall off the blanket if you hold it up and shake it. Dehus then admitted the fibers found on David's clothing that matched the blanket could have been picked up anytime when David was in Keith's trailer, but he did not have any firsthand knowledge of it. That concluded Dehus's testimony.

Again, Wayne Stephan dropped the ball during cross-examination of Larry Dehus. When Dehus said that he did not conduct any chemical analysis of the hair found on David Rowell's body, Stephan should have asked why. This fact could have planted the seeds of reasonable doubt in the mind of the jury by painting a picture that every piece of evidence was not properly analyzed. Apparently, Wayne Stephan and Robert Bostick did not realize that their job was to raise reasonable doubt in the prosecution's case.

The prosecution rested its case at this point. The testimony discussed was the significant testimony in this case. It took the Montgomery County Prosecutor over a week to present their case to the jury. Now it was the defense's turn. Wayne Stephan and Robert Bostick only called a handful of witnesses. The two key witnesses were John McGarvey and Charles "Keith" Wampler.

John McGarvey's Testimony

John McGarvey was called to the stand, and his direct examination was handled by Robert Bostick, defense attorney. McGarvey was Keith Wampler's next-door neighbor, and he met Keith in the summer of 1981. McGarvey was trying to clear out some of the thorn-bushes in the field, and Keith simply came out and began to help him. McGarvey pretty much kept to himself but did socialize with Cecil and Keith Wampler. McGarvey told the court that if there was any work needed done around his trailer, Keith would lend a hand and help. McGarvey attended law enforcement courses at Sinclair Community College and criminal justice courses at the University of Dayton. McGarvey identified Robert Langer, assistant Montgomery County prosecutor, as one of his instructors.

McGarvey knew Michael and David Rowell because they socialized with Keith. Michael Rowell sometimes came to his trailer looking for Keith. McGarvey told a story of when David Rowell came to his trailer looking for Michael Rowell. According to McGarvey, Keith and Michael Rowell were there, and when Michael found out it was David looking for him, Michael went and hid in McGarvey's bathroom. McGarvey said Michael asked him to tell David that Michael (he) was not there.

The knife the prosecution presented at the trial as being part of this case was actually McGarvey's. The last time he saw the knife was when he gave it to Sergeant Joseph Wynne. McGarvey claimed Sergeant Wynne tried to weasel the knife from him. McGarvey kept the knife in a secret place in his trailer and that even his fiancé did not know where the knife was kept. McGarvey hid his knives and guns because his parents were robbed and the robbers took his parents' hunting knives and guns. McGarvey said Sergeant Wynne asked him if Keith Wampler knew where the knife was kept, and McGarvey stated he told the police Keith did not.

McGarvey said he talked to Dennis Langer, assistant Montgomery County prosecutor, about this case. McGarvey was upset with the Moraine Police and the Montgomery County Prosecutor for taking his knife because it had nothing to do with this case. According to McGarvey, Sergeant Wynne promised to return the knife within two or three days after McGarvey gave it to him. McGarvey was furious when he learned that the knife was being used at this trial. He needed the knife for hunting and fishing. McGarvey used to trap rabbits when he lived at the Gem City Estates Trailer Park. Keith would help him set up the rabbit traps and check the traps. McGarvey asked the Rowell brothers about who was messing with his traps. According to McGarvey, nobody threatened the Rowells. He only wanted to know who was damaging his traps. McGarvey told Michael and David Rowell that if they continued to mess with his traps, he would have to call the police. At that point, according to McGarvey, the Rowell brothers admitted to messing with his traps.

McGarvey saw Keith on February 5. According to McGarvey, Cecil Wampler, Keith's father, was getting some supplies for a birthday party that McGarvey's fiancé was hosting for Keith. It was Keith Wampler's sixteenth birthday, and McGarvey's fiancé wanted to throw a nice party for him. McGarvey described how Keith was excited about getting his driver's license and how he studied the driving manual. On February 5, Keith Wampler was excited because Cecil would be taking Keith to the Wright-Patterson Air Force store to get supplies for the party. McGarvey knew Keith was waiting for his father to get home so they could go to the base. McGarvey saw Keith while he was loading up his truck to go to Vandalia. McGarvey told the jury his fiancé and he would go to her parents in Vandalia on Fridays or Saturdays to do laundry. McGarvey said Keith came out of his trailer and gave his fiancé something to drink. McGarvey had some wood in his truck because he was building shelves and Keith got a splinter in his hand from the wood. According to McGarvey, Keith removed the splinter and started to bleed. McGarvey saw Keith rub his hands on his jeans. McGarvey stated his fiancé and he were planning on doing their laundry and then coming home that night. However, their plans changed once they arrived in Vandalia, and they spent the night with his fiancé's parents. McGarvey said it was about 6:00 p.m. on February 5 when he last saw Keith that day.

If McGarvey was home on a Friday or Saturday night, then usually Keith Wampler would come over to hang out, according to McGarvey. This was especially true if Cecil, Keith's father, was spending the night with relatives in Waynesville. McGarvey stated that Keith did not go with his father and it was because McGarvey and his fiancé were going to be home and they were talking about going snowmobiling.

McGarvey and his fiancé did not return home until noon on February 6. Upon arrival, they got into an argument, and he left to play racquetball. When he returned, the police were in the field. According to McGarvey, Keith was running around trying to find things out to report back to McGarvey. Keith told him that some kid was found in the field.

McGarvey testified that he went to the movies accompanied by Keith Wampler, McGarvey's brother, and his fiancé, McGarvey's fiancé. After the movie, everyone returned to McGarvey's trailer to celebrate Keith's birthday. According to McGarvey, everyone was sitting around eating cake and talking but not much celebrating because of what occurred that day, when McGarvey noticed two men in suits approaching Keith's trailer. At that time, Keith and McGarvey approached the men, who identified themselves as police officers. The police asked Keith Wampler to identify some pictures, and Keith agreed, so Keith went back into McGarvey's trailer to get some cigarettes and tell his father. The police did not talk to Cecil, Keith's father.

It was 2:30 a.m. on February 7 when he received a telephone call. It was Keith, and he was calling from the police station. Keith wanted a lawyer because the police were trying to pin the murder on him.

Bostick asked McGarvey one more question, and it dealt with if he went to Keith's trailer on February 6. McGarvey went to Keith's trailer to get a bottle of vodka that Cecil bought for McGarvey's fiancé.

Dennis Langer, assistant Montgomery County prosecutor, handled the cross-examination of John McGarvey. Langer asked if McGarvey knew any of Keith Wampler's friends ever came to Keith's trailer. McGarvey said that Michael Johnson and the two Rowell brothers would visit Keith from time to time, as well as three girls.

McGarvey told Langer that he took Keith under his wing and showed him how to do things. McGarvey gave Keith advice on who to hang out with and who not. McGarvey said that he appreciated all the help Keith would give him and how he missed having Keith around because he is behind in his chores. McGarvey told the court that he never gave Keith Wampler a key to his trailer.

McGarvey repeated his earlier testimony that it was about 6:00 p.m. on February 5 when his fiancé and he left for Vandalia and that was the last time he saw Keith Wampler on February 5. Langer told McGarvey that McGarvey told the police that his fiancé and he left for Vandalia around 3:15 p.m., not 6:00 p.m. McGarvey denied saying that to the police. Langer read from Sergeant Joseph Wynne's report about McGarvey telling Wynne that McGarvey only waved at Keith. McGarvey said Sergeant Wynne is lying and he never said such a thing to the police.

McGarvey testified that she saw Michael Rowell in Keith Wampler's trailer on February 5, when he went to Keith's trailer to tell Keith that his fiancé and he were going to Vandalia. According to McGarvey, Michael Rowell was sitting on the couch. McGarvey further testified that is when Keith fixed his fiancé a drink and brought it to the truck.

Langer's cross-examination continued. His attempts to get McGarvey to change his story failed. McGarvey said he did not know the Rowell brothers that well, only by sight. He repeated his earlier testimony of how Keith Wampler would help him around the trailer. Langer then discussed the time Keith and McGarvey confronted the Rowell brothers over the traps. McGarvey stated that Keith was trying to find out who damaged the traps, but Keith was not threatening.

Langer's continued cross-examination did not yield any new information regarding the case. Stephan conducted redirect, which cleared up some minor points. Then John McGarvey was excused from the stand.

Charles "Keith" Wampler's Testimony

Now the defendant in this case, Charles "Keith" Wampler, was called to the stand by his attorney, Robert Bostick. Though not required by law to testify, Keith was called to present his side. Bostick did not spend much time on preliminary questions. He went right to the heart of the matter.

Keith Wampler testified that he did not have anything to do with the murder of David Rowell. When David went missing, nobody contacted him regarding his knowledge of David's whereabouts. According to Keith, the last time he saw David Rowell was at 5:30 p.m. on February 5, 1982, when David was talking to James Shipman Jr. on the front porch of the Shipman trailer, which was located across Cozy Lane from his trailer.

Bostick handed Keith Wampler the knife that the prosecution claimed was used in this crime, the knife that belonged to his neighbor, John McGarvey. Keith could not tell the court when was the last time he saw that knife. Also, he did not have access to the knife, nor did he know where McGarvey kept it. Bostick handed Keith another knife; this one was defendant's Exhibit A. Keith believed this was the knife he used to own in 1981. Keith said he gave it to his father, Cecil, because Cecil did not want him to have a knife.

Keith Wampler testified that the Moraine Police picked him up at 11:00 p.m. on February 6, when he was at John McGarvey's trailer celebrating his sixteenth birthday. According to Keith, plans were in the works for quite some time for this celebration. John McGarvey, McGarvey's fiancé, McGarvey's brother, Cecil, and he were present for the celebration. Nobody called the McGarvey trailer prior to the arrival of the police, as Detective Mullins stated. Detective Mullins did not speak to Cecil regarding taking Keith to the police station.

It needs to be noted that Detective William Mullins and Sergeant Joseph Wynne violated the Ohio Revised Code by not speaking to Charles "Cecil" Wampler, Keith's legal guardian, prior to taking Keith to the police station. Under the Ohio Revised Code, Section 2151.31, the police needed to inform Keith's father regarding their desire to take Keith Wampler to the police station. Obviously Detective Mullins and Sergeant Wynne were ignorant of the law they are sworn to uphold or they decided to ignore it. What is even more disturbing is the defense team never made an issue of it.

After he arrived at the police station, he was taken to a room. According to Keith Wampler, he was asked questions, and he answered those questions truthfully. Detective Mullins began to repeat the questions, and Keith said he gave the police the same answers as before. Sometime during the interview, according to Keith, Mullins turned off the tape recorder. Keith testified that he wanted to speak to an attorney after Detective Mullins began to accuse him of the murder.

Keith Wampler told the court that on February 5, he knew his father was going to Waynesville and Keith expected him home sometime that evening. Keith said that it was common for him to take the electric blanket back to his father's room and watch television when he'd realize his father would not be home that night, which is what he did on February 5.

According to Keith's testimony, on the afternoon of February 6, he was about to leave his trailer to take a bottle of vodka to McGarvey's trailer when he noticed the police in the field and Michael Rowell on his patio. Keith said that he put the vodka on the kitchen table and went outside to see what was happening. He asked Michael Rowell about what was occurring, and Michael said David was in the field and someone cut him up. Keith told the court that is when the police approached him. A little while later, according to Keith, he was in his trailer with Michael Rowell, and that is when Detective Mullins came to ask questions.

Prior to Detective Mullins coming to his trailer, Keith said he was talking with Michael Rowell and told him about Michael Johnson, Ted Ritchie, and the Shipman brothers being at his trailer the previous evening. Michael Rowell asked Keith not to tell the police about that. Keith did not know why Michael did not want the police to know, but he decided he would tell the police anyway.

Bostick went back to the police questioning Keith at the police station. Prior to the interview, according to Keith Wampler, Detective Mullins asked him to remove his boots and hat and place them by the door. Through this portion of the testimony, Keith said he did everything the police asked of him and cooperated until Detective Mullins accused him of murder. Keith said that he was not immediately advised of his rights. According to Keith, Detective Mullins advised him of his rights about an hour into the interview. Keith confirmed he was kept away from his father when he was at the police station.

Dennis Langer, assistant Montgomery County prosecutor, handled the cross-examination of Keith. Langer started his cross-examination with a question about the knife, defense's Exhibit A. Keith believed that was the knife he gave his father because his father did not want him to have a knife. Then Langer made an issue about the differences between knives and what Keith told Detective Mullins. Langer asked Keith if he truthfully answered Detective Mullins's questions and Keith said he did.

Langer wanted to know about when Keith Wampler started to use marijuana and drink beer. Keith said that he started smoking marijuana when he was ten and drinking beer when he was fifteen. Keith was asked to name his friends in the trailer park. Keith named John McGarvey, McGarvey's fiancé, Michael Johnson, James Combs, and Michael Rowell. Langer wanted to know why David Rowell was not named. Keith then said he considered David as a friend. Keith told the jury David was a smart-mouth to other people, but not to him.

Keith then told the court that on February 5, Michael Rowell showed up at his trailer around 4:00 p.m. The two boys were drinking grapefruit juice and vodka while talking and watching television. David Rowell arrived about 5:00 p.m., according to Keith. David came into the trailer, took a drink of Michael's cocktail, and sat down on a chair. At about 5:30 p.m., Keith said that he got up to use the bathroom. When he came back, Michael Rowell was leaving, and David was still sitting on the chair. Keith ran after Michael for a little way but could not catch up with him. When he turned to return to his trailer, he noticed David at the Shipman trailer talking to James Shipman Jr. He had no knowledge of where Michael was going because Michael did not say anything before leaving his trailer.

Langer asked Keith about when Michael Johnson, Ted Ritchie, and the Shipman brothers came to Keith's trailer. It was around 9:00 p.m. He gave the boys some beer, and they sat listening to music and watching television. At some point, James Shipman Jr cut his hand on a beer can. According to Keith, James Jr. was bleeding and did not feel well. James Jr. went to Keith's room to lay down. After some time, James Jr. came out from the back of the trailer and said it was getting late and that Joey and he needed to go home. The two Shipmans left to go home. Keith believed it was fifteen minutes later when Ted Ritchie and Michael Johnson left his trailer. After Ted and Michael left, he was alone in the trailer.

Langer then showed Keith a pink towel with the letter *A* on it. Keith could not remember if he ever saw that towel. Langer wanted to know if Keith ever looked at his towels, and Keith said he only used them to dry off and he never paid attention to them.

According to Langer, Michael Rowell said Keith and Michael got into a fight and that is why Michael left Keith's trailer. That was a lie, according to Keith Wampler. Langer then brought up Joey

Shipman's testimony in which Langer characterized Joey as saying he saw David go into Keith's trailer. Keith said that did not happen and that the last time he saw David was at the Shipmans' trailer. Langer talked about Michael Rowell's return to Keith's trailer at 7:00 p.m. and claiming he asked Keith about David's whereabouts. Keith told the jury that was not true.

Langer continued his badgering of sixteen-year-old Keith Wampler. Langer relayed a story Keith telling Michael Johnson that he drank vodka with David Rowell. Keith said that was not true. Then Langer wanted to know who Keith was talking about roughing up to Michael Johnson. Keith stated that conversation dealt with someone coming to the neighborhood looking for the person who stole a pit bull dog. Michael Johnson told Keith the dog was in West Carrollton, but Keith denied any discussion about roughing up anyone.

Langer asked about what was said between James Combs and Keith while the police were recovering David's body. Langer reminded Keith Wampler that James Combs testified Keith said David had been strangled. Keith stated that was not true. Langer then pressed Keith about the interview with Chief Carmichael, and Keith told Chief Carmichael that David was a "smart-ass." Keith said that never occurred.

Robert Bostick did re-direct examination of Keith Wampler. Bostick asked Keith about the conversation Chief Carmichael had with Keith. Keith said the police chief wanted to know about any queers in the trailer park. Keith said that he began answering Chief Carmichael's questions, but they were interrupted by Detective Mullins. According to Keith, Chief Carmichael did not ask him any questions regarding David Rowell.

Keith Wampler then explained the only way he knew David Rowell was in the field was when Michael Rowell told him. He did not have any prior knowledge of who was in the field, if anyone.

Bostick then addressed Michael Rowell's return to Keith's trailer at 7:00 p.m. on February 5. Michael Rowell wanted a cigarette and did not mention anything about David. The rest of redirect dealt did not deal with anything significant in this investigation. At that point, Charles "Keith" Wampler's testimony was over. Also, the defense rested their case.

The next step in the trial was closing arguments. The only significant thing about the closing arguments was the prosecution told the jury that someone else, Michael Johnson, was convicted in juvenile court of this crime. This was done in spite of Judge Kessler stating, at the opening, that Michael Johnson's conviction could not be mentioned unless he is called as a witness.

Late in the afternoon of July 27, 1982, the jury received the case for deliberation. The jury deliberated until 1:00 a.m. on July 28, 1982, when they returned to the courtroom and convicted Charles "Keith" Wampler on all counts. Judge Kessler was finally able to take his vacation. On August 24, 1982, a rested Judge John Kessler sentenced Keith to twenty years to life in the custody of the Ohio Department of Rehabilitation and Corrections. Keith Wampler, a sixteen-year-old boy, was sent to prison.

CHAPTER 5

The 2015 Investigation

The Overview

The first four chapters in this book discussed information that was obtained from official documents regarding this case. Those documents were police reports, forensic reports, the autopsy report, and trial transcripts. This chapter will refer to the previous chapters but will add information that was learned in the 2015 investigation, along with analysis. Unlike the original investigation, the 2015 investigation does not jump to conclusions based on "we think this person is dirty" but will use facts. You can draw your own conclusions.

This investigation started in June 2015, when Lori Wampler, Keith's wife, contacted Heartland Investigations through its website. She was seeking a private investigator to review her husband's case. Lori said she did not have any money because the money she saved was used to hire other private investigators, who simply obtained copies of police reports and charged her over two thousand dollars for them. I agreed to meet with her and said if a case existed, I would investigate it pro bono. At our meeting, Lori provided me with copies of police reports and trial transcripts. It should be noted that additional police reports were obtained from the Moraine Police

Division, so the previous private investigator did not provide her with everything available. I was able to talk with Keith, who called from the London Correctional Institution in London, Ohio. I made one rule, and that rule was, "Do not lie to me." If you lie, I walk. Everyone agreed to that; thus the investigation began.

The investigation started on June 16, 2015, and ended on September 15, 2015. Approximately two thousand pages of documents were reviewed. As stated earlier, these documents were police reports, the autopsy report, forensic reports, and trial transcripts. An interesting fact about the trial transcripts that is when Lori Wampler initially asked for them, the Montgomery County Clerk of Courts said they were destroyed and did not exist. It was through a friend of one of Lori's relatives that the transcripts were found in the basement of the Montgomery County Courthouse and were subsequently obtained. This is interesting because Ohio Revised Code, Section 149.43 (the Open Records Law), allows the public broad access to official records, such as trial transcripts from common pleas court. A recent check of the Montgomery County Clerk of Courts website indicates that this case is under review by Judge Mary Wiseman of the Montgomery County Common Pleas Court. One has to ask if the records do not exist, which was Montgomery County's initial response to the request to obtain the trial transcripts, then how could they be under review?

After the documents were reviewed, the field investigation began, which included reconstruction of the secondary crime scene and interviewing seventeen witnesses. Six of the witnesses no longer resided in Ohio. Therefore, trips to Kentucky, South Carolina, Alabama, and Florida were made to locate and interview them. Analysis was conducted on the witnesses' statements. The statements in the original investigation were compared to the trial transcripts and the statements made in the 2015 investigation. It was expected that minute details could be off due to the length of time, in this case thirty-three years. But the material facts should not differ. As you will see, in several key interviews, recollection of material facts differs greatly in 2015 as compared to what the witness said in 1982.

An open-minded approach to this investigation was used. Unlike Detective Mullins's investigation, this investigation would go where the evidence took it. A good detective follows the evidence and the clues to make inferences and not to try to make them fit a theory like trying to jam a square peg into a round hole. A good detective may develop a hypothesis, but that hypothesis cannot, and should not, be etched in concrete. The hypothesis must be fluid because it may change several times based on the evidence collected. That hypothesis may or may not become an established fact because the accumulation of additional evidence may not support it. A good detective is objective when approaching an investigation and never makes the evidence fit his or her hypothesis. If the detective has an open mind and has properly collected the evidence, then the who, what, why, when, and how will be answered. A good detective will then take a step back and ask whether or not these answers make sense. If it does make sense, then the case will be able to identify three key factors: motive, opportunity, and means. If it does not make sense, then a good detective will know that he or she is missing a piece of evidence, be it a statement or a piece of physical evidence. No matter what it is, a piece of the puzzle is missing, and a good detective will endeavor to find it. As a safety net, a good prosecutor will be doing the same exercise. In this case, none of that was done, thereby calling into question the professionalism of the Moraine Police and the Montgomery County Prosecutor, thus raising reasonable doubt.

The state's theory in this case was on February 5, 1982, at 5:30 p.m., David Rowell returned to Keith Wampler's trailer, 2753 Cozy Lane, where he was sexually abused, tortured, and murdered. Sometime during the late evening of February 5 and early morning of February 6, Keith Wampler disposed of David Rowell's body in a vacant field along Kreitzer Road. The state believed this crime was perpetrated by some deranged male with homosexual tendencies. This investigation will show there are other theories that make more sense than the one Dennis Langer and Robert Head, the prosecution team, presented to the jury. As you will see, the State of Ohio's own evidence does not, and did not, support the prosecution's theory of the crime. The 2015 investigation, at the minimum, raises reasonable doubt regarding Charles "Keith" Wampler's guilt in this case. Actually, the 2015 investigation exonerates Charles "Keith" Wampler and provides a stronger, more likely theory regarding this crime.

The Autopsy

The prosecution used the autopsy report as a guideline in establishing when the crime was committed. It is clear that the Moraine Police and the Montgomery County Prosecutor zeroed in on 1:00 a.m., plus or minus two hours, on February 6, 1982, and accepted this to be the time of David Rowell's death. Dr. Schaffer determined the time of death based on lividity (pooling of the blood after death) and rigor mortis (death stiffness). Not only did Dr. Schaffer put this in the official autopsy report but he testified to it at trial. This time frame for the death of David Rowell is certainly too restrictive and may well be totally inaccurate.

While lividity, livor mortis, and rigor mortis are important factors in establishing a window for a time of death, there are three other factors that a forensic pathologist must take into account. Those factors are body temperature (algor mortis), stomach contents, and presences of insects. It is standard international practice to use all five factors in establishing a time frame for the time of death. Unlike the popular television shows, forensic pathologists cannot give an exact time of death based on an autopsy alone. An autopsy gives a time frame in which death occurred. A properly conducted full field investigation, conducted by law enforcement, combined with the autopsy will narrow the window. In this case, an inaccurately restrictive autopsy played a key role in the state's theory of the crime.

It is clear that Dr. Schaffer did not factor in body temperature, stomach contents, or presences of insects. In the autopsy, David Rowell's body was described as being "cold to the touch, but not frozen." Just touching a body is no way to establish the body temperature. Upon preparing the body for an autopsy, the forensic pathologist must take the temperature of the victim's rectum and record it. Once the forensic pathologist obtains the temperature, he or she then applies the Glaister equation, which is 98.4°Fahrenheit minus rectal temperature divided by 1.5. A forensic pathologist has to factor in the stability and/or fluctuation of the ambient temperature, the thickness of clothing, the thermal conductivity of where the body was lying, the presence of drugs or disease (which may increase the body temperature), and the existence of temperature plateau (a period of time in which the body does not cool). The Glaister equation, coupled with the variants, gives a general idea as to when a time of death may have occurred. Keep in mind, this is one factor of a five-factor equation. Dr. Schaffer never recorded a body temperature in his autopsy report; therefore, a body temperature was never available for the Glaister equation. Without this critical piece of information, it would be impossible for any forensic pathologist to give a time of death as being 1:00 a.m., plus or minus two hours.

The green food substance that was found in David's stomach serves to indicate that the time of death was earlier than the estimate by Dr. Schaffer, which was 1:00 a.m., plus or minus two hours, on February 6, 1982. What was this substance? We will never know because the coroner's office failed to test it. What is disturbing being that even today, the current Montgomery County coroner stated that he would not test this stomach content. This green food substance is a vital clue. The fact that this substance was present in David's stomach indicates that he ate something two to four hours prior to this death. In the average person, it takes the stomach two to four hours to process food. This serves to indicate that David Rowell was certainly someplace other than Keith Wampler's trailer when he was killed. Would it make sense for a deranged killer with homosexual tendencies, like the prosecution tried to portray Keith as being, to take a break in torturing his victim to have the victim eat a salad? That is very doubtful. It is more likely that David Rowell ate this green food substance at his home, 2790 Kreitzer Road, approximately two to four hours prior to his death. If this information was made available to the jury during the trial, then reasonable doubt would be created in the minds of the jurors.

Finally, the fact insects were not present on the body when David was found or, later, at the morgue indicates that David Rowell was not dead for a lengthy period of time. The fact this crime occurred on a frigid February day would have slowed the maggot larva from forming in the various orifices, such as the nose. This indicates that David's body was discovered within twenty-four to thirty-six hours after the time of death.

Clearly, Dr. Schaffer's estimate was *not* based on solid scientific data at best. At worst, the estimate is chimerical. Did this inaccuracy mislead the police? That is doubtful because Detective Mullins already had Keith Wampler in custody. However, this inaccuracy did play a role in convicting Keith Wampler, and that cannot be overlooked. If the defense team of Wayne Stephan and Robert Bostick did their jobs, they would have discovered the problems with the autopsy. If these attorneys did their job correctly, they would have been able to raise a great deal of reasonable doubt regarding a critical piece of the state's case. A good criminal defense attorney would have the autopsy report reviewed by an independent forensic pathologist and enter those findings in as evidence for the defense. That was not done by Wayne Stephan or Robert Bostick.

Given what we now know, a more accurate window for the time of death would be from 7:00 p.m. on February 5, 1982, to 4:00 a.m. on February 6, 1982. This is an educated guess based on the factors we know. A key piece is missing: the body temperature. If we had that, then the time frame could be narrowed. Based on what we know from the police investigation, it is likely that David was murdered sometime after 9:15 p.m. on February 5. Remember, there is a witness who said that he saw David Rowell at the Moraine Civic Center's barbeque pit at that time.

The autopsy, more accurately Dr. Schaffer's trial testimony, tells us where David Rowell was murdered, and it contradicts the state's theory. Dr. Schaffer testified about a condition called cyanotic. To be more accurate, Dr. Schaffer's testimony talked about peripheral cyanosis, which is the bluish tint in the fingernails and toenails caused by the lack of oxygenated blood reaching these areas. One of the causes of this condition is exposure to the cold. In his testimony, Dr. Schaffer said in fair-skinned people, cyanotic conditions form when the place of death is a cold environment. It is a fact that Keith Wampler's trailer was not a cold environment. There are several witnesses who testified that Keith was not wearing a shirt at his trailer on February 5, 1982. The fact that peripheral cyanosis was present indicates that David Rowell was killed in a cold environment. In this investigation, aside from the outside wintry weather, three places were identified as being unheated: the abandoned house (former Michael Johnson residence, at 2791 Kreitzer Road in the Gordon's Trailer Park) and an unheated cellar and an unheated garage, both located at 2790 Kreitzer Road (the Rowell home). Dr. Schaffer's testimony of peripheral cyanosis indicates that one of these locations is likely to be the primary crime scene. We probably will never know because none of them were searched by the Moraine Police.

What do the injuries inflicted upon the body tell us? The autopsy report stated, and Dr. Schaffer testified, that there were bruises about the mouth that indicated a blow to this area. In simple terms, someone hit David Rowell in the mouth prior to death. Also, there is a blow to the back of the head, which may or may not have caused unconsciousness. These injuries are indicative of someone being angry with David. The bruising on the buttock also indicates anger. The way Dr. Schaffer described the bruises on the buttock tells us that David received some sort of whipping prior to death. We do not know what specifically caused the bruising. It could have been a leather strap, a leather belt, or the palm of someone's hand. That is not clear. However, these injuries serve to indicate that the killer was angry with David. The injuries tell us that the killer was angry and had a violent temper. The person who caused the bruising on the buttocks could have been someone other than the person who caused the death. Thus, reasonable doubt rears its head.

Now, we must ask, what injuries are missing? The state's theory of the crime is from 5:30 p.m. on February 5, David Rowell was being held against his will in Keith's trailer. If David is being held against his will, it stands to reason that some form of restraints would be used to secure him. Yet there is not one report of any ligature marks on the body. Therefore, the body lacked any indication of being restrained. There should have been some sort of ligature marks on the wrists and/or ankles. This could be the reason why the Montgomery County Prosecutor's Office dropped the abduction charge. There is no evidence that David Rowell was being held against his will or restrained. The defense team should have exploited this to create reasonable doubt. Instead, Wayne Stephan and Robert Bostick did not even attempt to chip away at the prosecution's case.

The autopsy report indicates that David Rowell had some tears in his rectum. Dr. Schaffer described these tears as "superficial." It is clear that the Montgomery County Prosecutor's Office used these tears to establish that a sexual assault occurred in this case. Based on the description of the tears, it is highly unlikely that a rape occurred. The fact the tears are superficial does not help the prosecution's case. Dennis Langer and Robert Head, both assistant Montgomery County prosecutors, went to lengths to portray Keith Wampler as some deranged killer with homosexual tendencies. Would the injuries inflicted by a deranged killer be only superficial? That is doubtful. The Montgomery County Prosecutor had the jury believing Keith Wampler tortured David Rowell prior to death. The autopsy report does not provide any evidence to support that claim. This accusation should have been attacked by Robert Bostick and Wayne Stephan, the defense team. Had these two officers of the court followed the Canons of Ethics and provided their client with an aggressive defense, then the seeds of reasonable doubt, especially regarding these tears, could have been planted in the jury's mind.

The state portrayed Keith Wampler as a deranged killer. Would a deranged killer want to inflict minimum or maximum pain upon the victim? If the killer is raping the victim, would the killer care if he is causing damage to David's rectum? The answer to those questions is no because a deranged killer cares about self-gratification, not the comfort of the victim. Also, the state failed to prove whether or not the tears were caused by a sexual assault. Could such damage to a small sixty-five-pound boy be caused by being bent over someone's knee and receiving a severe whipping? With him being bent over someone's knee and being nude, David's rectum would be exposed to whatever force and whatever instrument was used to whip him. If the whipping was conducted with an object, then this could possibly explain the superficial tears that were found.

Finally, the amputation of the penis indicates anger and humiliation. Dennis Langer and Robert Head, the prosecution team, wanted to paint the picture of this being a homosexual act. This indicates that the Montgomery County Prosecutor misread the crime. In *The*

Handbook of Psychology for Forensic Practitioners, Graham J. Towl and David Crighton discuss the psychology behind sexually motivated homicides. In their research, Towl and Crighton found that in these types of homicides, the sadistic sexual behavior occurs postmortem. The killer would defecate, urinate. or ejaculate onto the victim.[54] There is no evidence of that occurring in this case. The research also found perpetrators of these crimes have unstable or inconsistent employment patterns. Keith Wampler was a fifteen-year-old teenager on February 5, 1982, when David Rowell went missing, so employment is not a factor. However, it is documented that one person related to this crime did have an unstable employment history. The amputation was designed to dehumanize the victim. If this were a sexually motivated homicide committed by a deranged killer, the killer would have kept a souvenir.[55] Nothing belonging to David Rowell was found in Keith Wampler's trailer.

Research by the Federal Bureau of Investigation (FBI) indicates that crime scenes of sexually motivated homicides would show signs of disorganization. The vacant field along Kreitzer Road, where David's body was discovered on February 6, was described as the body being in one location, and the bag containing the neatly folded clothing is in another. There is nothing to indicate that this scene was disorderly. This indicates that, at the very least, the disposal of the body was planned. The murder may or may not have been planned, but the disposal of the body was planned. All this disproves the state's portrayal of Keith Wampler as being a deranged killer with homosexual tendencies.

Overall, a key piece of the state's evidence, the autopsy, is seriously flawed. The autopsy report provides an inaccurate time frame for the time of death. This time frame is too restrictive and is *not*

---

54   Graham J. Towl and David Crighton, *The Handbook of Psychology for Forensic Practitioners* (Routledge, 1996) 43.
55   Ibid.

based on inferences from solid scientific data but rather on guess-work from observations such as "cold to the touch, but not fro-zen." The prosecution either misread the autopsy or they decided to deliberately overlook key elements that disproves the prosecution's theory. What is even more astonishing is the defense team, Robert Bostick and Wayne Stephan, did not read the autopsy report or have it reviewed by a forensic pathologist. These self-proclaimed outstand-ing attorneys would have learned the autopsy indicates David Rowell was murdered in a cold environment, not a warm one, like Keith Wampler's trailer. We know this because of the presence of peripheral cyanosis. They could have used this to rip open the state's theory that David Rowell was killed in Keith Wampler's trailer. Had the defense team done their homework, they would have learned that you cannot determine the time of death based on lividity and rigor mortis alone. They could have questioned why the green food substance was not tested. Had they done their homework, Bostick and Stephan could have developed an alternate theory of the crime. They could have developed a theory that made more sense than the one the prosecu-tion presented. They most certainly could have developed reasonable doubt.

The Secondary Crime Scene

The secondary crime scene is the vacant field located in the 2900 block of Kreitzer Road. This is the field where David Rowell's body was discovered on February 6, 1982, at 3:50 p.m. Kreitzer Road runs from Dryden Road on the east and dead-ends at I-75 on the west. Gem City Estates Trailer Park is located along the north side of Kreitzer Road. Gem City Estates Trailer Park is parallel to Kreitzer Road for about a tenth of a mile. Past that tenth of a mile, a vacant field sat. Entrance to Gem City Estates Trailer Park is along Dryden

Road. Gem City Estates Trailer Park has various streets, such as Cozy Lane. Along Cozy Lane, which is at the western edge of the park, the trailer homes sit in cul-de-sacs. Each cul-de-sac could house five trailers. In 1982, Gem City Estates Trailer Park was filled to capacity, as compared to 2015, where most of the trailer park is vacant. Adjacent to and at the northwest corner of Dryden Road and Kreitzer Road sat Gordon's Trailer Park. In 1982, an abandoned home sat within Gordon's Trailer Park.

The south side of Kreitzer Road is home to several residences, such as 2970 Kreitzer Road, David Rowell's house. At the very western edge of the road and on the south side, the Moraine Civic Center is located. A sidewalk runs between the Moraine Civic Center and Moraine Meadow Elementary School, which is located on Holman Street. The sidewalk goes from Holman Street to the south to Kreitzer Road to the north. In 1982, the majority of the north side of Kreitzer Road consisted of a vacant field. In 2015, a light industrial complex is located on that field.

In 1982, a dirt path separated Gem City Estates Trailer Park from the vacant field. Today, a barbed wire fence and trees separate the two properties due to the existence of the light industrial facility. As stated earlier, in 1982, the field contained thornbushes, rabbit traps, a garden area, and trash. Keith Wampler's trailer, 2753 Cozy Lane, was on the very western edge of the trailer park, and the entrance faced the field. To go from David Rowell's house on Kreitzer Road to Keith Wampler's trailer on Cozy Lane, in the Gem City Estates Trailer Park, a person would cross Kreitzer Road and either walk through the vacant field or walk past a number of trailers. Approximately 500 feet separated Keith Wampler's trailer from David Rowell's house.

On February 6, 1982, at 3:50 p.m., David Rowell's body was found 77 feet southwest from Keith's trailer and 279 feet north of Kreitzer Road. A bag containing David's clothing was discovered 20 feet and 4 inches in a northeastern direction from the body. The green toilet seat lid, which was discovered a week after the body, was found 59 feet due north from the body.

From 5:00 p.m. to 10:30 p.m. on February 5, snow fell in the Miami Valley. A total of 0.2 inches of snow accumulated in Moraine. The snow fall is important for two main reasons. The first is if anyone was walking during, or after, this snow would leave footprints. The second reason is the snow fall indicates when various pieces of evidence were placed in the field, such as David's body.

Let's look at the footprints in this case. The only set of footprints that were documented by Officer Dennis Adkins and Detective William Mullins goes from Keith's trailer to the body. Where is the documentation of the other footprints found in the field? For example, there is no documentation of Robert Rowell's footprints. If Robert Rowell is telling the truth, there should have been several sets of his footprints in the snow. Remember, he was in that field at least three times since the snow started to fall at 5:00 p.m. on February 5 and finding David's body at 3:50 p.m. on February 6. Robert Rowell said he even past the area where David's body was found twice before he made the grisly discovery. Yet there is no documentation regarding his footprints.

What about Ted Ritchie's and Michael Johnson's footprints? Ted Ritchie testified that Mike Johnson and he left Keith's trailer at 11:00 p.m. on February 5, right after the snow stopped falling, and walked through the field in the direction of the Moraine Civic Center and onto Andrew Choate's house on Holman Street. Unless they sprouted wings and flew, they would have left footprints in the snow. As a matter of fact, the footprints that Officer Robert Schmidt discovered on February 6 matches exactly the path the two boys took the previous night.

What about Michael Rowell's footprints? He testified about visiting Keith Wampler's trailer at 10:00 a.m. on February 6 then going to the civic center from there. Michael stated he walked through the field. He would have taken the same path that Ted Ritchie and Michael Johnson took the night before. Yet there is no documentation of those footprints.

Another interesting point about the footprints is there is no documentation about the footprints going past the location where David's body was discovered. Three people took the same route going from Keith's trailer to the area of the Moraine Civic Center. There had to be footprints going from the location where David's body was discovered, in a southwestern direction, to Kreitzer Road. Yet there is no documentation of those footprints. There is a mention of those prints. Officer Dennis Adkins told the court it was possible for footprints to go past David's body, and it was hard, according to Adkins, to locate footprints past the body because of the terrain. At best, Adkins's testimony indicates a possible sloppy job in evidence collection. At worst, his testimony was geared to mislead the jury.

Here is another interesting point regarding the footprints. Officer Adkins and Detective Mullins testified that the footprints were leading from the trailer to the body and another set of prints went from the body to the bag containing the clothes. If the state's theory is correct, then Keith carried the body 77 feet in a southwestern direction from his trailer and where David was discovered. Then, according to this theory, Keith walked 20 feet 4 inches in a northeastern direction and at a 15-degree angle to the north to place the bag containing the neatly folded clothes on the ground. If this were true and the state's theory correct, where are the footprints going back to the trailer? Remember, Adkins and Mullins testified about footprints going from the trailer. Neither police officer mentioned any footprints returning to the trailer. It is shocking that the self-proclaimed best attorneys in Dayton did not ask any questions about the footprints.

Joey Shipman told the court he saw David Rowell return to Keith Wampler's trailer at 5:30 p.m. on February 5, 1982. Joey was seven years old at the time, and calling him a liar would be irresponsible. However, it was physically impossible for Joey Shipman to see anything past the entrance to his cul-de-sac, which was opposite of the cul-de-sac that contained Keith's trailer. Joey was inside his trailer. He testified to that. Being inside the trailer, all he could see was the parking area of his cul-de-sac, the trailers in his cul-de-sac, and the entrance to his cul-de-sac from Cozy Lane. He could not see past that. If he could, he could not see Keith's trailer because, at least, three other trailers would have obstructed his view. On top of that, he could not see the entrance to Keith's trailer. The east side of Keith's trailer was facing in the direction of Joey Shipman's trailer. The entrance to Keith's trailer was on the west side, facing the field. Therefore, Joey could not have seen anyone entering Keith's trailer. There will be more on this later in this book, but his statement does indicate possible prosecutorial misconduct by the Montgomery County Prosecutor's Office. Did the defense team bother to go to the Gem City Estates Trailer Park in preparation for the trial so that they could be familiar with the scene and thus be able to ask questions to raise reasonable doubt? The answer to that question is, "Doubtful."

Joey Shipman was one of the prosecution's key witnesses. His testimony placed David Rowell entering Keith Wampler's trailer, and we know that it was physically impossible for him to see David enter Keith's trailer. This issue needed to be addressed at trial, but it was not. Had the defense attorneys, Robert Bostick and Wayne Stephan, done their job, they would have seen the obvious. The sad thing is these two officers of the court, supposed seekers of the truth, did not do their job. Robert Bostick as much as admitted so on July 14, 2015, when he said he did not visit the secondary crime scene prior to trial. Had he done his job, he would have been able to impeach Joey's testimony. It should be noted that in the expense report Robert Bostick filed with the Montgomery County Common Pleas Court in order to be paid for representing Keith Wampler, he billed Montgomery County for visiting the secondary crime scene.

Adrian West, who resided at 2765 Cozy Lane, two trailers to the south of Keith's, testified that he saw the comings and goings at Keith's trailer on February 5. West even testified that he saw lights go on and off at Keith's trailer and said that he saw the reflection of Keith's television. Again, that was totally impossible. In 1982, a single-wide trailer occupied 2753 Cozy Lane. Adrian West's trailer was also a single-wide. The way West's trailer sat would have made it possible for him to see the lights of Keith's trailer, except for one thing—John McGarvey's trailer—which sat between West's trailer and Keith's trailer. West's kitchen and dining room would have been on the western side of his trailer. He testified that he sat there in the dark watching television. If this were true, then the only light he would have seen from Keith's trailer would have been the front porch light, and then he would have only seen reflections. John McGarvey's trailer, at 2759 Cozy Lane, blocked West's view of Keith's trailer. This leaves one conclusion regarding Adrian West's testimony: it was fabricated.

It is clear that the prosecution was able to get a curveball past the jury with Adrian West's testimony. Adrian West's testimony does prove one thing: Robert Bostick and Wayne Stephan did not even attempt to break a sweat in defending Keith Wampler. These two self-proclaimed outstanding Dayton attorneys (as Bostick described himself on July 14, 2015) could have impeached West's testimony by simply seeing the physical layout of the secondary crime scene. They would have seen that West's testimony was fabricated and could have impeached him. One has to assume that being a court appointed attorney relieves the outstanding lawyer from having to break a sweat for an accused sixteen-year-old boy.

In his testimony, West said that he was unemployed and he would stay up all night and sleep during the day. If the state's theory is correct and Keith placed David's body in the field sometime during the wee hours of the morning on February 6, then West would have seen Keith carry the body to the field. West had a view of the entrance to the field. He could have seen anyone coming from the direction of Keith's trailer and enter that field. The only people West testified about seeing entering that field were the two boys (Ted Ritchie and Michael Johnson), who left Keith's trailer at 11:00 p.m. on February 5. He never mentioned seeing anyone else entering that field.

As earlier stated, the body was found 77 feet southwest of Keith's trailer, 279 feet north of Kreitzer Road and approximately 400 feet northwest of 2790 Kreitzer Road, David's residence. If Dennis Langer and Robert Head are right and Keith Wampler killed David Rowell, then one has to ask if it makes sense for Keith to place David's body in, basically, Keith's front yard. If a killer wanted to dump a body, would they pick a place close to where they live or far from where they live?

The body being 77 feet from Keith's trailer raises another question. Why did it take everyone so long to find the body? With the body being 77 feet from Keith's trailer, anyone could look out into the field and see something was laying on top of the snow. If the state's theory is correct, then the body was placed in the field sometime during the wee hours of February 6, 1982. Yet Bobby Rowell was in that field at 7:00 a.m. on February 6, and he did not see David laying there. At 10:00 a.m. on February 6, Michael Rowell walked from Keith's trailer, through the field, toward the Moraine Civic Center. Unless Michael Rowell was blind, he could not have possibly missed his brother's lifeless body lying in that field. So when was the body placed in the field?

Dr. Schaffer's statement indicates that David was kept in a cold, but not frigid, place for several hours after his death. We know, based on Dr. Schaffer's testimony, that David was kept on his left side for at least six hours then moved to his back. We know this because of the lividity. We know the place of death was a cold place due to the presence of peripheral cyanosis in the fingernails and toenails. With all this, one could conclude that David Rowell was kept in the location where he was murdered for several hours until his body was placed in the field. Also, based on the description of the body by Dr. Schaffer, "cold to the touch, but not frozen," one can conclude that the body was placed in the field shortly before the police arrived at around 3:50 p.m. on February 6. Keep in mind, David had a gaping hole in his groin because his penis was amputated. If his body was exposed to the frigid conditions for any length of time, then there would be indications that this area was exposed to the elements, such as ice-like crystals forming around the wound. There is not one report to indicate that.

Officer Dennis Adkins testified about conducting a search of the field when David's body was discovered on February 6, 1982. He was looking for evidence and clues. Aside from the footprints, the bag containing David's clothing, some shopping bags, and beer cans, a question does arise regarding this search of the secondary crime scene: how could this trained evidence technician missed the toilet seat lid, which was fifty-nine feet north of the body?

Dennis Langer and Robert Head, the prosecution team, made a huge issue about the toilet seat lid. They wanted the jury to believe the toilet seat lid came from Keith's trailer and the bloodstains on the lid indicated that Keith propped David's body on the toilet in order to amputate David's penis because the toilet seat lid contained bloodstains. The blood evidence will be discussed later. The prosecution wanted the jury to believe this toilet seat lid played a role in the murder of David Rowell. Here is where Wayne Stephan and Robert Bostick really dropped the ball. A huge question arises about the toilet seat lid. If it played a role in the murder, then why did it take

Officer Dennis Adkins an entire week to find it? After all, he testified about searching the field for evidence when the body was discovered.

One could cut Officer Adkins some slack and say the toilet seat lid was covered with snow; therefore he missed it when he "searched" for evidence. If you do that, then you have to admit that the toilet seat lid had nothing to do with this murder because it would have been placed in the field prior to 5:00 p.m. on February 5, 1982, which is the time it began to snow in the Miami Valley. Remember, the coroner placed the time of death at 1:00 a.m., plus or minus two hours, on February 6, 1982. It snowed between 5:00 p.m. and 10:30 p.m. on February 5 with 0.2 inches of accumulation. If that toilet seat lid had any role in this murder, then why would it have been snow covered, thus causing Officer Adkins to miss it?

It is very clear that the toilet seat lid had nothing to do with this murder. If you believe Officer Adkins, then ask him how he could have missed it on February 6. Again, if it was snow covered, then it definitely could not have been involved in this case. If it was placed out there after 10:30 p.m. on February 5, then Officer Adkins should have seen it when he searched the field for evidence. That is, if he actually conducted a search of that field for evidence.

Quickly, let us go over proper police procedure for a crime scene search. Once David's body was discovered and the police were called, the field needed to be secured. Nobody, other than the police and the coroner, would be permitted into the field until a proper search was conducted. The body was found at 3:50 p.m. on a winter's day in Moraine. This means that the police had 90, maybe 120, minutes to conduct a search of the field before the sun would go down. That clearly is not enough time to conduct a thorough and proper search of the crime scene without flashlight or spotlights being used. Ideally, the search should be conducted during the day. This type of search would require the use of a grid search technique. The evidence technician would draw a map of the field and divide it into grids. The evidence technician would search a grid then, on the map, indicate what was discovered and when was it discovered. Then when the search of a grid is complete, the technician would document the date and the time of the completion. This would occur for each grid. Could this type of search be conducted in a short amount of time? The answer is obvious: no, it cannot. So the Moraine Police needed to seal off that field and assign two police officers, one at each possible entrance to the field, to secure the field until a proper and thorough search can be conducted. That was not done. As soon as the body was removed, the field was released. This meant the public had access to the field for a week. Here is a question to ponder: because the police did not secure the field between February 6, when David's body was discovered, and February 12, when the toilet seat lid was found, could it be possible that evidence was removed from that field during that time?

Another interesting point can be made about the toilet seat lid. In his testimony, Officer Dennis Adkins said the color of the toilet seat lid as being green, but a lighter shade of green than the toilet in Keith's trailer. Toilet seats are sold with a lid, which is a matching color. If the toilet seat lid was a lighter shade of green than the toilet seat in Keith's trailer, one can draw two possible conclusions. The first is the toilet seat lid came from another toilet seat, therefore from someone else's trailer or house. The second is the toilet seat lid faded because it was exposed to the sun for a lengthy period of time. Both conclusions show that the toilet seat lid had nothing to do with this crime.

This is being discussed because the toilet seat lid should not have been allowed into evidence or to be mentioned in this case. The Moraine Police and the Montgomery County Prosecutor's Office could not tell the court when this item was placed in that field. Keep in mind, the toilet seat lid was discovered on February 12, 1982, six days after David's body was found. From the time David's body was removed to February 12, anyone had access to that field. Again, the sad thing is these issues should have been brought up by the outstanding defense team of Robert Bostick and Wayne Stephan. One can only speculate why Dayton's best attorneys did not see the obvious issue with the toilet seat lid. At minimum, a motion to suppress should have been filed.

The crime scene tells us something else: the description of the clothes in the shopping bag. There is no documentation that the clothing, which belonged to David, was torn or ripped. There is indication that the clothes were neatly placed into the shopping bag. If Keith is this deranged killer with homosexual tendencies, like the Montgomery County Prosecutor portrayed to the jury, then the clothing would have been ripped or torn. Would Keith have taken the time to neatly fold the clothing and place it in the shopping bag? Would a deranged killer allow his victim to undress, or would the killer use a sharp object to rip off the clothes? The FBI tells us that deranged killers leave a messy crime scene. This crime scene was neat and organized. The fact the clothing was neatly placed in the shopping bag could serve to indicate that someone, close the David Rowell, wanted him to have some form of dignity and that person wanted to provide some sense of order. Does that sound like a deranged killer with homosexual tendencies?

Regarding the secondary crime scene, the prosecution's case has some serious issues, and if those issues were identified by the defense team, then reasonable doubt would have been established, and the outcome of this case could have been very different. The prosecution's key witness, Joey Shipman, could not have seen David Rowell return to and enter Keith Wampler's trailer at 5:30 p.m. on February 5, 1982. It was physically impossible given where he was in his trailer. Adrian West could not have seen activity at Keith Wampler's trailer because John McGarvey's trailer was in the way. The Moraine Police documented only one set of footprints, yet there had to be many others in that field. The prosecution's own witnesses testified they were in that field since the snow stopped falling at 10:30 p.m. on February 5. Why did the Moraine Police fail to document those footprints? If the toilet seat was such a big piece of evidence, then why did Officer Adkins miss it in his so-called search of the crime scene?

Then there is the nagging question about when was the body placed in the field. If we accept the prosecution's theory, then David Rowell was murdered at 1:00 a.m. on February 6. That would mean the earliest Keith Wampler could have placed that body in the field was 7:00 a.m. on February 6. Lividity tells us that David was dead for at least six hours. The body was moved from laying on the left side to laying on the back during that time. If the earliest time for Keith to place the body in the field is 7:00 a.m., then how could Bobby Rowell, David's father, have missed him? In his testimony, Robert Rowell said he was at that location at 7:00 a.m. on February 6, yet it took him almost nine hours later to find the body. Also, in the extreme cold, David's body would have been frozen solid in a short period of time. Thus, the body was not exposed to the elements for a very long period of time when David's father had his vision of bushes.

The 2015 Interviews

As with any investigation, or reinvestigation, witnesses must be interviewed. This case is no exception. Witnesses were reinterviewed. The 2015 reinterview is then compared to their statement to the Moraine Police and/or their trial testimony. All this is outlined in this section. The majority of the witnesses interviewed had a very good recollection of the material facts from 1982, as you will see. However, you will also see in some of the interviews some of the witnesses are telling bold-faced lies; therefore, their credibility and integrity comes into question. This leaves one to ask, did they lie in 1982, or are they lying in 2015? These lies do question the integrity of some of the actors' alibis.

Charles "Keith" Wampler

Charles "Keith" Wampler was interviewed on July 29, 2015, at the London Correctional Institution in London, Ohio. The interview lasted from 11:45 a.m. to 2:00 p.m. The interview occurred in an attorney's interview room within the visiting center of the prison.

Keith moved to 2753 Cozy Lane in Moraine, Ohio, sometime during the summer of 1981, approximately seven or eight months before the murder of David Rowell. Keith's father spent four thousand dollars for the single-wide trailer in Gem City Estates Trailer Park. Prior to coming to Moraine, Keith lived with some cousins in Kettering, Ohio. During this period, 1981–1982, Keith's parents were experiencing difficulty in their marriage and decided to divorce. Keith moved with his father, Charles "Cecil" Wampler. Keith remembered feeling like a pawn in his parents' troubles.

Keith did not attend Moraine public schools. As a matter of fact, he dropped out of school and spent most of his days at home. Keith was allowed to smoke and drink. Cecil Wampler, Keith's father, provided him with cigarettes and beer that were purchased at the store on Wright-Patterson Air Force Base. In the interview, Keith admitted to being a marijuana user during this time. According to Keith, he would smoke one marijuana cigarette a week. On February 5, 1982, Keith had one carton of cigarettes and plenty of beer in his trailer.

Cecil went to work and then went to visit family in Waynesville on February 5. Keith was expecting Cecil to return home later that day, possibly late afternoon or early evening. Keith kept busy on February 5 by cleaning out the shed behind his trailer. Keith found a rusty old grill in the shed and dumped it in the field. Keith said that many of the trailer park's residence dumped their trash in the field. Keith, in midafternoon, briefly talked to John McGarvey and his fiancé on February 5 while McGarvey was preparing to take his fiancé somewhere. Keith was expecting his father or John McGarvey to return that evening. Keith was going to hang out with either his father or John McGarvey.

On February 5 between 3:00 p.m. and 4:00 p.m., Michael Rowell came to visit. Keith considered Michael a friend, so when Michael entered Keith's trailer, Keith offered him some vodka and grapefruit juice. The two teenaged boys drank, smoked cigarettes, and watched television. About forty-five minutes to an hour after Michael arrived, David knocked on the door. Keith let David into the trailer. Keith remembers David taking Michael's drink and having a sip of it before Michael took it back. All three boys were watching television.

According to Keith, about thirty minutes after David arrived, Keith had to go to the bathroom. When he returned to the living room, he found Michael Rowell leaving and David still watching television. Keith wondered why Michael was leaving, so he decided to chase him to find out. He suspected Michael Rowell of stealing cigarettes and explained that in the past when Michael was left alone at his trailer, cigarettes would turn up missing. Keith described Michael as walking in a very fast pace to avoid Keith. Keith was wearing his jeans and cowboy boots and was not wearing a shirt. He followed Michael Rowell south on Cozy Lane to a little past the cul-de-sac that leads to James Shipman Jr.'s trailer, 2754 Cozy Lane. It was at that point Keith decided to go back home because he was getting cold. Keith saw David talking to James Shipman Jr. at the Shipmans' trailer. That was the last time he saw David Rowell. Keith remembered it was around 5:30 p.m. on February 5.

Keith returned to his trailer, where he took a nap and then washed his hair. It was around 7:00 p.m. when Michael Rowell returned to Keith's trailer. Keith described Michael's behavior as being strange and not being his normal self. Keith said that he thought Michael's strange behavior was because Michael Rowell felt guilty about taking some cigarettes earlier. Keith believed that Michael was attempting to find out if Keith suspected him of stealing. Michael was there for about five minutes, and he never mentioned David. According to Keith, Michael bummed a cigarette and chatted some small talk. Then Michael Rowell left.

At 9:00 p.m., Michael Johnson, Ted Ritchie, James Shipman Jr., and Joey Shipman visited Keith's trailer. Keith became friendly with Michael Johnson when he (Johnson) lived in the abandoned house in the Gordon's Trailer Park. Keith stayed in touch after Michael Johnson moved to West Carrollton, Ohio. Keith invited all four boys into his trailer, offering the three older teens some beer. This was the first time Keith met Ted Ritchie. The boys were hanging out in the living room watching television or listening to the stereo. James Shipman Jr. decided to tear a beer can in two, and in doing so, he cut his hand. James Jr. needed to lay down, so Keith allowed him to go to the back of the trailer to use Keith's bedroom. Keith said James's little brother, Joey, followed James back to Keith's room.

Keith said Michael Johnson and Ted Ritchie made a couple trips to Keith's room to check on James or to go to the bathroom, which was between Keith's room and his father's room. Keith never escorted his guests down the hall because he allowed them to have free access throughout the trailer.

It was about 10:30 p.m. when James Shipman Jr. and Joey Shipman came back into the living room. Keith remembers James saying Joey and he had to go home before their parents got home. It was not too long after that when Ted Ritchie and Michael Johnson left Keith's trailer. They each had a beer in their hand when they left to go to Andrew Choate's residence, 2628 Holman Street. Keith saw his guests walk in a southwestern direction through the field toward to the Moraine Civic Center.

After everyone left, Keith cleaned up the mess and threw away the empty beer cans. When the mess was cleaned up, Keith took the blanket, which was in the living room, and the portable television to his father's room, where he wrapped himself up in the blanket and an electric blanket and watched television. Keith figured his father was not coming home that evening, so he decided to use his father's room to sleep and watch television. When Keith woke up the next morning, his father was home.

Sometime in the late afternoon of February 6, Keith was in the process of taking some vodka to John McGarvey's residence to give to McGarvey's fiancé. Keith remembered opening the door to find Michael Rowell standing on the patio, looking out into the field. Keith noticed the police in the field, so he asked Michael what was happening. According to Keith, Michael Rowell told him about the police recovering David's body and "It looks like they are picking him up in pieces." Keith distinctly remembers that statement. To which Keith replied, "That's gross." Keith said Michael Rowell stayed at Keith's trailer for quite a long time while the police were recovering David's body, and during that time, Keith told Michael Rowell about Michael Johnson, Ted Ritchie, James Shipman Jr., and Joey Shipman visiting him at 9:00 p.m. the previous evening. Michael Rowell asked Keith not to mention that to the police should the police question Keith.

Keith said Detective Mullins came to his trailer to ask questions regarding the murder of David Rowell. He cooperated with Detective Mullins and told him about the events of the previous afternoon and evening. Keith told Mullins about David and Michael Rowell being at his trailer in the afternoon of February 5, and the last time he saw David Rowell was at 5:30 p.m. on February 5, when David was at the Shipman trailer. That is when Keith asked to speak to Mullins in private. Detective Mullins and Keith went to Mullins's police car, and Keith told Mullins about the four boys visiting him at 9:00 p.m. the previous evening. Keith informed Mullins that Michael Rowell did not want Keith to tell the police about that visit. That is when Keith provided the police with a written statement.

The next time Keith had interaction with Detective Mullins was around 11:00 p.m. on February 6, when Sergeant Wynne and Detective Mullins came to take Keith to police headquarters for questioning. It needs to be noted that Detective William Mullins and Sergeant Joseph Wynne, at minimum, did not follow proper police procedure and, in the worst case, may have violated Ohio law by not personally speaking to Keith's father, Cecil Wampler, prior to taking Keith to police headquarters. There was no reason why the police officers could not speak with Cecil Wampler because he was sitting a few feet away inside the McGarvey trailer. What is more troubling is that the defense team did not make an issue of this at pretrial or during the trial.

Upon arriving at police headquarters, he was lead to a room, where he was told to remove his hat and boots. He was instructed to place them by the door, outside of the room. Keith repeated his earlier story to the police. Keith said he does not recall being advised of the *Miranda* warning and several times he wanted to see his father, Cecil, and each time the request was denied. Keith remembers at 2:30 a.m. on February 6, he asked to talk to an attorney and wanted to make a telephone call. He called John McGarvey seeking help because McGarvey's fiancé's father was somehow involved in law or law enforcement. Keith remembers the police continued to question him after he expressed his desire to have an attorney present.

The next part of the interview dealt with Keith Wampler's relationship with other individuals involved in this case. Keith described David Rowell as being "a mouthy small guy." Keith had no idea that

David was thirteen years old and thought David was closer to being eight years old due to his size. That is why he did not let David drink or smoke at his trailer. According to Keith, when you saw Michael Rowell, David was soon to follow. Keith believed Michael Rowell was the only person who was friendly toward David. Keith knew nothing about David's friends. As a matter of fact, he knew nothing about David.

Keith never met Robert or Myrtle Rowell, David's parents. There were rumors about threats against the Rowell family, but Keith did not have any details. He learned of those rumors while David's murder was being investigated. Keith believed the threats had something to do with an incident in New Carlisle, but he had no details.

Michael Johnson was another one of Keith's friends. When Michael Johnson lived in Moraine, Keith and he would hang out on a daily basis. Keith remembers Michael Johnson living in an abandoned or condemned house in the Gordon Trailer Park, and at some point, Michael and his family was evicted from that house and moved to West Carrollton, Ohio. Michael Johnson's cousin, Judy Tabor, still lived in the trailer park, so from time to time, Michael would visit her then come to Keith's trailer to hang out. Keith considered Michael Johnson to be a good friend.

James Combs was another one of Keith's good friends. Combs lived at 2941 Schoolhouse Lane, in the Gem City Estates Trailer Park. Keith described Combs's parents as being strict with James. Keith saw Combs on the morning of February 6, prior to Combs leaving to attend a family function, and that was the only time he saw Combs that day. Keith stated that Combs's trial testimony about visiting Keith while the police were recovering David Rowell's body is a lie.

Keith described John McGarvey has being his closest friend in Moraine. Keith would work with McGarvey in fixing things around the trailer. He liked McGarvey's fiancé and even admitted to having a crush on her. McGarvey taught Keith how to do different things, such as trapping rabbits. Keith learned a lot from John McGarvey. In the evenings, Keith would either hang out with his father, Cecil, or with John McGarvey. Keith repeated that he expected Cecil or John McGarvey to return home on evening of February 5.

When asked about Lisa Collins to allegedly described Keith as being "weird" and "only hung out with little boys," Keith could not understand why she would say such a thing because he did not know Lisa Collins.

Keith described Scott Lombardo, who was questioned by the Moraine Police regarding Keith's character, as being a friend. Lombardo allegedly told the Moraine Police that Keith made sexual advances toward him. Keith denies that and stated Lombardo arranged for Keith to have sex with some girl named Shannon at Lombardo's house. Keith could not understand why Lombardo would make such statements to the police.

Keith was acquainted with Andrew Choate but was not friendly with him. Keith related a story about an incident, which Ted Ritchie overhead Keith telling Michael Johnson on the evening of February 5. According to Keith, Fat Mickey Wax, member of the Dayton Outlaws motorcycle gang, was looking for the person who stole his pit bull dog. Wax approached some teens in the area, including Keith, about the missing dog and said there was a one-hundred-dollar reward for the return of the dog or the name of the thief. Keith knew Andrew Choate had talked about stealing the dog, and he convinced Choate to return it. According to Keith, Choate lived behind the Moraine Civic Center on Holman Street.

Bad blood existed between Adrian West and Keith since Keith confronted West about threatening McGarvey's fiancé. West lived at 2769 Cozy Lane, two trailers from Keith's. Keith described West as being mean.

Regarding Ted Ritchie, Keith said February 5 was the one and only time he met Ritchie. He just remembers Ritchie was one of the boys who came to his trailer at 9:00 p.m. on February 5. The rest were Michael Johnson, James Shipman Jr., and Joey Shipman.

Keith told an interesting story about his father, Cecil Wampler, being approached by Ray Salunek. Keith knew Salunek from his days in Kettering, Ohio. According to Keith, Salunek approached Cecil and told Cecil the Moraine Police tried to get him to testify that the knife the police showed Salunek was given to him by Keith. Salunek told Keith's father he refused to cooperate because he knew it was a lie.

Keith could not explain how the towels got into the field. He said it was possible, and probably likely, they were taken by someone who visited his trailer. Keith and his father did not keep track of towels or anything like that.

When asked if it were possible to extract DNA from David's remains, would the authorities find his DNA on David's body? Keith said they would not. Keith said there would be no reason for his DNA to be on David's body, and he is willing to submit a sample of his DNA to the authorities. Keith repeated that he did not kill David Rowell and he does not know who did.

Every aspect of this case was discussed during the interview. Keith Wampler's demeanor was forthright and honest. He made no attempts to shy away from anything and was even willing to answer questions, which could be described as derogatory, such as describing his marijuana use. To further prove his candor during this interview, Keith could have told a story regarding the towels. He could have said they were stolen, and he could have named someone as the thief, but he did not. He simply stated he could not explain how those towels got into the field.

Keith's own recollection of the events surrounding David Rowell's murder confirms most of the prosecution's timeline of events. The major, and key, difference is whether or not David Rowell returned to Keith's trailer at 5:30 p.m. on February 5, 1982. Under our system of justice, it is the prosecution's job to prove he did. The defense does not have to prove he did not. Keith said David did not. As we will see later, David Rowell did not return to Keith Wampler's trailer. Had Wayne Stephan or Robert Bostick done some legwork, they would have been able to prove David Rowell did not return to Keith's trailer. However, for the two self-proclaimed outstanding court-appointed attorneys, that would be far above and beyond expectations on the behalf of a sixteen-year-old boy who faced losing his freedom for the rest of his life.

The next interview was very useful. This witness's statement totally disproves the prosecution's theory of the crime, and had the defense team decided to defend their client, he could have been a key witness for the defense. Also, had the police done their job, they would have pursued what this witness told them. Unfortunately, clearing cases advances the careers of those in the criminal justice system, not necessarily seeking the truth.

Bryan "Cappy" C. Canterbury Interview

On July 30, 2015, between 1:15 p.m. and 2:00 p.m., Bryan "Cappy" C. Canterbury was interviewed. Canterbury was eleven years old in 1982, when this crime occurred, and was friends with David Rowell. He described David as being a wiseass with the tendency to upset people. Canterbury described David Rowell as being small for his age and was often bullied by classmates and other children in the neighborhood.

Canterbury identified Michael Rowell as being David's older brother, who had the tendency to lose his temper with David. Canterbury witnessed several occasions where Michael Rowell totally lost his temper with David. Canterbury knew Michael associated with Keith Wampler. According to Canterbury, it was common for David to follow Michael around the neighborhood.

Canterbury had the opportunity of visiting David's house on a couple occasions, which Canterbury described as being at 2970 Kreitzer Road. Canterbury described Robert and Myrtle Rowell as weird. Canterbury said Myrtle always had her hair pulled back and wore long dresses. It was common knowledge that the Rowells were "religious nuts." Canterbury described the Rowell family as being sad all the time, and he could not remember ever seeing them happy.

According to Canterbury, the cool kid in the neighborhood was Keith Wampler. Canterbury said the older boys would hang out with Keith. The older kids knew they could drink beer and smoke cigarettes at Keith Wampler's trailer. Canterbury did not hang out with Keith because of the age difference, but he said Keith was always nice to him.

The bully in the neighborhood was Michael Johnson. Johnson would constantly pick on the smaller children. Canterbury told how Johnson would punch the smaller kids and throw ice at them in the winter. Canterbury described Johnson as rough and mean with a chip on his shoulder. Johnson was very poor and resided in an old home in Gordon's Trailer park. Canterbury knew about Michael Johnson being convicted of David Rowell's murder.

On February 5, 1982, Canterbury attended the movie at the Moraine Civic Center. His grandparents always let him go to the movies because they were free. It was about 9:00 p.m. when the movie let out and he was on his way home. Canterbury walked past the BBQ pit near the civic center when he heard David Rowell yell, "Hi, Cappy!" All of Canterbury's friends called him Cappy. Canterbury looked toward the barbeque pit and saw David Rowell there. That is when he returned the greeting by saying, "Hi, David." Canterbury did not stop to engage in conversation because he had a curfew and he needed to get home. David Rowell was known to frequent the barbeque pit at the civic center. Canterbury described David wearing a winter coat with fake fur on the hood. Canterbury recalled the coat as having silver on it.

Canterbury recalled the events of February 5, 1982, with remarkable clarity. He spoke of these events as if they occurred last night instead of over thirty years ago. Canterbury had no idea that Keith Wampler was in prison for this crime, and he was totally shocked because he said Keith was not capable of committing such a crime.

Why did the defense team ignore this witness? Bryan Canterbury could place David Rowell at the Moraine Civic Center at around 9:00 p.m., which happened to be the same time Keith Wampler was receiving four visitors. According to the state's theory, David Rowell was being tortured at Keith Wampler's trailer at this time. How could David be at the civic center and Keith's trailer at the same time? Well, the answer is simple: He was not at Keith's trailer. He was at the barbeque pit near the civic center. This was not presented to the jury by the prosecution because it would have created reasonable doubt and deny the prosecution their coveted conviction rate and boost their careers. As to the self-proclaimed outstanding defense attorneys, it can only be assumed that they never reviewed the police reports, which they should have received during discovery. That is the only logical reason why they did not call Bryan "Cappy" Canterbury to the stand to impeach the state's theory.

Lisa Collins Interview

The August 4, 2015, interview of Lisa Collins produced one surprise. The forty-five-minute interview shed some light onto the integrity of the Moraine Police investigation. On February 5, 1982, Lisa Collins lived at 2754 Quail Lane, Moraine, Ohio, which was a trailer in the Gem City Estates Trailer Park. Collins was sixteen years old at the time of David Rowell's murder. Collins knew David through Michael Rowell, David's brother. Collins described David as being small for his age with "a mouth bigger than him." She thought of David as being annoying and said he had a knack for upsetting people. According to Collins, David always followed Michael around, and Michael Rowell told her this was beginning to upset him.

Collins knew the Rowells resided at 2970 Kreitzer Road and said she knew the parents, Robert and Myrtle Rowell. She described the parents as being weird. According to Collins, Myrtle Rowell was a Pentecostal lady, who wore her hair back and long dresses. Robert Rowell was described as being a strict father. Myrtle Rowell upset Lisa Collins a couple days after the discovery of David's body, when Collins went to pay her respects upon the Rowell family. According to Collins, Myrtle Rowell told Collins, "If you didn't live here, this would not have happened."

Although she never met Keith Wampler, Collins described him as weird. Collins believes Keith Wampler killed David Rowell, but she did not provide any information to support her belief. Michael Johnson was described as being way off and mean. Collins was friends with Alice Johnson, Michael's sister.

On February 5, 1982, Collins said the only time saw Michael Rowell at 10:00 p.m., when Michael came to her trailer looking for David. This is where the interview gets interesting. Collins was reminded of her statement to the police on February 10, 1982, when she was interviewed by Detective William Mullins, Moraine Police, where, according to the report filed by Mullins, she supposedly said that Michael Rowell visited her at 5:30 p.m. on February 5 and he was intoxicated. Lisa Collins, in a clear and concise manner, said, "That's a lie."

Collins did not see David Rowell on February 5, 1982. She was read the portion of Detective Mullins's report where she claimed David Rowell said, "This is the last time you are going to see me. I'm going to die." Collins appeared genuinely shocked when this was read to her. She said that never told that to Detective Mullins. Collins said if David Rowell ever said that to her, she would immediately go to inform Myrtle Rowell about it. Collins repeated she did not see David Rowell on February 5.

Due to the conflicts between what was in Detective Mullins's report and what Lisa Collins was saying, Collins was shown Detective Mullins's report from 1982. After she read the police report, she said the entire report is false. She knew nothing about David getting into trouble on the school bus, which was a claim that Detective Mullins made. She repeated her denial that Michael Rowell came to her trailer at 5:30 p.m. on February 5. The only time she saw Michael Rowell was at 10:00 p.m. on February 5, when he was looking for David.

Collins said the entire statement about Michael Rowell telling her that Keith Wampler grabbed his genitals was false, as well as the statement regarding her knowledge about Keith having a knife. Collins denied telling Detective Mullins about David Rowell having access to various drugs or Robert Rowell having a heart condition. Collins repeated her earlier statement about the entire police report being false.

Collins described Detective William Mullins as having a bad reputation among the people of Moraine. Collins claimed it was common knowledge that Mullins would frame people for crimes they did not commit.

Collins remembers seeing Michael Rowell at noon on February 6, when he came to her residence. According to Collins, Michael Rowell said, "They found my brother's body." It should be noted that David's body was not discovered until 3:50 p.m. Also, according to Collins, it was well-known that David's clothing was found neatly folded in the shopping bag in the field. There were no tears in the clothing.

This interview is, at least, damning to the integrity of the Moraine Police investigation. Lisa Collins said the entire report regarding her interview was false. If that is in fact the case, then one has to ask the following: What else did the Moraine Police fabricate? What other reports are mere fiction?

Lisa Collins, as earlier stated, was genuinely upset after reading the Moraine Police report filed by Detective William Mullins regarding the February 10, 1982, interview. Collins firmly maintained the report was fabricated. In his own documentation, Detective William Mullins said he was doing a telephonic interview with Robert Rowell at the same time he was interviewing Lisa Collins. If that documentation is correct, how could Detective Mullins be a two places at the same time?

In his report, Detective William Mullins claimed that Collins told him about Michael Rowell returning to her residence on Friday, February 5, 1982, as *Fantasy Island* was coming on the television. This is clearly fabricated because *Fantasy Island* was not shown on Friday, February 5, 1982, or any other Friday. *Fantasy Island* was shown by ABC-TV on Saturday nights. This fact was confirmed by WKEF-TV, the ABC affiliate in Dayton. When asked if was possible for WKEF-TV to be showing a previous episode of *Fantasy Island*, the response was simply no because the station is committed to showing the network programs during the prime time. According to WKEF-TV, if they had to replay a program because it was missed due to a special report, then that program would have to be shown after the late-night news. This fact does give some credibility to the claim about this particular report is fabricated. If this report is fabricated, then the integrity of the entire investigation comes into question, thus creating reasonable doubt.

John McGarvey Interview

On August 6, 2015, at 12:30 p.m., John McGarvey agreed to be interviewed for this investigation. McGarvey lived at 2759 Cozy Lane, next door to Keith Wampler's trailer. McGarvey lived there with his fiancé.

McGarvey did not really know David or Michael Rowell. He knew the Rowell boys would visit Keith once in a while but did not know them other than that.

McGarvey described Keith Wampler as being a "good kid," who would help him with handyman projects. McGarvey taught Keith how to trap rabbits and how to repair things. Keith liked to hang out at McGarvey's trailer at night. Keith would usually hang out with either Cecil, his father, or McGarvey. McGarvey was shocked that Keith was convicted of this crime because he believes that Keith is not capable of committing such an offense. When told that Keith was still in prison for this crime, McGarvey showed signs of being genuinely upset.

On February 5, 1982, McGarvey remembers seeing Keith. McGarvey was putting laundry in his truck to take to his fiancé's parents' house in Vandalia, Ohio, where they did their laundry. McGarvey had no intention of spending the night there. His plans were to do laundry, have dinner, then come home. The decision to spend the night in Vandalia was made while they were doing laundry and at the last minute. Keith had no idea they were staying in Vandalia, and he had expected them to return.

McGarvey remembers when Keith was arrested. He said sometime after the police took Keith away, Keith called his trailer asking for a lawyer and some legal help. McGarvey's fiancé's father was a military police officer at Wright-Patterson Air Force Base. McGarvey called his future father-in-law, who made some discrete inquiries. His fiancé's father told him, "It was a good thing you weren't there, or they would have had you." McGarvey said he interpreted that statement as meaning the Moraine Police was going to charge someone in the trailer park with murder, regardless of the evidence. McGarvey claimed the Moraine Police did not have a good reputation in 1982.

The police questioned him several days after David Rowell's body was discovered. This is where the interview became fascinating. According to McGarvey, the police asked him about a hunting knife. The police tried to associate the knife with the murder, but that is impossible because the knife was hidden in his trailer. Nobody knew, or knows, where he keeps his knives, and that included his fiancé at the time. He does not allow anyone access to his home and remembers that his trailer did not show signs of being burglarized. When the police asked about it, he walked directly to his office in the trailer and to the spot where he kept his knives. He retrieved the hunting knife for them and handed it to them. The knife was used to clean rabbits that he trapped.

Two huge pieces of the puzzle were learned from this interview. The first regards the knife. Detective William Mullins must explain how the knife, which the state alleges was used in this crime, could be in a place where Keith Wampler did not have access? Keep in mind, it is the state's job to prove the knife was involved. It is not Keith Wampler's job to prove it was not. Later, in the Salunek interview, you will see how this knife was used, by Robert Head, assistant Montgomery County prosecutor, in an attempt to solicit perjured testimony.

Second, we get a glimpse into the mind-set of the Moraine Police. Apparently, it was common knowledge throughout the Miami Valley law enforcement community that the Moraine Police was going to pin this crime on someone in the Gem City Estates Trailer Park. John McGarvey stated, in the 2015 interview, that his fiancé's father told him that it was a good thing McGarvey was not home on night of February 5, 1982, because the Moraine Police was going to charge someone in that trailer park with murder. John McGarvey's fiancé's father worked as a law enforcement officer at Wright-Patterson Air Force Base and made several inquiries about the case. Instead of following the evidence to see where it goes, the police were going to manipulate the evidence and make it fit their theory. That is not how proper, transparent criminal investigations are conducted in the United States.

Andrew Choate Interview

At 12:15 p.m. on August 10, 2015, an attempt was made to interview Andrew Choate in person as his residence. That attempt was not successful, so a voicemail was left for him. At 4:05 p.m., Andrew Choate returned the voicemail and agreed to be interviewed, via telephone. Choate provided some very interesting information, as well as contradicting his original statements to the police.

Andrew Choate was friends with Michael Rowell and knew David as being Michael's little brother. Choate described David Rowell as being a good kid. Choate spent the night at the Rowell's home from time to time. Choate said the Rowells were Pentecostal people. Choate remembers two days after David's body was discovered, Michael Rowell came to his house to give him a winter coat. According to Choate, Michael told him to take the coat because Michael would not be needing a winter coat anymore. That was the last time he saw Michael Rowell or the Rowell family until the trial in July 1982. Choate claimed Bobby Rowell took David's murder very hard. According to Choate, rumors circulated about the neighborhood that David Rowell was Robert's biological son and Michael Rowell was not. Choate said Myrtle Rowell was both boys' mother, but they had different fathers.

Choate described Keith Wampler as being "an evil son of a bitch." Choate first met Keith in the fall of 1981, and they socialized for only a few months. Choate claims that in December 1981, Keith tried to grab Choate's crotch. According to Choate, this happened on Keith's patio, and Michael Johnson was present for it. Choate believed Keith was trying to molest him, and he immediately went home. Choate never told his parents about this.

The alleged molest attempt was not the last time Choate saw Keith Wampler. Michael Johnson, Keith, and he got into a fist fight near the Moraine Meadows Elementary School. This occurred two weeks prior to David's murder. According to Choate's recollection of events, Michael Johnson was talking trash to him when Choate took a swing at Johnson. At that point, Michael Johnson and Keith proceeded to beat up Choate. Choate claims the fight was over "kids' stuff."

Choate remembers Keith Wampler carrying a hunting knife, and he kept it in a sheath on his hip. Choate does not remember if Keith ever pulled the knife from the sheath. Keith never had a sword. When Choate's statement to the Moraine Police regarding Keith having a sword was read back to him, he denied ever telling the Moraine Police such a story.

Michael Johnson and Andrew Choate were good friends before Keith Wampler moved to Moraine, according to Choate. Michael Johnson began hanging out more and more with Keith, which created a strain in the Johnson-Choate friendship. Johnson reestablished the friendship several days after David's murder. It was not long after that when Johnson was arrested, charged, and convicted for David's murder. Choate confirmed that Michael Johnson was convicted in Montgomery County Juvenile Court. According to Choate, Michael Johnson and he spoke about once a year. Choate believes Johnson could not have committed this crime.

Here is where the interview gets really interesting. According to Andrew Choate, he was home during the evening of February 5, 1982. He said he did not have any visitors. Choate denied ever meeting Ted Ritchie. This statement contradicts what Ted Ritchie testified about in court, when he said Michael Johnson and he left Keith's trailer and walked to Andrew Choate's house. Above all, it contradicts Choate's own trial testimony, where he stated that Michael Johnson and Ted Ritchie came to his house at about 11:15 p.m. and stayed until about midnight. It also contradicts Choate's statement to the Moraine Police.

When asked how did the police know to interview him, Andrew Choate said someone in the trailer park claimed Choate was involved in the murder of David Rowell. Choate does not have a clue as to who would tell the police such a story.

Choate described Detective Mullins and Sergeant Wynne as being assholes. Choate claims the Moraine Police were always trying to charge people there with crimes because the people living there were poor.

In his interview, Choate came off as holding some sort of grudge against Keith Wampler. Even though the interview was conducted telephonically, it was very clear Andrew Choate was being deceptive. It cannot be overlooked that his statements conflict with each other. He either lied in 2015 or in 1982. His statements regarding whether or not Ted Ritchie and Michael Johnson visited him on February 5, 1982, are at total opposite ends of the spectrum. This raises a huge integrity issue regarding the prosecution of Keith Wampler. If he lied in 2015, then Andrew Choate just showed he knows more about this murder than he is telling. If he lied in 1982, he committed perjury, which is a crime in the State of Ohio.

If the Andrew Choate interview muddied the waters of this investigation, then the next interview really stirred up the dirt. The Montgomery County Prosecutor's Office wanted to paint Keith

Wampler as being a deranged killer with homosexual tendencies. They looked into Keith's activities while he was living in Kettering, Ohio. In doing so, they found Scott Lombardo.

Scott Lombardo Interview

The research into Lombardo's background revealed he is the president and founder of Medicare Solutions, which, according to his website, is located at 10501 Success Lane, Suite 200, Dayton, Ohio. On August 8, 2015, an attempt to locate and interview Scott Lombardo occurred at the so-called location for Medicare Solutions. The term *so-called* is being used because it does not exist there. An abandoned set of offices were found on the second floor of the building located at 10501 Success Lane. Suite 200 is the entire second floor. The owners of the building were located and said Medicare Solutions moved out in the middle of the night sometime in either February or March 2015 without paying the owners several thousand dollars of rent.

On August 8 and August 10, 2015, attempts were made to interview Lombardo at his home. Those attempts were unsuccessful, and a message was left for him to call. At 8:55 p.m. on August 10, 2015, Scott Lombardo returned the message and agreed to be interviewed. The interview was conducted telephonically.

Lombardo remembered Keith Wampler from Keith's days in Kettering. Lombardo said Keith lived on Dorothy Lane in Kettering during that time. Lombardo claimed to have known Keith for a period of six months to eighteen months—Lombardo could not remember exactly. Lombardo said Keith drank and smoked marijuana while he lived in Kettering. He described Keith as being weird. When asked about what he meant, Lombardo could not give any details.

The June 10, 1982, police report, filed by Detective William Mullins, was read to Lombardo. This report documented Detective

Mullins interview with Scott Lombardo. In a police report, a statement was made that Keith masturbated in front of Lombardo. The report credited Lombardo with telling the police this story. When questioned about it, Lombardo said, "It could have happened." Lombardo repeated his statement about Keith being weird. Lombardo does not remember talking to the police about this case. When confronted with the report indicating that Lombardo was taken to Dennis Langer's, assistant Montgomery County prosecutor's, office, Lombardo said he does not remember that occurring, but further stated he does not deny it either. Scott Lombardo's excuse for not remembering being interviewed by the police or being taken to the Montgomery County Prosecutor's Office is, "I was high most of the time." It should be noted that there is no documentation indicating that Detective Mullins spoke with Scott Lombardo's parents to gain their permission for Scott to be interviewed by the police, as required by Ohio Revised Code, Section 2151.

This interview brings into question the integrity of this character witness. It is hard to believe that a fifteen-year-old boy would not remember being questioned by the police or the prosecutor about a murder. That is a huge event in a teenager's life. If he was high, like he claims, then it is plausible he does not remember and that he was as much of a delinquent as Keith Wampler. If he was high and the interview occurred, one has to ask why Detective Mullins, this highly trained police officer, did not pick up on the fact he was questioning an impaired individual?

It was clear Scott Lombardo was being evasive and, at times, tried to be cute during the interview. What Scott Lombardo did not realize was a complete background check was conducted on him, and everyone else, prior to the interview. The more evasive he was, the more his background, to include criminal history, showed.

Officers of the court are sworn to seek the truth. As a matter of fact, it is a crime to knowingly and willingly provide false information to the court. The next interview gives a hint that a fraud may have been perpetrated upon the court. This fraud was not committed by the defense team but by the Montgomery County Prosecutor's Office.

Raymond T. Salunek Interview

Raymond T. Salunek was interviewed on August 12, 2015, at his residence. The interview lasted seventy-five minutes and covered his relationship with Keith Wampler. Salunek knew Keith for about a year when Keith lived in Kettering, Ohio. Salunek claimed Keith would introduce himself as Chuck Wampler. This is disputed by Keith, who says he always went by the name of Keith. Salunek described Keith as being weird and a loose cannon, but not violent. Salunek clearly said Keith was not capable of murder. According to Salunek, Keith had a poor family situation and was being abused by an older brother. It should be noted that Keith did have an older brother, who never resided in Ohio. The older brother lived and died in Louisiana in 1982.

Keith Wampler used drugs and drank while he was in Kettering, according to Salunek. Most of the people Salunek socialized with, including Scott Lombardo, drank and smoked marijuana. Some of them even used harder drugs, such as quaaludes. Salunek admitted he too smoked marijuana and drank.

Salunek was approached by the Montgomery County Prosecutor's Office regarding testifying at Keith's trial. It was some-time in the spring of 1982. Salunek remembers this because he was living in Chillicothe, Ohio, at the time and his parents were separated. Someone, Salunek could not remember who, from the Moraine Police came to Chillicothe and drove him the seventy-seven miles to Dayton to meet with Robert Head, assistant Montgomery

County prosecutor. Salunek remembers clearly it was Robert Head because he thought it was a strange name.

In the meeting, Head showed Salunek a buck knife and told Salunek it was used in the murder of David Rowell. Head accused Salunek of giving the knife to Wampler and demanded that Salunek testify to that in court. Salunek told Head he never saw the knife before and he was not going to testify in court because that would be a lie. Head wanted him to tell the court that he gave the knife to Wampler. Again, Salunek repeated that he never saw the knife before the meeting with Head. According to Salunek, Head became hostile and threatened him with jail if he did not do as the prosecutor wanted. Salunek still refused to testify and was never called to the stand in Keith's trial. The knife Salunek described matches the description of the knife that belonged to John McGarvey, Keith Wampler's next-door neighbor in Moraine.

Salunek added he thought it was strange that Keith Wampler's attorneys did not call him to testify. Salunek said if the prosecutors were trying to create a story around this knife, his testimony would be used to dispute the prosecution's claim. Robert Bostick or Wayne Stephan never called Salunek.

Salunek had communicated with Keith Wampler while Keith was sent to prison. According to Salunek, he quit communicating with Keith because the two had a falling out over Salunek's fiancé at the time.

Salunek's interview brings into question the honesty of the prosecution's case. Salunek's interview alleges not only misconduct by the Montgomery County Prosecutor's Office but illegal activity as well as incompetence by the defense team. It is quite possible that Robert Head made an attempt to suborn perjury in this case, which is the most serious fraud that an attorney can inflict upon the court. It was clear that the forensic evidence did not support the state's theory of the crime, so Robert Head wanted some help to ensure a conviction.

AND THEN THERE WAS REASONABLE DOUBT

The most disturbing thing is in 1984, Mr. Head lost his law license for subornation of perjury. The license was returned in 1988.

As a part of the investigation, attempts were made to locate David Rowell's friends in order to get the complete profile of the victim. In many homicide cases, clues as to the suspect's identity are often found in the victim's background. The interview of Bryan "Cappy" C. Canterbury gave some good information into David's background. There were two other friends mentioned in the police reports: Roy Elam Jr. and Randall Hendricks. Roy Elam Jr. was known to be David's close friend, but interviewing him turned out to be impossible. Roy Elam Jr. died in 2002 while in the custody of the Ohio Department of Rehabilitation and Corrections. He was serving a two-year sentence for robbery. Better luck was had in locating Randall Hendricks.

Randall Hendricks Interview

Interviewing Randall Hendricks was important not only to learn more on David Rowell's background but Michael Rowell claimed, in his testimony, Hendricks helped him look for David on February 5, 1982. On August 12, 2015, at 2:00 p.m., an attempt was made to interview Hendricks at his residence in Monroe, Ohio. That attempt was not successful, and a message was left for Hendricks to call. At 5:45 p.m., Hendricks called. At first, his demeanor was confrontational and insulting. When the purpose for the interview was explained, he changed his attitude and agreed to the interview.

Hendricks claimed that he was one of David's close friends. Like Andrew Choate, who said he would spend the night at the Rowell residence from time to time, Hendricks would also spend the night because of his friendship with David. Hendricks called David a jokester, who had the tendency to upset people. He remembers a prank that David pulled at the Dayton Mall that included goldfish and a hot tub that was on display. Hendricks described the Rowell family as being Pentecostal in their religious beliefs, with Myrtle Rowell being extreme. Hendricks thought Bobby Rowell, David's father, as being a nice person, and he described the workshop that Robert had in the garage.

Hendricks remembers learning about the reason the Rowell family moved to Moraine from New Carlisle. According to Hendricks, the family received death threats because Myrtle Rowell was being accused of informing the police about some neighbors' illegal drug activities. Hendricks described Myrtle Rowell as being a protective mother to the point of being paranoid about her children.

Hendricks recalled the events of February 5, 1982. He was a member of the Moraine Baptist Church, who sponsored an open gym at Moraine Meadows Elementary School. Hendricks attended those open gyms. It was sometime between 7:30 p.m. and 8:00 p.m., when he left the school to return home. While he was leaving the school, he was approached by Michael Rowell, who asked Hendricks if he saw David. Hendricks remembers telling Michael that he had not seen David, and that was the only time he saw Michael Rowell that evening. Hendricks never went looking for David that night.

Hendricks knew nothing about Keith Wampler and never met him. However, Hendricks knew Michael Johnson. Hendricks described Johnson as having "a mean streak." Hendricks avoided contact with Michael Johnson, but that was difficult because Hendrick's older brother was one of Johnson's friends. Hendricks recounted a scenario in which Michael Johnson, without provocation, pushed Hendricks to the ground one day. The neighborhood knew Michael Johnson as being a bully. Hendricks went on to describe other acts of delinquency committed by Michael Johnson, to include theft and animal cruelty.

Hendricks had a clear memory of February 6, 1982. In the late afternoon, word was spreading throughout the neighborhood that the police were recovering David Rowell's body from a field on Kreitzer Road. Hendricks remembers walking to Kreitzer Road to watch the police activity. At the end of the sidewalk, which runs beside the Moraine Civic Center, Andrew Choate, Choate's stepfather, and Michael Johnson were standing there watching the police. According to Hendricks, Michael Johnson made a statement that came out of the blue. Johnson said, "I had nothing to do with this. I spent the night at Andrew Choate's house."

Hendricks considered Andrew Choate to be a thief, and he proceeded to give examples of how Choate allegedly stole things and tried to sell them to Hendricks. Choate and Johnson were close friends. Hendricks believes Michael Johnson and Andrew Choate know more about this murder than what they are telling, to include Johnson's involvement. Hendricks could not provide an opinion regarding Keith because he did not know Keith Wampler.

Hendricks's information is useful. However, it should be noted that since the interview, several issues arose regarding Randall Hendricks. On several occasions, late at night, Hendricks made calls demanding to have copies of reports from this investigation. When he was told that could not be done, he became threatening and began harassing Lori Wampler, Keith's wife. The harassment included threats of bodily harm and got so bad that she had to call the Dayton Police. The complaint was forwarded to the Montgomery County Prosecutor's Office, who issued a civil Do Not Contact order. Apparently, the Montgomery County Prosecutor's Office does not enforce Ohio Revised Code, Section 2917, Telecommunications Harassment. It looks as if they view it as a civil issue, not a criminal one.

It should also be noted that Mrs. Wampler had a battle on her hands for someone to take the complaint. When she called Dayton

Police, they dispatched an officer to her residence. That officer refused to take the report and made several derogatory statements regarding Keith Wampler. When this occurred, Lori Wampler was advised to file a complaint with the Office of the Chief of Police. To Dayton Police Department's credit, a lieutenant took over the case and took the report. The unprofessional police response, coupled with the prosecutor turning a criminal matter into a civil matter, makes one question the quality of justice for those who are not affluent in the Miami Valley.

In 1982, James Combs resided at 2941 Schoolhouse Lane in Moraine, which was on the southern edge of the Gem City Estates Trailer Park. Moraine Police interviewed James Combs regarding the events of February 6, 1982. On August 16, 2015, James Combs agreed to be interviewed regarding the murder of David Rowell. The latest interview lasted seventy-five minutes.

James Combs Interview

Combs knew David Rowell, Michael Rowell, Michael Johnson, and Keith Wampler. Combs attended school with Michael Rowell, whom he considered as being a friend. Through that friendship, he became familiar with David and the other members of the Rowell family. Combs described David Rowell as being a normal and good kid. Combs hung out with Michael and David at the Moraine Civic Center. Bobby and Myrtle Rowell were strict parents, according to Combs. Combs knew the parents were religious but could not recall what denomination. However, the parents were strange. Combs recalled how the Rowell family just up and left in the middle of the night from their home at 2970 Kreitzer Road, after David's murder. The family left without notice or warning. Combs believed it was within a day or two after David was discovered.

As for Keith Wampler, Combs described him as strange at times and further clarified that by saying Keith was a loner. Keith was the new kid on the block. It was common knowledge among the kids in the neighborhood that if you wanted to smoke cigarettes or drink beer, you went to Keith's trailer because he would share his with anyone. Combs knew that Michael Johnson and Michael Rowell were common visitors to Keith's trailer.

Combs did not have any derogatory things to say about Michael Johnson. Combs confirmed that Johnson did reside in a condemned house in Gordon's Trailer Park. Johnson's cousin, Judy Tabor, resided in Gordon's Trailer Park as well. Michael Johnson's close friend was Andrew Choate, whom Combs described as being weird. Combs further described Choate as being a heavy marijuana user.

James Shipman Jr. was also considered weird by Combs. Combs remembers that James Shipman Jr. and Joey Shipman, James's little brother, were often left alone by their parents. Combs saw James Jr. and Joey always together in the neighborhood. Combs thought it was strange that the Shipmans left the neighborhood immediately after David Rowell's murder.

Combs said many people in the neighborhood had hunting knives because several neighbors trapped rabbits in the vacant field adjacent to the Gem City Estates Trailer Park. The field were David Rowell's body was discovered.

Combs was grounded on February 5 and February 6, 1982. He was not allowed to go to visit with friends or have visitors. Combs was home all night on February 5. On February 6, he did not have any visitors because of his punishment. Combs left his home at 11:00 a.m. to go to Farmerville, Ohio, to attend a family function. It was late in the afternoon of February 6 when Combs returned home. According to Combs, his father always parked along Kreitzer Road, behind his trailer. As his father was parking, Combs noticed the police cars on Kreitzer Road. As his parents went into the trailer, Combs, knowing he was violating his punishment, ran over to Keith's trailer to find out what was happening. Combs asked Keith about what was happening, and Keith either said "Someone killed David Rowell" or "Someone strangled David Rowell." Combs cannot remember Keith Wampler's exact words.

Combs believes Keith Wampler did not commit this crime because Keith is not capable of committing such a crime. Combs further believes that Michael Johnson did not kill David Rowell; however, he believes Johnson is withholding information, as well as James Shipman Jr. Combs thinks Andrew Choate could be capable of killing David Rowell.

Then Combs said members of the Rowell family could have killed David. Combs repeated his claim about the family being strange, and he thought it was odd that Bobby Rowell, David's father, found the body. Combs opined about how odd it was that the father found the body, and soon after, the entire family left the area. He repeated his belief about it being possible the family had something to do with the murder of David Rowell.

Combs said the Moraine Police interviewed him a couple days after David's body was found. Combs remembers the interview clearly because prior to the interview, he pulled a knife on Sergeant Joseph Wynne. The entire neighborhood was on edge for weeks, and his father gave him a knife for protection. According to Combs, Sergeant Wynne snuck up on him, and Combs did not realize who this person was, so he pulled out his knife.

Combs described Sergeant Joseph Wynne and Detective William Mullins as being assholes. Detective Mullins did not have a good reputation in Moraine. Combs further stated the community did not have much respect for the Moraine Police in 1982. Combs claimed he did not meet with the Montgomery County Prosecutor's Office prior to his trial testimony.

Combs recollection of the events surrounding this case was pretty good, except for one area: he firmly states he did not meet with the prosecutor prior to his testimony. However, his trial testimony tells another story. Under oath, he told the court he did meet with the Montgomery County Prosecutor prior to trial. If he forgot such important meetings, then it is possible that he forgot about Keith Wampler visiting him on February 6, which Keith claims and Combs denies.

The two-hour interview of Michael Johnson on August 19, 2015, could be described as fruitful. Michael Johnson was arrested, charged, and tried, as a juvenile, for the murder of David Rowell. The way Michael Johnson was handled by the Montgomery County Prosecutor raises many fascinating questions. One of the most important question is, why did Johnson get tried as a juvenile while Keith Wampler got tried as an adult?

There were two main purposes to interview Michael Johnson. The first was to seek his cooperation in releasing his juvenile court record, which he denied. The second was to get his recollection of the facts in this case. In doing so, you will find that Michael Johnson destroyed his own alibi.

Michael Johnson Interview

Michael Johnson confirmed that he lived in a condemned house in the Gordon Trailer Park, which was adjacent to the Gem City Estates Trailer Park, in 1982 and claimed that his family did not move to West Carrollton, Ohio, until after he was arrested for David Rowell's murder. This statement contradicts police reports and trial testimony from various witnesses, to include members of his family, who said that in February 1982, Michael Johnson lived in West Carrollton. One has to wonder what other fascinating tales would be told during this interview given the fact that contrary to everyone else's recollection, Michael Johnson would lie about where he was living on February 5.

That wonder turned to total amazement when Michael Johnson contradicted himself regarding his relationship with Keith Wampler. At first, Johnson denied ever knowing Keith Wampler or ever visiting Keith's trailer. Then he admitted that he drank beer with Keith on a regular basis. Later in the interview, Johnson said, "Keith didn't do it." Johnson claimed the prosecution had no evidence regarding Keith's involvement in David Rowell's murder. Those are pretty bold statements from a person who started the interview out by saying he did not know Keith Wampler.

Johnson constantly contradicted evidence that was presented in court regarding his whereabouts on February 5, 1982. Though claiming to be living in the Gordon Trailer Park, Johnson said he spent the night at Andrew Choate's house. This is in spite of the fact that Choate stated Ted Ritchie and Michael Johnson came to his house at 11:15 p.m. and stayed until midnight. Johnson could not understand why Choate would tell such a story in court. Johnson was not told that during his interview, a week earlier, Choate claimed he did not see Johnson at all on February 5, 1982. Maybe Michael Johnson can ask Andrew Choate about it. After all, in his own admission, Michael Johnson is friends with Andrew Choate to this day and they talk at least once a month.

Johnson totally denies Randall Hendrick's claim about, on February 6, 1982, while the police were recovering David's body, Johnson saying, "I had nothing to do with this. I was at Andy Choate's all night." On top of that, Johnson cannot remember if the police were in the neighborhood on February 6.

When confronted about his visit to Keith Wampler's trailer at 9:00 p.m. on February 5, 1982, accompanied by Ted Ritchie, James Shipman Jr., and Joey Shipman, Johnson denied it ever happened.

Again, this totally contradicts statements by many witnesses, to include members of his own family. Johnson denied ever knowing James Shipman Jr., Joey Shipman, or Ted Ritchie.

Johnson denied ever knowing the Rowells, though changed his story to say that he knew Michael Rowell and they were friends because they attended the same school. Johnson said he never met David Rowell.

Johnson did confirm the fact that Judy Tabor is his cousin and she lived in a trailer in the Gordon Trailer Park but denies ever being at her trailer on February 5, 1982. Johnson described his relationship with Tabor as being strained and claimed that most of the family broke off contact with her because of "the way she is."

Johnson was shown the police report Detective William Mullins filed on March 3, 1982, regarding Johnson's interview with the police. Johnson said, contrary to the report, Detective Mullins spoke to his mother at their home and then took Johnson to police headquarters. Johnson's mother was not present in the interview room when he was questioned. Johnson did confirm that his mother was disabled but denies Detective Mullins's claim about her being a "functioning illiterate." Johnson said the entire police report is fabricated.

Johnson remembers Detective Mullins as starting and stopping the tape recorder, but he could not remember the questions he was asked or the answers he provided. Johnson claims Detective Mullins told him if he answered questions in a certain way, the police would let him go home. Detective Mullins suggested answers to Johnson. Keep in mind, Johnson cannot remember the questions or his answers, but he remembers Detective Mullins suggesting answers.

Regarding the police report dated February 9, 1982, regarding Johnson's initial interview with the police, Johnson denied it ever happened.

Johnson claims his childhood is a blur, especially this terrible period. He drank and smoked a lot of marijuana during this time.

He cannot remember his trial in juvenile court. He described his trial as "surreal."

Johnson opined that the Moraine Police were going to prove that someone in the trailer park committed this murder. Johnson said Detective William Mullins did not have a good reputation. However, Johnson claimed that several years later, Detective Mullins approached his father and apologized for "railroading your son." Johnson claimed Mullins made the statement that the police were "out to get Wampler." When asked if his father would like to make a statement for this investigation, Johnson claimed he would, but as of yet, Johnson's father never called to provide that statement.

Johnson cleared his voice prior to saying "I didn't kill David Rowell." Johnson's main desire is to clear his name. However, it should be noted that Johnson was told if he cooperated, findings of this investigation could be shared with him in order to clear his name and it would not cost him anything because the case is being investigated pro bono. Johnson refused to be honest and refused to release his juvenile court record.

Throughout the interview, Michael Johnson kept claiming he cannot be tried again for this crime. Of course, that is very true, because of double jeopardy. Given that double jeopardy is attached, one has to ponder the true reason as to why he does not want his juvenile record released. One can speculate that there are things in that record that may exonerate Keith Wampler. One can also ponder that Michael Johnson was involved in this crime and he does not want the world to know. Is it possible also that Michael Johnson lied to the police and the prosecutor?

For a person who wants to clear his name, his demeanor through-out the interview indicated the opposite. He appeared more like he had something to hide. Aside from his bold-faced lies, he was nervous throughout the interview. This interview occurred on Johnson's own turf, in his backyard. The fact that Andrew Choate and Michael

Johnson changed their statements since 1982 and cannot get their stories straight definitely wrecks their credibility. Unfortunately for Choate and Johnson, the subsequent interviews will make their statements, and them, look ridiculous.

The next phase of the investigation was to locate and interview witnesses who reside outside of the state of Ohio. This required two trips: one to Kentucky and South Carolina, the other to Alabama and Florida. Ted Ritchie, Darrell Doan, Judy Tabor, James Shipman Jr., Joey Shipman, Robert Rowell, Michael Rowell, and Myrtle Rowell all needed to be interviewed.

Some information learned on the trips supports a hypothesis that was developed in this investigation regarding who really murdered David Rowell. Other pieces of information support suspected misconduct by the Montgomery County Prosecutor's Office. Also, some information learned supports allegations that were made in 1982 about witnesses withholding information.

The first trip lasted four days, and the first stop was Jessamine County, Kentucky, which is located southwest of Lexington. The first stop was the Jessamine County Sheriff's Office, where the sheriff and his staff were hospitable and extended every courtesy.

Ted D. Ritchie Interview

On August 26, 2015, Ted Ritchie was located and agreed to be interviewed regarding this case. The thirty-five-minute interview was informative and, to an extent, sad. Ted Ritchie was led to believe the prosecution's theory on this case is true. This has haunted him since 1982.

Ritchie confirmed he was residing in Orlando, Florida, in 1982 and came back to Ohio in January 1982 to attend his brother's funeral. Ritchie was staying with his mother for a while because of the tragic nature of his brother's death. His mother lived in Gordon's Trailer Park at the time. It was in January when he met Michael Johnson. Ritchie really did not know Michael Johnson that well and they only hung out a few times. Ritchie remembers visiting Keith Wampler's trailer on February 5. He described Wampler as "quiet" and "not outgoing."

Ritchie talked about Michael Johnson, another teenager, and he were at Keith's trailer. Ritchie could not remember the other teenager's name. He could not remember whether or not a younger boy was with them. They were all drinking beer while at Keith's place. Ritchie remembers having to use the bathroom and Keith told him where it was. Ritchie described the trailer as having two bedrooms with the bathroom between them. Ritchie noticed the door was closed to the back bedroom and he did not think anything of it. Ritchie believed he could have gone anywhere in the trailer without restriction. Michael Johnson and he stayed at Keith's trailer for about two hours before leaving to visit another one of Michael Johnson's friends.

Ritchie remembers leaving Keith's trailer and walking through the vacant field along Kreitzer Road. He followed Michael Johnson down a sidewalk that went between Moraine Civic Center and a school. Ritchie could not remember the friend's name, but he remembers staying for about an hour. He said the friend could have been Andrew Choate but could not remember his name. Michael Johnson and his friend were playing with knives while he was at the friend's house.

After Michael Johnson and Ritchie left the friend's house, they went their separate ways. He does not know where Michael Johnson went, but he went to Judy Tabor's trailer. Tabor was one of Michael Johnson's relatives. That was the last time he saw Michael Johnson. Michael Johnson was wearing some kind of boots but could not remember the style.

When asked about the police report claiming that Michael Johnson, David Rowell, and Ted Ritchie were seen together on Kreitzer Road at 7:00 p.m. on February 5, 1982, Ritchie firmly stated that the report is false. Ritchie has no idea who David Rowell was, nor did he ever meet any of the Rowell family on February 5. Ritchie's only contact with the Rowell family was during the trial of Keith Wampler because the Rowell family and he were staying at the same hotel. He repeated that he never had any contact with them prior to the trial.

Ritchie repeated he did not find anything unusual about Keith's trailer. He felt he could have gone anywhere in the trailer and Keith would not have objected. He did not believe anyone else was in the trailer, other than Michael Johnson, another teenager, Keith, and him. Ritchie expressed his willingness to provide DNA, fingerprints, or anything else required to help clear up this case. He said this has haunted him for all these years. According to Ritchie, the Montgomery County Prosecutor's Office told him that David Rowell was in the trailer, not the other way around. He said they convinced him that was true.

Ritchie's demeanor throughout the interview indicated his willingness to cooperate. Overall, he was truthful. When he was asked a question and he could not remember, he simply said he did not remember. One could say Ted Ritchie is another victim in this crime. While David Rowell's suffering came at the hands of his killer, Ted Ritchie's suffering came at the hands of the so-called educated attorneys at the Montgomery County Prosecutor's Office, who led him to believe that David Rowell was tied up in the second bedroom in the trailer while Ted Ritchie was in the living room drinking a beer.

The next stop was Mount Vernon, Kentucky, where the next morning would be spent tracking down Darrell Doan, who resided at the Gordon Trailer Park in 1982 and was friends with Judy Tabor and Michael Johnson. The search for Darrell Doan turned out to be quite colorful. The first place visited was the Rockcastle County Sheriff's Office. It was here where it was learned that Darrell Doan is well-known to the law enforcement community in Rockcastle County. Apparently, it was during one of his encounters with the local constabulary where he stole the personal information of the local sheriff and began to use it. After several hours of going to one false address after another, a lead was developed, through the Mount Vernon Police Department, that Darrell Doan was known to reside at an old rundown motel called the Blue Grass Inn.

To describe the Blue Grass Inn as a rundown motel would be kind and possibly an insult to rundown motels. The residents of the Blue Grass Inn were hanging out with the doors of their rooms open. Several were smoking, while others were drinking beer. The only folks that were cooperative was the young couple who took over Darrell Doan's room. The couple said Darrell Doan left Mount Vernon, Kentucky, for parts unknown, possibly Louisiana.

With the attempt to locate and interview Darrell Doan being a failure, it was off to South Carolina to locate and question Judy Tabor. On August 28, 2015, she was located in Cherokee County, South Carolina, which is located in the northwest corner of the state. Her residence was located, and it proved to be quite challenging. The residence, a rundown mobile home, is on a steep hillside with a narrow dirt driveway. Since 1982, Judy Tabor got married, and her last name is now Offill.

Judy Tabor-Offill Interview

Offill confirmed she is Michael Johnson's cousin and she resided in Gordon's Trailer Park in 1982. Offill remembered Michael Johnson and his sister, Alice, coming to her trailer on February 5, 1982. She could not remember what time they arrived. Offill said Michael

Johnson was living in West Carrollton, Ohio, at the time because they were forced to leave a condemned house where they were living in Gordon's Trailer Park. Michael Johnson was at her trailer for a few minutes after he arrived, then he left, and she did not know where he went. Alice Johnson and she went looking for Michael Johnson after he was gone for quite a long time. Offill was not clear on how long. They failed to locate Michael Johnson.

It was at this point where the interview began to get interesting. Offill would be asked certain questions and then claim she could not remember. Her trial testimony was then read back to her, and she was questioned about it. In her testimony, she said Michael Johnson and Ted Ritchie came to her trailer. Today, Offill denies knowing Ted Ritchie. When she was read her testimony regarding Michael Johnson, Ted Ritchie, and Alice Johnson drinking beer at her trailer, Offill said that could have happened. Then she repeated her claim that she does not know Ted Ritchie. Offill does not remember Ted Ritchie's mother visiting her trailer on February 5. When read her testimony regarding that, Offill cannot recall. Then Offill was asked about her testimony regarding Michael Johnson telling her that Ted Ritchie and he were going to Andrew Choate's house. Offill does not remember testifying about that and claimed she could not have testified about it because she does not know Andrew Choate. Offill claimed she was unaware of Choate's name until it was mentioned to her during this interview.

In most of the interview, Offill kept claiming she does not remember or that did not happen. She recalled being interviewed by the Moraine Police. She could not remember the name of the police officer who questioned her, but she felt pressured to provide certain answers. She said when she would say one thing and the officer did not like the answer, he would pound his fist on the table. Offill remembers the police wanted certain information from her and were hostile if that information was not forthcoming.

One could chalk up Offill's lack of memory for not wanting to cooperate, but that would not be correct. It is very possible that Offill's lack of recall is due to years of substance abuse. She was not trying to hide anything. Unsolicited, she spoke of her struggles with the authorities in Ohio and how the State of Ohio took her children away and declared her an unfit mother, as well as having one of her children serving time in an Ohio prison. It would be hard to believe that someone would try to be deceptive in their answers yet out of the blue give up information such as that. It is not impossible, simply hard to believe. The one thing learned, and it was not even asked, is the Moraine Police exercised aggressive tactics when questioning Offill. This, as we have seen, is a common theme from people interviewed in this investigation.

As with any investigation, a detective may receive unsolicited information. It was an hour after leaving Judy Tabor-Offill's residence when another source of information called. This source is related to both Offill and Michael Johnson. She said after the interview with Offill, Offill called her to tell her about it. This source, who will remain anonymous, relayed a story that her mother told her regarding the murder of David Rowell.

According to the source's mother, David Rowell was sexually assaulted with a drill and his penis was amputated. The story goes that an older boy was behind the murder of David Rowell and he forced the other boys to participate and to dispose of the body. One of the boys who participated was Michael Johnson, according to the source. The source further said the story she was told has the murder occurring in the condemned house in Gordon's Trailer Park, where Michael Johnson used to reside. Source opined that she believes Michael Johnson was involved.

Granted, most of the information the source provided is secondhand, hearsay. However, this is a story that was circulating in the streets of Moraine, Ohio, in 1982. Though most of the story is not supported by the evidence, one has to admit that the Moraine Police and the Montgomery County Prosecutor never firmly established the primary crime scene or, in other words, where the murder actually occurred. It is possible that the murder could have occurred in the condemned house? We will never know because the house was never searched. Hearsay information cannot be used in court, with a limited list of exceptions, but it can be used by investigators in building a case, as long as they have evidence to support the information.

Because Michael Johnson was less than cooperative and truthful in his interview, interviewing his sister, Alice Johnson, became necessary. The investigation revealed that Alice Johnson is married, and her married name is Alice Pannell.

Alice Johnson-Pannell Interview

On September 2, 2015, Alice Pannell was contacted regarding this case and agreed to be interviewed. It was a telephonic interview. The information Pannell provided contradicts other witnesses' stories. It should be noted that there is no record of Alice Pannell ever being interviewed by the Moraine Police regarding the murder of David Rowell.

Pannell confirmed she used to live in a condemned house in the Gordon Trailer Park with her mother and brother, Michael Johnson. Judy Tabor, Pannell's cousin, lived in a trailer in the same trailer park. The Johnson family was forced to move to West Carrollton when the authorities found the house to be an unsafe structure. On February 5, 1982, though condemned and abandoned, the house was still standing in Gordon's Trailer Park.

Pannell recalls arriving at Judy Tabor's trailer sometime in the late afternoon or early evening of February 5. David Johnson, Pannell's oldest brother, drove Michael Johnson and her to Tabor's trailer that evening. Shortly after arriving at Tabor's trailer, Michael Johnson left. According to Pannell, Michael Johnson wanted to go to Andrew Choate's house on Holman Street. After several hours of Michael Johnson being gone, Tabor and Pannell began to look for him. Their search yielded no results, so they returned to Tabor's trailer and remained there for the rest of the evening. Pannell went to sleep on the couch in Tabor's living room, and when she awoke on February 6, Michael Johnson was sleeping on the floor, near the couch. Pannell does not know what time Michael Johnson returned to Tabor's trailer, but she was very clear on the fact he was sleeping on the floor on February 6.

Pannell claimed she did not know anybody by the name Darrell Doan and did not recall Darrell Doan coming to Tabor's residence on February 5. When Pannell was read the Moraine Police report that stated Darrell Doan took Michael Johnson from Tabor's trailer to his trailer, Pannell said that did not occur. As for Ted Ritchie, Pannell did not recall knowing him and was not sure if Michael Johnson knew him or not. Michael Johnson could have known Ritchie. Pannell did not recall Ritchie coming to Tabor's trailer on February 5 but claimed it could have occurred while she was asleep on the couch. It was midday, around noon, when Michael Johnson and Pannell returned to West Carrollton, Ohio.

As for Keith Wampler, Pannell remembered him and said she did not like him. Pannell thought Keith was a bad influence on her brother. Pannell claimed she had a verbal altercation with Keith about how he was a bad influence on Michael Johnson. Pannell said she warned Keith to stay away from Michael Johnson. Keith Wampler denied this altercation ever occurred.

Pannell did not have any praise for Detective William Mullins. Pannell thought Detective Mullins's behavior was deceptive and he willfully took advantage of her mother, who was disabled. According to Pannell, her mother suffered a stroke while in delivery with one of her children. The stroke caused brain damage that affected her ability to comprehend complicated issues, such as legal matters. Detective Mullins took full advantage of the situation to get her mother to sign various documents. Detective Mullins told her mother if she signed the various forms, Michael Johnson could go home. Instead, Michael Johnson was arrested.

Though Pannell believes her brother was not capable of murder, she provided information regarding violent behavior in the Johnson and Tabor families, to include allegations of abuse against an elderly person perpetrated by Judy Tabor. Pannell believes Michael Johnson did not smoke marijuana or drink alcohol as a teenager.

Pannell described her present relationship with her brother as severely strained. When interviewed, Michael Johnson and Pannell had not spoken to each other in over two years, in spite of both of them residing in the Dayton area.

Pannell's mood during the interview was depressed. Several times, she broke down during the thirty-minute interview. The information obtained in the interview contradicts Michael Johnson's and Andrew Choate's recall of the events on February 5, 1982. If this interview establishes one thing, it would be that Andrew Choate and Michael Johnson are deceitful. When you couple their deception with the other major issues in the prosecution's case, nothing but reasonable doubt exists regarding Keith Wampler's involvement in the murder of David Rowell.

The field investigation was into the home stretch at this point. One more trip needed to be made, and several more witnesses needed interviewed. These interviews would be key and actually turned out to be vital in this investigation. The Shipman brothers and the Rowell family needed interviewed. Joey Shipman would be the vital interview because he was the prosecution's key witness against Keith Wampler. The information Joey Shipman shared would be upsetting, but not shocking.

The other key interview would be with the Rowell family. What was learned during this interview would be earthshaking and cannot be ignored by any law enforcement agency. The surprising contradictions and statements made really put a cloud over the family instead of clearing up this case. If reasonable doubt did not exist before this interview, it sure does after it.

Sometime after 1982, the Shipman family moved to Escambia County, Florida. The family still resides in the metropolitan Pensacola area. This is where the Shipman brothers, Joey and James Jr., were found and interviewed.

Joseph "Joey" Shipman Interview

On September 9, 2015, Joseph "Joey" Shipman was found at his home near Pensacola, Florida. When the purpose of the interview was explained, Joey Shipman appeared to genuinely want to help; therefore, he agreed to be interviewed. At the time of David Rowell's murder, Joey Shipman was a seven-year-old boy living at 2754 Cozy Lane in the Gem City Estates Trailer Park. His trailer was in the opposite cul-de-sac from Keith Wampler's trailer.

Joey Shipman remembers February 5, 1982. He was sitting in his living room watching television when David Rowell knocked on the door. Joey Shipman cannot recall the exact time but knew it was late in the afternoon. According to Joey, his brother, James Jr., opened the door and talked to David. The boys were home waiting for their parents to get home from work.

Joey remembers David Rowell standing at the base of the steps leading to the trailer. David asked for a cigarette and then talked to James Jr. for about five minutes. After that, David left, and Joey did not know where he went. Joey saw David Rowell walk as far as the end of the cul-de-sac. From there, he could not say where David

Rowell went. According to Joey Shipman, it was impossible for him to see Keith Wampler's trailer from his trailer due to several trailers blocking the view and the entrance to Keith's trailer was on the opposite side from Joey's trailer. Joey said it was *impossible* for him to see anyone entering Keith Wampler's trailer.

The only time Joey Shipman was ever in Keith Wampler's trailer was during the evening of February 5, 1982. Joey remembers his older brother, James Jr., being intoxicated that evening. James Jr. knew Keith and knew Keith had beer. James Jr. continued to drink beer while visiting with Keith, and it was during this time when James Jr. decided to tear open a beer can. In his attempt to prove how strong he was, James Jr. cut his hand on the sharp edge of the can. Joey remembered his older brother wanting to lay down, so Keith Wampler showed them to his room and allowed James Jr. to use his bed to rest. Joey did not see anything unusual or sense anything was wrong while he was at Keith's trailer. James Jr. laid down, while Joey was standing in the doorway to the bedroom watching his older brother. Keith, after showing James Jr. where the room was located, returned to the living room, where other teenagers were. James Jr. rested for a while and then decided to go home. Joey denied ever hearing a scream or anyone yelling, as stated in a report filed by the Moraine Police.

Joey did not socialize with Keith Wampler because of the age difference, but his brother was friends with Keith. Joey did not know David Rowell, Michael Rowell, Michael Johnson, or Ted Ritchie.

On February 6, 1982, the Moraine Police came to Joey's trailer and interviewed other members of his family, but not him. Twice, prior to trial, Joey was interviewed by someone in the Montgomery County Prosecutor's Office. Joey believes he was coerced to testify in a certain manner. Joey said, "The prosecution wanted me to say certain things." Looking back, Joey believes the prosecutor twisted his story and influenced his testimony.

Joey Shipman's statement verified the findings that were discussed in the July 14, 2015, review of the secondary crime scene regarding Joey's inability to see David Rowell entering Keith's trailer. Maybe Dennis Langer, assistant Montgomery County prosecutor, and Robert Head, assistant Montgomery County prosecutor, should explain how, in 1982, Joey Shipman saw David Rowell enter Keith Wampler's trailer, when a review of the secondary crime scene in 2015 and a statement by their key witness in 2015 refutes that claim? The bottom line fact is, Joey Shipman's testimony was totally fabricated. It was produced by the prosecution, not the witness. Coercing a seven-year-old boy into testifying a certain way shows how low the prosecution would stoop to get a conviction. They had no physical evidence. They had no forensic evidence. They only had a seven-year-old boy. What is even more distressing being it took three decades for this to come out. Had Wayne Stephan or Robert Bostick, the self-proclaimed best attorneys in Dayton, done their job, they could have questioned the authenticity of Joey's testimony. Instead, they sat back and collected their six-thousand-dollar pro bono fee from the court.

The other point about Joey's statement is he did not sense that anything unusual was happening at Keith's trailer during his visit. He did not see or hear anything out of the ordinary, as portrayed by Detective Mullins. In his statement, Joey Shipman brings another Moraine Police report into question. It makes one wonder how many other reports are not based on fact.

The September 9, 2015, interview of Joey Shipman may have produced a bombshell in this investigation. His brother's interview a day later will only muddy the waters a little and create some more doubt in the state's case against Keith Wampler.

James Shipman Jr. Interview

Less than cooperative would be diplomatic in describing James Shipman Jr.'s attitude on September 10, 2015, when he agreed to be interviewed for this case at his parents' home in Escambia County, Florida. Upon arrival at the trailer, James Jr. was seen sitting on a couch in the enclosed porch watching television. He was smoking cigarettes and drinking beer. It took several knocks before he finally answered the door. Upon entering the enclosed porch, several empty cans of beer were noticed near where James Jr. was sitting.

James Jr. confirmed he lived at 2754 Cozy Lane in Moraine, Ohio, on February 5, 1982. James Jr. could not remember what time David Rowell came to his trailer but was sure David stopped to bum a cigarette from him. James Jr. did not know from where David came or to where he was going. According to James Jr., the visit was a short one.

That afternoon, Joey and James Jr. were alone at their home waiting for their parents, who worked in Piqua, Ohio, to come home. James Jr.'s parents managed SOHIO gas stations in Piqua and Sydney.

James Jr. confirmed that Joey and he went to Keith Wampler's trailer sometime during the evening of February 5. According to James Jr.'s recollection of the evening, it was Keith Wampler, Joey, and he at Keith's trailer. He claimed nobody else was there. This contradicts his trial testimony, where he stated Michael Johnson and Ted Ritchie were also present at Keith's trailer. James Jr. said he drank beer at Keith's trailer and cut his hand on a beer can. He asked to lay down, and according to James Jr., Keith allowed him to use his room. James Jr. rested for about twenty minutes and then left Keith Wampler's trailer to return home with Joey. James Jr. did not sense anything strange happening at Keith's trailer, nor did he notice anything out of the ordinary. James Jr. said the police report that stated he heard a scream is false.

The reason for James Jr.'s hostility throughout the interview is not clear. His attitude is opposite of the one his brother, Joey, displayed on the prior day. In his statement on September 10, 2015, he discredited his own trial testimony in 1982. One developed a sense that he knows more than he is willing to tell.

Robert "Bobby" D. Rowell Interview

The Rowell residence was located in Mobile, Alabama. Not only did Robert "Bobby" D. Rowell and Myrtle Rowell live there, but also their daughter, Krista, who was a ten-year-old girl at the time of David's murder. Kristi answered the door, and soon her mother, Myrtle, was in the living room. It was clear that the years took their toll on Myrtle Rowell. The prim and proper, devote, Pentecostal woman, as she was described in 1982, was now a tired-looking, cigarette-smoking older woman. Kristi went to the detached garage to get Bobby Rowell. The desire to interview Michael Patrick Rowell was also explained. When Bobby Rowell arrived from the garage, where he maintained a workshop, Bobby Rowell said Michael Rowell was dead. Kristi and Myrtle confirmed it.

After a brief explanation for the interview, everyone sat down in the enclosed back porch of the Rowell home. At the beginning, nobody could predict just how challenging this ninety-minute interview would be, and how volatile it would become, but it did yield some very damaging information for the Moraine Police and Montgomery County Prosecutor's Office. It also yielded some very damning information regarding Robert "Bobby" Rowell.

Bobby Rowell claimed the last time he saw David was at 7:30 a.m. on February 5, 1982, which was the time David left for school.

Bobby stated that he returned home at 5:00 p.m. to find Myrtle and Krista the only family members in the house. It was 5:30 p.m., according to Bobby, when Michael came home. Bobby described Michael as being high. After arriving at the house, Michael went straight to bed and stayed there all night. When confronted with his testimony about Michael searching for David, Bobby said it was a lie. Bobby continued to deny he ever said such a thing in court. Bobby, in a raised voice, insisted Michael Rowell spent the entire night in bed.

When presented with his testimony about being unemployed at the time of David's murder, Bobby Rowell denied ever telling the court such a story. Bobby claimed he was working for a friend in Huber Heights, Ohio. When confronted with his trial testimony, Bobby again denied ever saying that in court. When told he testified about being unemployed and having to take David to school because David was thrown off the school bus, Bobby Rowell said, "You don't know what you are talking about." When he was told it was his trial testimony, he rolled his eyes.

When asked about the statement he gave the coroner's investigator about seeing David at 5:30 p.m. on February 5, 1982, Bobby Rowell became totally flustered and started waving his arms. He claimed he never said such a thing. When asked why would the coroner's investigator lie about that in his report, Bobby repeated his claim that he never told that to the coroner's investigator, and he became more agitated.

Bobby said that he started looking for David around 7:00 p.m. He searched the civic center, near I-75, the vacant field, and through the trailer parks. He claimed he saw Wampler's neighbors get into a pickup truck and leave. When confronted with the fact that Wampler's neighbors left earlier, around 3:30 p.m., Bobby said that was a lie. He said they were leaving around 7:00 p.m. When told this was their statement to the police, as well as their trial testimony, Bobby said, "You don't know what you are talking about." Bobby denied searching Keith's car, as he stated he did in his trial testimony. Bobby searched the condemned house in Gordon's Trailer Park, which he did not testify about at Keith Wampler's trial. When asked about the barbeque pit at the Moraine Civic Center, Bobby Rowell claimed he did not know where it was, in spite of his testimony to the opposite at trial.

Then Myrtle Rowell, out of the blue, came back into the covered porch. She pointed at Robert "Bobby" D. Rowell and said, "He killed David. He cut his dick off. He killed David. He killed Mike. He murdered my boys." Myrtle continued, "He was there behind Mike Johnson at the Civic Center, and you beat him and killed him." At that point, Bobby Rowell exploded like a volcano. His response was violent and loud. He flew out of his seat and began yelling at Myrtle Rowell, the mother of a murdered boy. He threatened to end the interview if she did not leave. Krista immediately forcibly pulled her mother out of the room.

After Myrtle Rowell was removed from the enclosed porch by her daughter, Bobby Rowell returned to his chair. Bobby called his wife nuts and claimed she has been treated for mental illness. According to Bobby, Myrtle suffers from bipolar disorder and schizophrenia. "She hasn't been right since David died," Bobby said.

Bobby Rowell restarted the interview by talking about his search for David. Bobby admitted that he did not knock on any doors or ask anyone if they saw his son. He remembers helping a stranded motorist while he was driving around looking for David. Bobby said she was coming from Dayton International Airport. When asked how would Bobby get to the airport from Moraine, he denied knowing where the airport was but claimed he used it on a couple occasions to fly to Mobile, Alabama.

Regarding hearing any screams during the night of February 5, 1982, Bobby Rowell claimed he did, but it was close to his house.

According to Bobby, the Moraine Police told him that children were playing near his house.

On the morning of February 6, 1982, Bobby Rowell stated that he went for a walk through the field and saw nothing. According to Bobby, he left his home to go to Huber Heights to a friend's television repair shop, where he stayed until 1:00 p.m. When he got home, Bobby found he was the only person there. Bobby denied going to the basement, as he said in his trial testimony. When confronted with his trial testimony, Bobby Rowell said he never went to the basement, and if anyone said he did, they would be lying. Bobby was reminded about his vision of bushes and a doll, which he testified about in court. Bobby Rowell denied it ever happened.

At this point, the interview became strange. Bobby Rowell gave a description about the condition of David's body when he discovered it. It was as if he was describing a totally different crime. Bobby Rowell described his son, David, as being decapitated with an arm amputated. Bobby said David's head was in a bag. When confronted with the coroner's description of David's body, Bobby became agitated and said it was not accurate. Bobby really became upset when he described the towels found near David's body as being bloody. When told that David only lost 10 cc of blood, therefore the towels could not have been bloody, Bobby Rowell was about to explode again. Then Bobby began to talk about a trail of bloody footprints that ran from Keith's trailer to the body. Again, he was confronted with the police reports, which never stated a trail of bloody footprints. Bobby Rowell's face tensed up and was a little closer to a full eruption.

When asked about how many sets of footprints he remembered seeing in the snow, Bobby Rowell denied it had snowed on February 5, 1982. When told about the National Weather Service and the Moraine Police reporting snow from 5:00 p.m. to 10:30 p.m. with 0.2 inches of accumulation, Bobby called the National Weather

Service and the Moraine Police liars. Bobby Rowell became indignant when asked how he could have seen bloody footprints if there was not any snow on the ground. Yelling, Bobby said there was not any snow on the ground and the reports were wrong. "You weren't driving around that day" was Bobby's explanation for sticking with his claim of no snow on the ground.

Bobby Rowell described Michael Johnson as being bad and evil. Bobby told a story of how Michael Johnson jumped in front of his van and claimed Michael Johnson wanted Bobby to hit him with the van. Bobby remembers Michael Johnson living in a condemned house, which he searched while looking for David.

Bobby Rowell did not know Keith Wampler but is sure that Keith killed David. When asked how he could be sure, Bobby claimed the Moraine Police told him that Keith signed a fourteen-page confession. When told Keith never confessed and there is no fourteen-page confession, Bobby again become indignant. It was suggested that the confession, if it did exist, could have come from Michael Johnson. Bobby, again, yelling, claimed it was Keith Wampler.

Bobby Rowell denied David was ever banned from the bus. Bobby was reminded about his court testimony, where he said David was kicked off the bus the previous December and again the day David was murdered. Bobby was reminded how he testified about being inconvenienced by having to take David to school. Bobby said it never happened. When asked to explain his trial testimony to the contrary, Bobby Rowell had no explanation.

As with other parts of the interview, the next part was confrontational. Bobby Rowell, throughout this interview, contradicted everyone, to include his own sworn testimony. Now he took a swipe at the autopsy report. This is strange because he mentioned it. He was not questioned about it. He brought up the green vegetable in David's stomach. When a witness, or suspect, opens a door, a good detective will walk in and pursue information. So here we go. Bobby was reminded that the Montgomery County Coroner did not test the substance and only listed it as a green food substance. Bobby Rowell insisted it was a vegetable. When asked how he knew it was a vegetable, he could not answer that question. He continued to insist it was a vegetable. When pressed if David had dinner that night, Bobby said he could not remember. If his statement about the last time he saw David was 7:30 a.m. on February 5 was true, then the answer to that question should have been no, and not that he could not remember because David would not have been home. Bobby Rowell maintained the substance in David's stomach was a green vegetable. Makes one wonder, how he can be so sure?

When asked about how he punished his children, Bobby Rowell would not provide a direct response. He asked for scenarios. Bobby was asked about the time he caught his sons smoking. He confirmed the story that another witness told about David and Michael being locked in a closet and told to smoke. Bobby had hoped they would get sick and quit, but that never happened. Bobby did not answer what he would do if one of the boys broke a window. He did not say what he would do, but he made a point that he would never hit his boys.

Bobby Rowell admitted to having a $3,500 life insurance policy on David at the time of David's murder. The policy had a double indemnity clause, which made it worth $7,000 in case of violent death. Then Bobby began to talk about the insurance money. In 2015, Bobby Rowell is still upset that he had to use some of the insurance money to pay a mortuary to transport David Rowell's body from Dayton, Ohio, to Mobile, Alabama. Bobby expressed how upset he was when the coroner would not release his son's body to him. Bobby Rowell wanted to put David's body in the back of his van and drive it to Mobile, Alabama. Bobby claimed he could not afford to use the insurance money on a mortuary.

When asked about Michael, Bobby claimed Michael died of a drug overdose in February 2000. Bobby claimed Michael was mixing painkillers with alcohol. According to Bobby, Michael seriously hurt his back while working for a drywall company. It should be noted that, according to Alabama law, all drug overdose deaths are investigated by the Alabama Medical Examiner's Office. A check with the Mobile District of the Alabama Medical Examiner's Office revealed no records for a drug overdose death investigation regarding Michael Patrick Rowell. Death records in Alabama are not public record until twenty-five years after the reported date of death.

As you can see, the interview of Bobby Rowell totally contrasts his trial testimony and contradicts official records in this case. Robert "Bobby" D. Rowell displayed a short, violent temper throughout the interview. He showed no compassion toward his wife, whom he claims is mentally ill. He contradicts police reports yet claims they are accurate. At minimum, Bobby Rowell's interview tore apart his credibility. He either lied in 2015 or on the stand in 1982.

Myrtle Rowell claimed Bobby is the murderer. That may be true. Myrtle was not interviewed because of the claim made by Bobby that she is mentally ill. It is best to error on the side of caution and not interview her unless a mental health professional, such as a psychiatrist or psychologist, is present. Is she telling the truth? We may never know because there is no evidence that the family was ever investigated by the Moraine Police Division. In fact, the only report indicating that any member of the family was interviewed is a report filed by Detective William Mullins on February 10, 1982. In that report, Detective Mullins claimed he telephonically interviewed Bobby Rowell, who was already in Mobile, Alabama.

Conclusions

A lawyer without history or literature is a mechanic, a mere working mason; if he possesses some knowledge of these, he may venture to call himself an architect."
—Walter Scott

The previous chapters dealt with facts. Some comparisons and conclusions are peppered in those chapters. This chapter will do comparisons of the 1982 investigation and trial with the 2015 investigation. To say there is plenty of information here would be an understatement. Some of these issues, such as the autopsy, were previously chronicled in detail and will only be briefly recapped here. Other issues, such as the integrity of the actors, will be discussed in detail in this chapter.

The State's Theory

The state of Ohio's theory in this case is at 5:30 p.m. on February 5, 1982, David Rowell returned to Keith Wampler's trailer, where Keith raped, tortured, and strangled David Rowell. The state believes the time of death to be 1:00 a.m., plus or minus two hours, on February 6, 1982. Sometime during the night, Keith Wampler placed the lifeless body of David Rowell into the vacant field along Kreitzer Road. The cause of death was manual strangulation.

On the surface, this seems like a pretty straightforward, except when you scratch past the surface you discover the Montgomery County Prosecutor's Office, namely Dennis Langer and Robert Head, had nothing. They did not have fingerprints. Their own forensic reports were inconclusive. The integrity of their witnesses were questionable, at best. So they put on their tap shoes and danced while selling this fairy tale to a jury because they pulled Judge John Kessler, who was more worried about going on vacation than ensuring a sixteen-year-old defendant received a fair trial. Keep in mind, Judge Kessler's vacation desires are part of the trial record. The same trial record that the Montgomery County Clerk of Courts Office claims does not exist, except a copy was subsequently obtained through other channels.

Now mix in two of Dayton's best attorneys, Robert Bostick and Wayne Stephan, who did nothing to disprove the prosecution's theory. In short, the Montgomery County Prosecutor's Office had a cakewalk. The fact is the state's theory had more holes than the *Titanic*. If everyone did their jobs properly, this case should have sunk quicker than the famed ship. Instead, the pungent smell of the *Good O' Boy* network permeated throughout this case. The same *Good O' Boy* network that exists, to this day, in every courthouse in all eighty-eight counties of Ohio.

We also must remember that a second person, Michael Johnson, was convicted for this crime. He faced the same charges as Keith Wampler, but his fate was decided in Montgomery County Juvenile Court, not Montgomery County Common Pleas Court. What is fascinating, and quite frankly illegal, is Dennis Langer and Robert Head based their prosecution of Michael Johnson and Keith Wampler on two different theories of the crime. In the case against Michael Johnson, the prosecution argued that Johnson and Wampler were codefendants in killing David Rowell. However, in Keith Wampler's case, they claimed he acted alone. Dennis Langer and Robert Head, which is it? This begs several questions. The first being why were they not both codefendants in one trial either in juvenile court or common pleas court? The second is why did the prosecution argue so forcefully to keep any mention of the trial in juvenile court out of Keith Wampler's trial in common pleas court. The third being why was the prosecution (and not the defense) allowed to mention the juvenile trial during closing arguments.

Now let us look at each part of the state's theory of the crime. Let us dissect it and examine each piece. Again, some of these have already been discussed, but it is important to review them again.

The Autopsy

As stated earlier, the autopsy is good for determining the cause of death, but as for the time of death, it is inaccurate. Dr. Schaffer determined the time of death based on using only two of five factors: lividity and rigor mortis. He failed to use body temperature, stomach contents, and whether or not insects were present. Instead of the time of death being 1:00 a.m., plus or minus two hours, on February 6, 1982, a more accurate window for the time of death would be 8:00 p.m. on February 5 to 4:00 a.m. on February 6, with evidence indicating that death may have occurred sometime after shortly after 9:15 p.m. on February 5. The time of death clearly occurred two to four hours after David Rowell ate a green food substance, which his father insists was a vegetable.

Now if we accept Dr. Schaffer's determination on the time of death as being accurate, this disproves the prosecution's theory of the crime. The prosecution contends David Rowell was being sexually assaulted, tortured, and murdered in Keith's trailer. Based on the autopsy, the earliest time of death could be 11:00 p.m. on February 5. This so happens is the time that Ted Ritchie and Michael Johnson left Keith's trailer to go to Andrew Choate's house. Prior to that, for two hours, Keith Wampler had four visitors at his trailer. In those two hours, not one visitor reported seeing anything out of the ordinary or felt anything strange happening in Keith's trailer. As a matter of fact, James Shipman Jr. and his brother, Joey, spent twenty minutes, unsupervised, in the back portion of the trailer, while James Jr. was lying down in Keith's room. Again, neither James Shipman Jr., Joey Shipman or Ted Ritchie reported anything unusual in Keith's trailer. They did not tell the police in 1982 that they saw anything unusual, and in 2015, they repeated that claim.

The autopsy does not report any ligature marks being present on the body, especially the wrists and ankles. One could speculate in a crime of this nature that some sort of restraints would be used to immobilize the victim while the perpetrator did something else, such as entertaining guests. Also, no drugs were detected in the toxicology report that could have rendered David Rowell unresponsive. Keep in mind, the autopsy stated the earliest time of death to be 11:00 p.m. on February 5. This means if David Rowell was in Keith Wampler's trailer at 9:00 p.m., when Michael Johnson, Ted Ritchie, James Shipman Jr., and Joey Shipman arrived at Keith's trailer, he would have been alive. If Keith Wampler was doing unspeakable things to David Rowell, one would think he would use something to restrain David to ensure that David would not be seen in his trailer. Also, if he was doing unspeakable things to David, why would he invite visitors into his single-wide trailer? This would especially be true when Keith suddenly was confronted with unexpected guests appearing at his door. Yet there is no evidence that David Rowell was being restrained. The reason Keith Wampler did not worry if David Rowell was or was not restrained because David Rowell was not in Keith Wampler's trailer at 9:00 p.m. on February 5, 1982, like Dennis Langer and Robert Head told the court. David Rowell was likely at the barbeque pit near the Moraine Civic Center. Remember, Bryan Canterbury stated that David and he exchanged greetings near the barbeque pit at 9:15 p.m.

The autopsy also tells us that David Rowell was in a cold place at the time of his death. This is known because of peripheral cyanosis in his fingernails and toenails. Again, as earlier stated, peripheral cyanosis occurs when a fair-skinned person is in a cold place at the time of death. There are other factors that could result in peripheral cyanosis, such as drug usage and disease, but they are not relative to this case. Dr. Schaffer described David as being fair-skinned. David's toenails and fingernails had a purplish-blue color. Keith's trailer was a warm environment. During the afternoon and early evening of February 5, he was walking around without a shirt. Sometime before 7:00 p.m., he even washed his hair. Now we must ask ourselves, who would walk around without a shirt and with a wet head in a cold trailer? So the trailer had to have been warm. If David Rowell was killed in Keith Wampler's trailer, peripheral cyanosis would not have been present in David's body. Therefore, it stands to reason that David Rowell was killed in a cold environment, such as an unheated garage, an unheated cellar or a condemned house. Here is another aspect in which the state's own autopsy report disproves the State's theory of the crime.

There are other major issues with the autopsy, and those issues were discussed earlier in this book. Another issue regarding the autopsy, and it has nothing to do with Dr. Schaffer or the staff at the Montgomery County Coroner's Office. It has to do with Wayne Stephan and Robert Bostick, the defense attorneys. The issue is whether or not these attorneys had actually read, reviewed, and understood the autopsy report. A good attorney takes every piece of evidence and places it under a microscope. He or she attempts to tear it apart in order to show weaknesses in a prosecutor's case. A mediocre attorney reviews the prosecution's evidence and makes an attempt to question it. A lazy and/or incompetent attorney sits back and does nothing. It is evident that Wayne Stephan and Robert Bostick made no attempt to have the report independently analyzed, which is permitted by law. We know this because of the application, entry, and certification for assigned counsel fee report filed by Robert Bostick with the Montgomery County Common Pleas Court on August 27, 1982, three days after sentencing. The cost for independent analysis of the autopsy that would have been covered by the court would have been listed on the fee report. That is, if the court takes its role as being truly objective seriously.

The time of death was an important part of the prosecution's case and, based on how Dr. Schaffer determined it, was the Achilles' heel in the autopsy results for prosecution. It is quite possible that forensic pathologists at the Miami Valley Regional Medical Center in Dayton, the Ohio State University Medical Center in Columbus, or the University of Cincinnati Medical Center in Cincinnati may have been able to present another possibility on the time of death. We will never know because these self-described well-educated and experienced attorneys did not question the autopsy.

The Moraine Police Investigation

What is fascinating about the Moraine Police investigation is they had a suspect in custody before any evidence was analyzed. In Detective William Mullins's own testimony, he admitted he determined that Keith Wampler was a suspect within the first forty-five minutes of Keith's interview with the police. This means at 11:45 p.m. on February 6, 1982, Keith Wampler was considered a suspect by Detective Mullins. That is nine hours and forty-five minutes before the autopsy was conducted by Dr. Schaffer at the Montgomery County Coroner's Office and days before the Miami Valley Regional Crime Laboratory conducted any analysis of the forensic evidence. Detective Mullins had a suspect in custody before a proper search of the field was conducted by any evidence technician or a proper search of Keith's trailer was conducted. Either Detective Mullins is the greatest detective since Sherlock Holmes and solved this crime with his cunningness and skill or else Detective Mullins took a shot in the dark and thought Keith Wampler did it, and in doing so, he molded the rest of his investigation to prove his theory while ignoring the possibility of any alternative theories and/or suspects. The later appears to be the case.

On February 6, 1982, at 3:50 p.m., the Moraine Police was handed a very disturbing and difficult case to investigation. In a case of this nature, the police are required to slow down, take a look around, and methodically examine potential suspects. That was not done. In crimes such as this, the members of the victim's family are usually the first ones examined. The police will either clear them or charge them, because, as the FBI statistics show, in the majority of murders in the United States, the victim has a relationship with the killer. We know only one interview occurred between Detective Mullins and Robert "Bobby" Rowell, and that interview occurred several days after David's body was discovered, and it was conducted by telephone because the family had already left the state of Ohio without being questioned and have moved back to Mobile, Alabama.

On February 6, 1982, members of the Rowell family should have been separated and questioned individually by the police. This was not done. If it was done, then where are the reports of those interviews? If it was done, where are the reports related to Myrtle

Rowell's statement and transcripts of her court testimony? The reason is she was not interviewed. The Moraine Police took Bobby Rowell's initial verbal statement about finding David's body, and that was it. No more interviews were conducted until the family was in Mobile, Alabama.

Detective William Mullins and Officer Dennis Adkins (now Judge Adkins) need to explain why David's house was not searched. At a bare minimum, David's room should have been searched for clues. There is not one report of any police officer searching 2970 Kreitzer Road, the Rowell home. Proper police procedure, and a thorough investigation, dictates that an attempt be made to search the victim's residence for clues and/or evidence. This could have been accomplished by seeking consent from either Bobby or Myrtle Rowell. That was not done. Failing receiving consent from the family, a search warrant should have been obtained.

A good detective would have recognized the field where David Rowell's body was discovered as a secondary crime scene. A good detective would have realized the immediate need to find the primary crime scene that is where the murder occurred. One possible location of the primary crime scene stared Detective William Mullins and Officer Dennis Adkins in the face and they looked right past it: the condemned house in Gordon's Trailer Park. At minimum, a cursory search in the immediate area around the house should have been conducted. Ideally, the police should have contacted the owners of Gordon's Trailer Park and obtained their consent to search the condemned house. None of this was done. Remember this was the residence of Michael Johnson, the juvenile court defendant, who was also convicted in this case.

On the topic of searches, the search of the secondary crime scene, the field where David's body was discovered, was amateurish at best and incompetent at worst. This scene was released by the police immediately following the removal of David's body by the

Montgomery County Coroner. A thorough search of the field was not conducted for another week. Frankly, this is inexcusable. Proper police procedure requires the scene be secured until it is thoroughly searched for possible evidence. Keep in mind, this is where the body of a thirteen-year-old boy was discovered. One would think the police would want to be careful and methodical in this investigation. It is very clear that was not the case.

If Detective Mullins and Officer Adkins were serious about conducting a proper homicide investigation, they would have made sure the field was secured overnight. From the time the body was discovered to sunset, the police had, maybe, ninety minutes to search the field. That is not enough time, unless they brought in spotlights to illuminate the field. The alternative was to post police officers on the perimeter of the field overnight to secure it. Then on February 7, conduct a grid search of the field. Again, there is no indication that was done. The only time the Moraine Police went back to the field was on February 12, when Officer Adkins supervised a US Army Reserve unit use a metal detecting device in searching the field.

An interesting point needs to be made regarding the February 12 search. Officer Adkins testified that the purpose of the search was to locate a knife. It was almost a week after David Rowell's body was discovered, and the police still did not have a weapon used in the crime. In his testimony, he said a knife was not found, but they discovered a toilet seat lid. The fact that Officer Dennis Adkins said the purpose of the search was to find a knife indicates the Moraine Police were desperate to find some sort of knife to present in court. This explains why the police took the knife from John McGarvey, who had nothing to do with this crime, and presented that knife in court as evidence against Keith Wampler. The Moraine Police could not legitimately find a knife, so by God, they were going to produce one regardless and under Ohio law that is perjury.

On the topic of searches, what did the Moraine Police and the Montgomery County Prosecutor's Office learn from the multiple searches of Keith's trailer? The answer is absolutely nothing! All the shopping bags seized from the trailer only indicated where Cecil Wampler did his grocery shopping. There was not any blood or fingerprints found on the shopping bags. The lab tested the bags for fingerprints and the results were negative. The police failed to find David's blood in Keith's trailer. They did find spots of blood, but those spots were only typed by the Miami Valley Regional Crime Laboratory, enzyme tests were not conducted on them. The blood that was found was discovered on the front door and on an end table in the living room. The blood type matched James Shipman Jr., who cut himself by tearing a beer can in half. This occurred near the end table. Also he used the front door to leave Keith's trailer. But of course, the self-described best attorneys in Dayton did not feel it was necessary to point out to the jury that this blood was almost certainly from the cut hand of James Shipman Jr.

The prosecution believed Keith Wampler amputated David Rowell's penis in Keith's bathroom. Where is the blood? The prosecution thinks, and quite frankly failed to prove, that David Rowell's body was propped up on the toilet seat while Keith amputated the penis. If that were the case, then David would have lost more than 10 ccs of blood. According to the autopsy, he lost only 10 ccs. There would have been blood spots on the floor from Keith picking David's body up off the toilet. Yet no blood was found. Also, no blood was found in either bedroom, so that rules out the bedrooms as being the place where the amputation occurred. The four searches of Keith's trailer, by the Moraine Police, yielded nothing and failed to identify 2753 Cozy Lane as being the primary crime scene.

Another interesting issue regarding the Moraine Police investigation is the integrity of the reports. During the 2015 investigation, several witnesses refuted the information in the police reports regarding interviews with Detective Mullins. For example, Lisa Collins said the entire report filed by Detective Mullins regarding her interview with him was false. In this particular report, Detective Mullins's own timeline indicates that Ms. Collins's refutation is truthful because the time that Detective Mullins documented in the report for the interview with Lisa Collins is the exact times that Detective Mullins was at Moraine Police Headquarters talking to Bobby Rowell, who was in Mobile, Alabama. Reading the date and time of each report, which were filed by Detective William Mullins, proves that. Also, there are reports filed by other officers where the witnesses were not identified or the time, date, and place of the interview was not documented. This development leads one to wonder what other reports are the figment of Detective Mullins's imagination? When a police report is filed documenting a statement by a witness without even identifying that witness then the professionalism of the officers and the supervision of the department has to be called into question.

It is very clear that John McGarvey's knife being associated with this crime was an imaginative leap of Olympic portions by a prosecution desperate to present a weapon to the jury. John McGarvey's knife had nothing to do with this crime. Yet Dennis Langer and Robert Head presented the knife as being the one used to abuse David's corpse. When asked about a knife by the police, John McGarvey went into his trailer and recovered it from the spot where he routinely had it hidden. Nobody knew where that knife was kept except for John McGarvey. The microscopic specks of blood found on the knife could not be identified as human. According to the crime lab, it could have been animal, which makes sense because McGarvey used the knife to clean rabbits.

Detective William Mullins and Officer Dennis Adkins were so desperate to find a knife that they latched on any knife they could find and presented it as evidence. Fabrication of evidence is in fact perjury, according to Ohio law. The Moraine Police investigation failed, and failed miserably, in putting this knife in the hands of Keith Wampler. They wanted this knife to fit this crime so badly that Robert Head bullied and coerced teenagers in an attempt to get them to testify that they saw Keith Wampler with this knife. Head went as far as to threaten to jail a teenager if the teenager did not go allow with this fable. It shows that the Moraine Police and the Montgomery County Prosecutor's Office was so desperate to prove a lie that they would suborn perjury. The scary thing is two of the actors in this fable are currently sitting judges on the Montgomery County Common Pleas Court.

It is very clear that in 1982, the Moraine Division of Police was in way over their head regarding the David Rowell murder investigation. It is quite clear they did not have a clue regarding the proper procedures in investigating a murder of this nature. Instead of calling for assistance from agencies with more experience, such as the Dayton Police, the Ohio Bureau of Criminal Investigation (BCI), or the Federal Bureau of Investigation (FBI), the Moraine Police fumbled its way through this case. Instead of following the evidence to see where it goes, the Moraine Police, led by Detective William Mullins, forced the evidence to fit a suspect. In a true, transparent, and properly conducted criminal investigation, the opposite is true. A good detective gathers the evidence and follows it to a suspect. This investigation by the Moraine Police could rightly be characterized as a farce except for the fact that the real perpetrator of this crime is free and someone who had nothing to do with this crime has spent more than three decades in prison. And that makes this a tragedy.

Defense Counsel

Were Robert Bostick and Wayne Stephan aggressive advocates for their client? The answer to that question is a giant no. On May 12,

1982, Judge John Kessler appointed Robert Bostick and Wayne Stephan to represent Charles "Keith" Wampler because Keith was declared indigent. Prior to this date, Keith was represented by the Montgomery County Public Defender's Office. Keith probably would have done better with the public defender. At least they put their hearts into their cases.

Based on the application, entry, and certification for assigned counsel fee form completed by Robert Bostick and filed with the court on August 27, 1982, Bostick and Stephan were paid $6,057.50 each to represent Keith. According to his paperwork, Robert Bostick, between May 12, 1982, and August 27, 1982, of the 180 3/4 hours he claimed to have spent on this case, Bostick spent a whopping three-and-a-quarter hours meeting with Keith in preparing for this trial, and most of those conferences were conducted by telephone.

The telephone played an enormous role in Robert Bostick's defense of Keith Wampler. Except for when he needed to be in court, everything else regarding this case was done by telephone. Bostick interviewed witnesses by telephone. A good detective and a good lawyer knows you interview witnesses by telephone as a last resort. You should always try to conduct interviews in person because a good detective and a good lawyer knows how to read body language and can tell if a person is being deceptive. Granted, in-person interviews are not always possible and a good detective and a good lawyer has to deal with that. But to say, every interview in this case had to be conducted by telephone is a huge stretch. It definitely shows a lazy streak.

The one thing Ohio law permits in court appointed cases is the hiring of a private investigator by defense counsel. It is very clear that Robert Bostick and Wayne Stephan had no interest in having someone else take a look at this case. After all, as Bostick said on July 14, 2015, he is Dayton's best attorney.

Had defense counsel actually followed the Canons of Ethics in defending their client, they would have hired a private investigator to investigate the entire case. An experienced private investigator would have identified the problems with the state's theory and provide evidence to discredit the prosecution's case. A private investigator would have identified problems with the autopsy. A private investigator would have discovered Joey Shipman could not have possibly seen David Rowell enter Keith Wampler's trailer. A private investigator would have learned that Bobby Rowell had a $3,500 life insurance policy, with double indemnity clause, on David. In short, a private investigator would probably have conducted a more thorough investigation than the Moraine Police. We will never know because Robert Bostick and Wayne Stephan never properly investigated this case. They simply accepted the State's theory. Maybe if they had this properly investigated, Bostick would not have resorted to lecturing the jury about the king's cloak of innocence in his opening arguments.

What is more troubling is Robert Bostick's attitude toward this case. Attempts were made to review Wayne Stephan's and Bostick's files regarding this case. Keith granted a power of attorney to this investigator, which allowed a review of these files. It was learned, on July 14, 2015, through Bostick, that the files were destroyed. In the conversation with Bostick, he said, "Wampler did it." When pressed for information regarding evidence to support that claim, Bostick developed a case of amnesia. It is a pretty bold statement for a defense lawyer to claim his client is guilty but cannot provide one shred of evidence to support that claim. It is even bolder to make that claim after being confronted with the fact the State's key witness, Joey Shipman, could not have possibly seen David Rowell enter Keith's trailer, which he should have known if he really did visit the crime scene on July 11, 1982, as he claimed in his bill to the court. This is the kind of justice $6,057.50 gets you in Montgomery County, Ohio.

Alternate and More Accurate Theory

Based on the evidence, the state's theory of the crime, as it relates to Keith Wampler, could not have occurred. If Dennis Langer and Robert Head are honest with themselves, they know their theory had no credence. If they had the courage of their convictions regarding this case, they would have tried Keith Wampler and Michael Johnson as codefendants in one trial. They would not have presented one theory in common pleas court and a different theory in juvenile court. Not only does it indicate they did not have a case, but it reeks of dishonesty, which cannot be tolerated by the court or society. To be frank, they should not have gotten away with it. But they pulled Judge John Kessler, who was paying more attention to travel brochures and leaving for his vacation on time than to safeguarding the rights of a sixteen-year-old boy, who is supposed to be innocent until proven guilty beyond a reasonable doubt.

Now, let us reenact a more likely scenario, which is based on the original investigation, the trial testimony, and the 2015 investigation. This scenario is developed after hours of thorough analysis of the evidence and information. This scenario factors in the who, what, when, why, and how. This scenario answers questions regarding means, opportunity, and above all, motive. Remember, in his opening arguments, Dennis Langer said motive is not important. This is where he is absolutely wrong.

On February 5, 1982, between 3:00 p.m. and 3:30 p.m., Keith Wampler talked to John McGarvey and his fiancé in the driveway outside of John McGarvey's trailer. Keith gave McGarvey's fiancé a drink, and they chatted about the upcoming sixteenth birthday party she was planning for Keith, which was going to occur the next day. John McGarvey and his fiancé left for Vandalia, Ohio, to do laundry and have dinner, with all intentions of returning later that evening. Earlier in the day, Cecil Wampler left for work and then, after

225

work, went to Waynesville, Ohio, to visit with family. He too had all intentions to returning home that evening. After John McGarvey left for Vandalia, Keith returned to his trailer expecting his father or his friend, McGarvey, to return.

At 4:00 p.m., Michael Rowell came to 2753 Cozy Lane to visit Keith. The fact that Michael Rowell came to Keith's trailer at this time discredits the State's theory, as well as conflicts with Michael's trial testimony. Remember, Michael testified that several days earlier Keith was bullying David and him, to the point that Keith made David cry. If this event occurred, does it make sense for Michael to go to the house of someone who bullied him? Unless Michael Rowell was a sadomasochist, he would stay away from Keith. So at 4:00 p.m., Michael Rowell visits Keith Wampler. The two teenagers sip grapefruit juice and vodka while watching television. Michael drinks to the point of intoxication.

At 5:00 p.m., David Rowell visits Keith's trailer looking for Michael. If David could not hang out with his friends, he would hang out with his big brother. He knew he could find Michael at Keith's trailer. Keith lets him into the trailer. David proceeds to take a sip of Michael's drink, at which point Michael retrieves his drink. David sits down on top of a blanket that Keith uses to wrap himself with when he is watching television.

The three boys watch television until 5:30 p.m., when Keith goes to the bathroom. Upon returning, Keith notices Michael leaving his trailer. Keith wonders why Michael abruptly left, so without wearing a shirt, he begins to follow Michael. He follows Michael to Cozy Lane and a little distance past the cul-de-sac that contained his trailer and the opposite cul-de-sac that contained James Shipman Jr.'s trailer. Keith decides to return home because it is cold and is just beginning to snow. Keith notices David Rowell, who has already left Keith's trailer, and is standing at the front steps of James Shipman

Jr.'s trailer. Keith returns home, wraps himself in his blanket, and takes a nap.

Meanwhile, David Rowell is bumming a cigarette from James Shipman Jr., with Joey Shipman standing inside the trailer. After a brief conversation, David Rowell, with cigarette in hand, leaves the Shipman trailer and walks out to Cozy Lane. According to the prosecution, Joey Shipman claimed to have seen David go to Keith's trailer. The 2015 investigation, examination of the secondary crime scene and Joey Shipman's own statement, on September 9, 2015, indicates that is false. It would have been physically impossible for Joey Shipman inside his trailer to have seen David Rowell enter Keith's trailer because of intervening trailers and the entrance to Keith's trailer was on the opposite side, out of view, of Joey Shipman's trailer. Joey would have to be Superman with x-ray vision to accomplish that task.

Because he was looking for his brother and it was getting close to suppertime, it is more likely that David Rowell walked south on Cozy Lane to where it intersects with Schoolhouse Lane, crosses Schoolhouse Lane, between two trailers, proceeds to Kreitzer Road, where he crosses the street and arrives at his house, 2970 Kreitzer Road.

Myrtle Rowell prepared supper, and everyone—Myrtle, Michael, David, and Krista—are waiting for Bobby Rowell, the father, to arrive home before they ate. Bobby Rowell comes home, and the family has supper, which is in the 6:00 p.m. hour. One can speculate that one of the suppertime discussion topics was David's failing grades and the fact he was, again, banned from the school bus. During supper, David asks to go to the movies at the Moraine Civic Center. Myrtle denies the request, and in his usual form, David throws a temper tantrum and storms out of the house. Keep in mind, it is documented that when David did not get his way, he would go off and hide somewhere. Also keep in mind we know David had supper. We know this from the state's own witness, Dr. Schaffer, who conducted the autopsy. In his autopsy report, Dr. Schaffer said David's stomach contained a green food substance. Bobby Rowell, in September 2015, insisted repeatedly and vehemently it was a vegetable. How would he know it was a vegetable, unless he was there watching David eat it?

At 7:00 p.m., Bobby sends Michael out looking for David. This contradicts Bobby's statement on September 10, 2015. Then again, the September 2015 statement contradicts his own trial testimony. One would think a parent would remember the details surrounding the death of their child. It is remarkable how his September 10, 2015, statement is totally different than this trial testimony. The one thing that was observed on September 10, 2015, is that Bobby Rowell has a short, violent temper. For example, several times during the September 2015 interview, Bobby Rowell would flail his arms and scream and his face would turn bright red. It is very likely that Bobby Rowell was angry on February 5, 1982. He was likely very upset that David stormed out of the house in defiance of his mother. He was likely very upset about David getting thrown off the bus again, which meant he (Bobby) would have to drive David to and from school. Remember, Bobby testified, at great lengths, about how David getting thrown off the school bus a couple of months earlier had greatly inconvenienced him and, if David got in trouble again, "God help him." It is likely he wanted David home in order to inflict some sort of punishment.

At approximately 7:00 p.m., Michael visits Keith's trailer. He is supposed to be looking for David, yet he does not ask Keith about David. Michael, in his testimony, said he did ask Keith about David. Keith denies Michael ever asked about David. Unfortunately, according to the Rowell family, Michael is no longer around to clear up this story. Keith does say that Michael bummed a cigarette and his visit was short. We do know Michael left Keith's trailer and walked to the Moraine Civic Center then onto Holman Street in Dog Patch. At 7:30 p.m., he encounters Randall Hendricks, who was leaving Moraine Meadows Elementary School. Michael asks Hendricks about David. Contrary to Michael's trial testimony, Hendricks does not help Michael search for David.

It is worth repeating that Michael's activities are different from what Bobby claims today. On September 10, 2015, Bobby said Michael came home drunk and went to bed. Bobby said Michael stayed in bed all night. That contradicts Michael's trial testimony and his own trial testimony. That leads one to conclude that Bobby Rowell is either lying in 2015 or he lied in 1982. If he lied in 1982, he committed a crime—perjury.

Sometime around 8:00 p.m., Michael returns home. Bobby was taking a bath. Upon exiting the bath, he learns Michael did not find David. So Bobby gets dressed, and at approximately 9:00 p.m., he starts looking for David. Bobby searches the field, along I-75, and then finally the area around the Moraine Civic Center. What is interesting here is Bobby Rowell wants people to believe he searched a steep embankment along I-75 on a snowy and cold night. The embankment is at a forty-five-degree angle and the interstate is elevated above the neighborhood. It is possible but does not seem likely.

While Bobby is searching for David, David is hanging out at one of his old haunts, the barbeque pit beside the civic center. At 9:15 p.m., Bryan "Cappy" Canterbury leaves the civic center after watching *Benji*. As Canterbury is passing the barbeque pit, he hears David Rowell, his friend, call out his name. The two boys exchange greetings, and Canterbury continues home to comply with his curfew. Canterbury told this to the police in 1982 and repeated exactly the same story in 2015. He even described the coat David Rowell was wearing on the night of February 5, 1982. Why Bryan Canterbury was not on the defense witness list boggles the mind. It reeks of total laziness or, worse, incompetence on behalf of defense counsel. The question is begged that the self-described Dayton's best attorneys attempt to interview the witnesses and persons with information listed in the police reports? The answer is no because there is no evidence that they did.

Based on his own court testimony, this is also about the time Bobby Rowell walks toward the civic center looking for David. Evidence suggests that unemployed, angry Bobby Rowell encountered David Rowell, his son, near the civic center sometime after 9:15 p.m. It is very likely the larger Bobby Rowell forcibly grabbed the four-and-a-half-feet tall, sixty-five-pound David Rowell and dragged him home in order to punish him. Once home, Bobby began to inflict a very violent and very abusive punishment upon David. The autopsy report tells us the injuries inflicted upon David's body were indicative of anger, not perversion. They were indicative of rage, not sex. The injuries were indicative of a killer that is releasing frustration and rage upon the victim, not that of a deranged killer with homosexual tendencies, as Dennis Langer and Robert Head wanted people to believe about Keith Wampler.

The punishment was long and severe. It was so severe that sometime after 10:00 p.m., David Rowell lets out a bloodcurdling scream, which was heard by Amy Hudson, the daughter of Gwen Hudson, who was residing in a trailer along Schoolhouse Lane on the southern edge of Gem City Estates Trailer Park and practically across the street from 2970 Kreitzer Road. A scream that was confirmed by Bobby Rowell on September 10, 2015. A scream, which he claims Moraine Police told him was caused by children playing. Children playing on at 10:00 p.m. on a very frigid night in Moraine, Ohio? That is highly unlikely to say the least. A thirteen-year-old boy receiving a "God help him" punishment is more likely the source of that bloodcurdling scream.

The punishment got out of control. It was during this punishment and quite possibly immediately after the scream that Bobby

Rowell put his arm around David Rowell's neck and squeezed the life out of him. David loses consciousness and slowly dies. This occurred in either the unheated cellar at 2970 Kreitzer Road or the unheated garage at 2970 Kreitzer Road, the Rowell family home. These two locations are likely because of the peripheral cyanosis present during David's autopsy. When he died, he had to be in a cold place. Also, the pinkish color in the lividity indicates David was kept in a cold place after death. Bobby Rowell, in his trial testimony, places himself in both the garage and the cellar when he stated that after his initial search of the neighborhood, he decided to search the house.

After he died, David was placed on his left side propped up against something, such as a worktable. Remember, there were indentation bruises indicative of the body being placed against something. David was kept in this position for at least 30 minutes. He was then placed on his back, where the remaining clothing was removed and his penis was amputated, which was meant to throw suspicion off of the family. The clothing was neatly folded and placed into a shopping bag. The fact the clothing was not torn and was neatly placed in the bag indicates that Myrtle Rowell participated in this aspect of the crime. She may not have been there for the actually murder, but she was present for the cover-up because it is very unlikely that a physically abusive and very angry Bobby Rowell would have neatly folded the clothing.

Now it is time to start establishing alibis. Bobby Rowell conducts another search of the neighborhood not only to establish an alibi but to look for a spot to place his son's body. Myrtle Rowell calls the police in order to give the appearance of being a concerned parent. Did the Rowell family call the police when David ran off before? The answer is no. However, this time, they made sure they filed a police report. After his second search of the neighborhood, again without knocking on anyone's door to ask about David, Bobby Rowell gets into his van to start a vehicle search of the area. One of the places he goes is the Dayton Mall, which is closed at this time. He also goes to places David was not known to frequent, such as the Holiday Inn, located at Dryden Road and I-75.

While he is out driving around, he catches a break. He stumbles upon a stranded motorist. He pulls over and offers assistance. Bobby gives her a ride and out of the blue mentions he is looking for his son. Mentioning this to a stranger was a stroke of genius because she could verify that Bobby was a concerned father looking for a missing son. After helping this motorist, Bobby returns home and the family calls it a night.

At 7:00 a.m. on February 6, Bobby Rowell takes another trip to the field with the family dog. He walks around there looking for a place to dispose of his son's body. He may have even considered disposing of it then, but there was a flea market at the Moraine Civic Center. People were coming and going. Keep in mind, he said he was at the spot where David's body was found later that day. David's body obviously was not there. This too disproves the state's theory of Keith Wampler placing David's body in the field sometime during the night. If David was placed in the field and was there at 7:00 a.m., Bobby would have found him. His body would have stuck out like a sore thumb against the freshly fallen snow. Yet the body would not be discovered for almost another nine hours.

Bobby Rowell returns home long enough to get into his van to drive to Huber Heights. With his son missing, he decides to go to Huber Height to visit a friend, who operates a television repair shop. Was he there to work or to visit? One can only speculate because Bobby Rowell gave conflicting statements on the matter. In Montgomery County Common Pleas Court in 1982, he said he was unemployed. At his home in Mobile, Alabama, in 2015, he said he was working.

While Bobby was in Huber Heights, Michael Rowell goes to Keith's trailer. He said that he is looking for Keith. It's 10:00 a.m.,

Keith is not home, but he speaks with Keith's father, Cecil. Michael leaves Keith's trailer, walks through the field, passes the spot where his brother's body will be discovered, and goes to the civic center. It is obvious that David's body was not in Keith's trailer because his father would have found it, and it was not in the field because Michael would have found it. Here is the question in which the Moraine Police should have examined, where was the body at 10:00 a.m. on February 6?

After leaving the civic center, Michael decides to hang out at a friend's house. While he goes to a friend's house, Myrtle, his mother, calls Bobby, who is still in Huber Heights, and tells him she is going to Kettering. This leaves nobody home in the event that the Moraine Police, who are supposedly looking for David because of the missing person report, finds David and returns him to his parents. There was nobody home to receive him from the police. There was nobody home because Bobby and Myrtle Rowell knew exactly where David was.

Bobby returns home around 1:00 p.m. and fixes some coffee. Here again is where he either lied in 1982 or in 2015. In 1982, he said he went to the cellar and had vision of bushes. In 2015, he said he never went to the cellar. If his 2015 statement is the truth, then he again committed perjury in 1982 because that statement was given under oath. Once he received these vision of bushes, he proceeds directly to the field where he finds David's body. It is highly likely he went to the field carrying David's body. Remember, David's small body of only sixty-five pounds could have easily been carried inside a large trash bag or wrapped in a blanket. He places the body and the bag containing David's clothes in the field, returns home, and calls the police. He was lucky that he had a police department with officers who cared more about their clearances than about seeking justice for a dead boy or discovering the truth.

While the police were recovering David's body, his brother, Michael, is wandering the neighborhood. First, he is at a friend's house, then he is hanging out at Keith's trailer. Maybe the reason Michael Rowell did not want to be home with his family is because he knew someone in the family had something to do with the murder of his brother, David. One can only speculate now because, according to the family, Michael also is dead. Bobby claims Michael died of a drug overdose, though the Alabama Medical Examiner's Office has no record of a drug overdose investigation in the name of Michael Patrick Rowell. It would take a court order to verify the death through death certificate search because, under Alabama law, death certificates do not become public record for twenty-five years after a person's death.

A couple interesting incidents occurred after David's body was discovered on February 6. These facts are quite troubling and apparently skipped the attention of Detective William Mullins. The first is how quickly the family moved to Alabama after David's murder. It was not weeks or months. It was days. As soon as David's body was released by the Montgomery County Coroner's Office, the Rowell family was en route to Alabama not just to bury David but to change residence. In the 2015 investigation, witnesses stated the family simply up and left Moraine. Remember, Andrew Choate said Michael Rowell gave him a winter coat two days after David's body was discovered. According to Choate, Michael said he would not be needing it anymore.

The other troubling incident, and it has Bobby still upset, is Bobby Rowell's anger over having to use some of David's insurance money to pay a mortuary to transport David's body to Alabama and not allowing him to transport David's remains in the back of the family van, as if it were a piece of luggage. After 33 years, Bobby Rowell is still upset over this and he went at great lengths on September 10, 2015, to talk about it. Forget about compassion. Forget about it was his son. He is more upset about spending a part of the $7,000 he received from the insurance company. At minimum, this should raise a few eyebrows because that is not under the rubric of what would be considered normal.

The only time the Rowell family would return to Montgomery County, Ohio, was in July 1982 because Bobby and Michael testified at Keith Wampler's trial. They had an all-expense paid trip to Dayton, which was paid for by the Montgomery County Prosecutor's Office.

The case against Robert D. "Bobby" Rowell is circumstantial. However, it is a much stronger case than the case against Keith Wampler, which Dennis Langer and Robert Head presented. Remember, Langer and Head did not have one piece of physical evidence or forensic evidence to link Keith Wampler to the crime. They relied upon the gestapo tactics of Detective William Mullins, whose street reputation left quite a bit to be desired, to provide them with evidence. In his opening arguments, Langer told the jury that a motive is not necessary. Why he said that is obvious, he did not have a case. The State of Ohio could not come up a reason why Keith Wampler would kill David Rowell. All they presented were hints and innuendos.

As for the other convicted killer in this case, Michael Johnson, his role is not clear. Is it possible he had something to do with David Rowell's murder? It is possible but unlikely. Was he railroaded like he claims? It is possible. It is quite possible the Moraine Police saw a chance to get a neighborhood bully off the street and took advantage of his disabled mother to do it. Michael Johnson wants to clear his name but passes on opportunities that could possibly exonerate him. Instead, he decided to wrap himself in a blanket of narcissism and expect people to believe he was persecuted. What Michael Johnson needs to realize is he is free. He was able to get on with his life. Keith Wampler, on the other hand, is still in the custody of the Ohio Department of Rehabilitation and Corrections. For a man who claims his innocence, Michael Johnson's activities and recollection of the events in this case raises more suspicions about his involvement than answers.

Lies, Lies, and More Lies

The state's case against Keith Wampler was built on a house of cards. Had Robert Bostick and Wayne Stephan been good lawyers, as Bostick claims he is, they could have dismantled this house. Instead, they went along with the program. Their crime in this travesty of justice is being lazy and incompetent. The State of Ohio's crime is much more sinister. The State of Ohio's crime in this matter shakes the very bedrock of our legal system. The Moraine Police and the Montgomery County Prosecutor's Office committed the most unforgiveable crime upon the court. They knowingly and willingly presented a case that was based upon lies, lies and more lies. Under Ohio law, that is perjury.

We already examined the integrity of the police reports. Those reports are seriously flawed. Several witnesses seriously questioned the accuracy and truthfulness of what Detective Mullins reported regarding their statements. Remember, Lisa Collins said the entire report regarding her statement is false. The date and time of her statement matches the date and time of Bobby Rowell's statement to Detective Mullin. Again, how could Detective Mullins be at two places at the same time? Also, that report had one huge mistake in it. His report said Michael Rowell returned to Lisa Collins's trailer on Friday February 5, 1982, while *Fantasy Island* was on television. We know for a fact that was a lie because *Fantasy Island* was never shown on Friday nights, according WKEF-TV in Dayton and ABC network in New York.

The evidence also indicates Detective William Mullins, Dennis Langer, and Robert Head were not familiar with the Ohio Revised Code. Regarding the so-called scratches on Keith's lower arms and hands, Mullins testified they were not photographed because the police did not have a court order from a juvenile judge. This is coming from the same police officer who questioned a juvenile suspect without the presence of a parent or the *Miranda* warning. He did not need a court order according to the Ohio Revised Code. According to Ohio Revised Code, Section 2151.313, Fingerprints, photographs require consent of juvenile judge, there are exceptions which apply in this case. Ohio Revised Code section 2151.313(A)(3) states, "This section does not apply to a child to whom either of the following applies: (a) The child has been arrested or otherwise taken into custody for committing, or has been adjudicated a delinquent child for committing, an act that would have been a felony if committed by an adult or has been convicted of or pleaded guilty to committing a felony. (b) There is probably cause to believe that the child may have committed an act that would be a felony if committed by an adult." In the State of Ohio, murder is a felony whether you are a juvenile or an adult.

So where are the photographs of the scratches? The answer to that question is simple. There are no photographs of the scratches because the scratches did not exist. This explains why it took Detective Mullins four months to document them. On top of that, the Ohio Revised Code does not say that a police officer cannot document injuries on a juvenile suspect. There is not one report from around February 6 that documents any scratches. Why? They did not exist. The only documentation is the May 1982 report. One can only speculate that Detective Mullins authored that report after consultations with Dennis Langer or Robert Head, lawyers who have a history of suggesting evidence.

Given these facts, along with those already examined, one can conclude that Detective William Mullins is less than honest. That is not an attribute you want lacking in a law enforcement officer. It would take more than several Hail Mary's to absolve his soul of these sins. The sad thing is his superiors and colleagues at the Moraine Police Division are just as guilty. Their lies and incompetence sent an innocent sixteen-year-old boy to prison to live his entire adult life behind bars.

Detective William Mullins is not the only one within the Moraine Police Division to be ashamed. Chief of Police Glen Carmichael shares some of the blame for this miscarriage of justice. The facts are clear; the Moraine Police Division was over its head in this case. Chief Carmichael, once realizing what kind of crime this was, should have called in assistance from agencies with more experience in investigating homicides. At least he should have called in an agency with more experience in processing the crime scene, such as the Ohio Bureau of Criminal Investigation (BCI). BCI then, and today, processes crime scenes on a daily basis. Can that be said of Officer Dennis Adkins, who had evidence collecting as a secondary duty?

Common sense for anybody who has watched even a few investigative television shows tells us not to release a crime scene until it has been properly searched. The "professionals" in this case did not hold the scene. Was the weather too cold and too dark for these professionals to conduct an adequate search for evidence? A proper and thorough search of the field was not conducted until a week later. This is when Officer Adkins found a faded-green toilet seat lid. In a properly managed courtroom, that toilet seat lid would never have been mentioned because the police could not say when it was placed in the field. The only reason the toilet seat was entered in this case is because defense counsel was either stupid, lazy, or both. The defense could have challenged anything discovered in the field after the initial search. What other articles of trash were discovered in the field? We do not know because there was no list kept. Could something have been exculpatory? We do not know. Could something have pointed suspicions in other direction than Keith Wampler that we do not know? It was Chief Glen Carmichael's responsibility to ensure that his officers were following procedure. He failed in this case and he failed miserably. President Harry Truman had a sign on his desk in the Oval Office that read, The Buck Stops Here. The buck, in this case a sloppy police investigation, stops with Chief Glen Carmichael.

"The primary duty of a lawyer engaged in the public prosecution is not to convict, but to see that justice is done. The suppression of facts or the secreting of witnesses capable of establishing the innocence of the accused is highly reprehensible." This quote is from Canon Five of the Canons of Ethics that regulates how attorneys are to conduct themselves. It is very clear that the Montgomery County Prosecutor's Office, namely Dennis Langer and Robert Head, ignored this canon. It is clear they were seeking a conviction, not justice. It is clear they were creating evidence that did not exist. It is very clear that pressure was placed on witnesses in this investigation. One cannot overlook Raymond Salunek's statement regarding being threatened by Robert Head to testify a certain way regarding a knife. A knife that belonged to John McGarvey, not Keith Wampler. A knife that the Moraine Police took from John McGarvey after he retrieved it from his trailer, not Keith's trailer. Head knew about the origins of the knife. Instead of not considering it as being part of the crime, he bullied a teenager. He may deny this, and he may deny it all day long, but his record speaks for itself. Remember, he was disbarred for subornation of perjury two years after this case.

The sad thing is Dennis Langer should have joined Robert Head in the penalty box because Langer knew the origins of the knife as well. He learned about it from the owner, John McGarvey. It was his responsibility to ensure the integrity of this case. After all, he was the senior prosecutor. Dennis Langer knew very well he did not have a case against Keith Wampler. He knowingly and willingly perpetrated a fraud upon the court. A fraud that cost a sixteen-year-old boy his freedom. It makes one wonder, if Robert Head suborned perjury while at the Montgomery County Prosecutor's Office, then was Dennis Langer party to it? Is Dennis Langer lucky in that he did not get caught?

Canon Four says, "A lawyer assigned as counsel for an indigent prisoner ought not ask to be excused for any trivial reason, and should always exhort his best efforts on his behalf." While there is no evidence to indicate Robert Bostick or Wayne Stephan asked to be excused from this case, there is evidence to suggest they either did not exhort their best efforts or they were too incompetent. The first piece of evidence to indicate Dayton's best attorneys did not exhort their best efforts is the failure to call Bryan Canterbury to the stand. Canterbury would have raised serious doubt regarding the prosecution's case. Canterbury saw David Rowell at 9:15 p.m. on February 5, 1982, when, according to the prosecution, David was supposed to have been restrained in Keith's trailer. Yet according to the trial transcripts, there is no evidence Canterbury was called. Let us suppose the prosecution did not tell Bostick and Stephan about Canterbury. If that is the case, then Robert Head and Dennis Langer thumbed their noses at the United States Supreme Court, who in 1963 ruled in *Brady v. Maryland* that withholding exculpatory evidence from the defense violates the due process clause of the Fourteenth Amendment to the United States Constitution. If this was the case, then the remedy, as we saw in *Brady*, would be a retrial of Keith Wampler. However, one really has to consider that Bostick and Stephan knew about Canterbury and made the unethical decision of not calling him to the witness stand. This decision is a clear violation of Canon Four of the Canon of Ethics. The remedy for this violation of the Canon of Ethics is a retrial of Keith Wampler based on incompetent and unethical counsel.

Now let us back up to Raymond Salunek. Robert Head interviewed Salunek at the Montgomery County Prosecutor's Office. As we saw in that interview, Head attempted to coerce this teenager into providing false testimony in court. Whether or not Salunek went along with Head's caper is irrelevant. Dennis Langer and Robert Head were required, by *Brady v. Maryland*, to turn it over to defense. If they did not, then the Montgomery County Prosecutor's Office clearly violated Keith Wampler's rights under the due process clause of the Fourteenth Amendment. As stated earlier, the remedy for this violation is the retrial of Keith Wampler. If the prosecution did comply with *Brady*, regarding Salunek, then this is evidence that Bostick and Stephan violated Canon Four of the Canon of Ethics, which proves they are either incompetent or unethical. Again, the remedy for that is a retrial of Keith Wampler. But after thirty-four years of what passes for justice in the State of Ohio, there is no retrial of Keith Wampler.

During his campaign for the 2016 Republican Presidential nomination, Governor John R. Kasich stated that when he died he wanted the guardians of heaven to know he did whatever he could for those less fortunate than him. Surely Keith Wampler would fit this description as a man who has spent his entire adult life in prison after being convicted in a demonstrably unfair trail without competent defense counsel. However, after being presented with the facts of this case, the Honorable Governor Kasich has refused to even order the case to be reviewed.

CHAPTER 7

Remedy and Corrections

True patriotism hates injustice in its own
land more than anywhere else.
—Clarence Darrow

It is easier to win a one-billion-dollar lottery than it is to overturn a wrongful conviction. This travesty of justice was allowed to happen because our courthouses are managed on the *Good O' Boy* system. What is the *Good O' Boy* system? It is prosecution, defense, and judges getting together to work out which cases go to trial and which ones will not. It is judges picking their buddies and pals to work pro bono cases. It is defense attorneys picking and choosing which cases to defend to the full extent of the law and which ones to push through the court based on the client's ability to pay, as well as an attorney's desire to kiss up to a judge. It is a system in which judges reward those attorneys who kiss up to them. It is a system where the indigent, the most vulnerable in society, receives a raw deal. It is a system in which the desires of the founding fathers, when they authored the Bill of Rights, are ignored, thus creating a black hole that sucks in the most vulnerable regardless of guilt or innocence. It is a system in which if you have the cash that can help your attorney purchase his or her brand-new BMW sedan and vacation in the south of France, you will receive justice. It is a system that does not severely punish misconduct by an attorney yet passes harsh judgement on the rest of society.

Do not believe that the *Good O' Boy* system ends at the courthouse steps. Keith Wampler has been fighting it every day for the past three decades. In 2004, twenty-two years after the conviction, he was given a glimmer of hope. The Ohio Innocence Project at the University of Cincinnati School of Law agreed to tackle Keith's case. On October 28, 2004, they filed an application for DNA testing with the Montgomery County Common Pleas Court. The Ohio Innocence Project wanted the evidence in this case analyzed for DNA. On December 9, 2004, James R. Levinson, assistant Montgomery County prosecutor, filed a response with the court stating the evidence in this case was destroyed on January 27, 1997. On December 29, 2004, the court rejected the application based on the evidence being destroyed. The ruling was made by none other than Judge John Kessler.

Keith sought help from the Wrongful Convictions Section of the Ohio Public Defender's Office. The request for help was rejected because, at the time of Keith's request, Robert Head was working for the Ohio Public Defender; therefore, a conflict of interest existed. Robert Head went to work for the Ohio Public Defender sometime after his license was reinstated. It should be noted that Robert Head and the Ohio Public Defender's Office have parted ways. As a result, copies of reports from the 2015 investigation were provided to them.

When a wrongfully convicted person enters prison, he or she has a better chance of being hit by lightning while simultaneously being run over by a runaway train than they are in receiving justice. There are some organizations and agencies, such as the Wrongful Conviction Project at the Ohio Public Defender's Office, that are dedicated to review wrongful conviction cases. These organizations and agencies are under financed, short staffed, and overworked. As a result, they pick their battles, which often minimizes a wrongfully convicted inmate's access to these organizations and agencies. This results in some wrongfully convicted inmates never receiving justice and those who do are considered lucky. Luck should never be a factor in the administration of justice in a nation that was conceived with the proposition that all men are created equal.

Since the acceptance of DNA evidence and testing, innocence project clinics have popped up in law schools across the country. These clinics are helpful if you were convicted since the early nineties, when DNA was collected in criminal investigations. If you were convicted of a crime prior to that, you are out of luck. These organizations are not interested. In this case, the Ohio Innocence Project, at the University of Cincinnati, showed interest for about three months in 2004. As earlier stated, the evidence in this case was destroyed and the Ohio Innocence Project lost interest. This investigation did contact the Ohio Innocence Project. A representative from that organization referred to Keith Wampler as being an asshole. The same representative was patronizing toward this investigation and the credentials of the investigator. It appears that these organizations only want to field ground balls and not seek out justice for those who do not have DNA evidence. It makes one wonder if these organizations are in this to correct an injustice or for the fifteen-second sound bite on the six o'clock news?

If a wrongfully convicted person has money, they may be able to hire a private law firm to handle their case. Then again if the person had money, chances are they would not be in prison. Keith Wampler did reach out to various law firms hoping they would consider his case and take it pro bono. Reviewing the responses from these law firms is quite troubling. It appears that tact is not taught in law schools. For example, Keith Wampler received a response from Carpenter, Lipps

& Leland LLP in Columbus, Ohio. In that letter, the attorney stated, "I think you have an uphill battle but if you have concrete evidence of another killer, I will consider it and get back to you as my time permits." What Kort Gatterdam really meant to say was, "Bugger off because you don't have the cash." Mr. Gatterdam cannot dispute this translation because, early in the letter dated January 7, 2013, he emphasized Keith's financial situation and he stated he does not work pro bono cases. The same can be said for Kerger & Hartman LLC response to Keith's inquiry. Richard Kerger, in his June 27, 2014 response, pointed out that he cannot handle pro bono cases but did state he would do his best to find an attorney who could help Keith. Keith is still waiting for that attorney. So much for attorneys giving back to the community!

One has to admire Carpenter, Lipps & Leland's frank response to Keith's inquiry. One cannot admire attorneys who play with inmate's emotions. They grant the inmate a glimmer of hope, only to turn around and snuff it out. Normally, these attorneys are looking for cases that will get them invited to appear on *Nancy Grace*. If your case does not meet that criteria, then they are not interested. This was the tone of the exchanges between Keith Wampler and Kathleen Zellner, of Downers Grove, Illinois. In her August 9, 2013, letter to Keith, she said she could not take his case due to caseload constraints. However, she has since told Lori Wampler, Keith's wife, it is due to the fact she no longer handles cases in Ohio. One has to ask, which is it? Since the release of *Making a Murderer*, Ms. Zellner is representing Steven Avery. Maybe if someone did a television cable show about Keith's case, Ms. Zellner would show some interest.

It is very clear that unless a wrongfully convicted person can finance an attorney's new luxury sedan and country club home, attorneys do not care about justice. Unless a client is willing to mortgage their home, attorneys show no interest in seeking the truth, which is the simple definition of justice. Nobody expects attorneys to take every case pro bono. However, there are cases in which an injustice has occurred. When this type of case is brought to an attorney's attention, they have an obligation to act. After all, they apply their trade in taxpayer financed facilities, courthouses. The people, through their tax dollars, pay to construct, secure, and maintain courthouses in all fifty states and the federal system. Yet the average citizen cannot have access to those courthouses due to the high cost of attorneys. God help the average middle-class citizen who gets accused of a crime because chances are they do not qualify for a public defender. They are expected to put their property in hock to pay the fifteen-thousand-dollar retainer and three-hundred-dollar per hour fee of an attorney. Many of those same attorneys, who turn their back on injustice because of a client's inability to pay, received their law degrees from state subsidized law schools. Those subsidies come from tax dollars. Because some attorneys obtained their law degrees from taxpayer-subsidized law schools and practice their trade in taxpayer financed arenas, one could consider the legal profession to be publically subsidized, like PBS. Unlike PBS, the legal profession does not give a return to the public, unless an individual member of the public is willing to pay a little more.

One has to wonder if these same law firms would change their tune if they examined this case and saw a potential civil rights lawsuit with a huge pay out? It is clear if that were possible, they would be circling over this case like buzzards over a dead bison. In wrongful conviction cases, millions of dollars are often paid out by the states. For example, on June 25, 2014, as a result of a federal civil rights lawsuit, the Illinois State Police agreed to pay the Dixmoor Five forty million dollars. In 1991, these men were wrongfully convicted of killing a teenager in Dixmoor, Illinois, a suburb of Chicago. One can only imagine a law firm taking Keith's case gets the verdict overturned and wins a civil rights lawsuit with a forty-million-dollar settlement. That law firm would bank thirteen million dollars for taking a chance.

While the law firms live up to the lawyer stereotype, as only being interested in fame and cash, politicians and government agencies support the image of them being corrupt, ruthless, and incompetent. In this case, politicians are not the people of honor, as they wish the public to believe on election day, while bureaucrats get gleeful pleasure in toying with inmates' emotions. The behavior of the Office of the Governor, the Ohio Parole Board, and the Ohio Department of Rehabilitation and Corrections is at the very least questionable in this case.

Keith Wampler was sentenced to serve twenty years to life in prison. In 2003, Keith made his first appearance before the Ohio Parole Board. His parole was denied, and he had to wait until 2013 for another hearing. In the meantime, Keith married Lori, who took up the cause to correct this injustice. Prior to the July 18, 2013, parole hearing, Lori Wampler contacted Trayce Thalheimer, member of the Ohio Parole Board. Mrs. Wampler wanted to know the steps Keith needed to take in order to receive parole. Ms. Thalheimer told Mrs. Wampler that if Keith would admit to the crime, then his chances of being paroled increases. Mrs. Wampler convinced Keith to do just that—tell the parole board he did it. Picture a person serving a twenty to life sentence for a crime he did not commit. He spent the last three decades trying to clear his name and thereby obtain a release from prison. He kept his nose clean and is viewed as a model prisoner. Now the same authority that has him in custody is dangling a carrot in front of him. This is his chance for freedom. In his parole hearing, Keith reluctantly listened to his wife and said he did the crime. He made this admission not because he did it but because it was a chance to taste freedom. The parole board not only denied parole but maxed out the time for his next parole hearing, which is ten years. Keith Wampler played the Ohio Parole Board's game and lost.

One could consider this a cruel turn of events. Ms. Thalheimer giving suggestions to an inmate's spouse regarding what to do in order to get released from prison then pulling the rug out from under the inmate. This cruel event was compounded by the behavior of Director Gary C. Mohr, Ohio, Department of Rehabilitation and Corrections. Mrs. Wampler contacted his office to find out what happened at Keith's parole hearing and to find out why he was denied parole. When Mrs. Wampler received the bureaucratic runaround, she told Director Mohr she would sit in his outer office until she received answers. The next thing that occurred sends chills down the back of every democracy-loving American. One day, two troopers from the Ohio State Highway Patrol knocked on Mrs. Wampler's door. They were there because Director Mohr perceived Lori Wampler as being a threat. The troopers determined no threat existed, yet Mrs. Wampler was still considered a threat by the Ohio Department of Rehabilitation and Corrections. She was denied access to see her husband and was forced to threaten a lawsuit against the department if the classification was not changed. The Ohio Department of Rehabilitation and Corrections reversed their decision and her visitation privileges were reinstated.

One of the cornerstones in a democracy is the ability of the people to question their public servants, whether they are appointed or elected. When the people become afraid to question their public servants because they will end up being investigated by the authorities, you no longer have a democracy—you have a police state. It appears that Director Mohr and the Ohio Parole Board are well versed in World War II history, especially the part on the gestapo. This is the type of behavior expected from a socialist dictatorship like the former Soviet Union, not the United States of America.

In September 2013, Keith Wampler applied to the Office of the Governor for clemency. Governor John Kasich's office did receive the request and provided Keith with steps on how to apply for clemency. On May 15, 2014, Samuel H. Porter III, assistant chief counsel, wrote Keith to acknowledge that the Governor's Office did receive his application for clemency. On August 19, 2015, Kevin O'Donnell Stanek, assistant chief counsel, wrote Lori Wampler to express the governor's appreciation for her support of Keith during this process and that the governor would be happy to receive letters and documents to support Keith's application for clemency. What Mr. O'Donnell Stanek failed to point out in his letter is that the Ohio Parole Board met on September 17, 2014, and recommended against clemency. The less-than-transparent behavior of Governor Kasich's office really shown through in this matter. On October 6, 2015, a copy of the 2015 investigation was sent to the governor's office. It is very apparent that Governor Kasich, Mr. Porter, or Mr. O'Donnell Stanek never read the report because on May 6, 2016 the Governor denied Keith's request for clemency based on the recommendation, dated September 24, 2014, from the Ohio Parole Board. Requests to have the copy of the 2015 investigation returned have fallen on deaf ears. Why would Governor Kasich want a copy of a report he never read? After all, his mind was made up way before May 2016.

It is crystal clear that the hugs and compassion John Kasich showed in his failed bid for the White House was a facade, a gimmick to win votes. If he is the compassionate governor as he claims, he would have had questions raised by the 2015 investigation. He would have taken the time to review information uncovered in the latest investigation, instead of simply relying on the recommendation of the Ohio Parole Board. If he relied simply on the parole board's report, then Governor Kasich should have been decent enough to inform Keith of his decision in 2014. Instead, and for some callous reason, Governor John Kasich decided to drag out the decision until

May 2016. The American people showed they are more compassionate than the governor because they did not make him wait twenty months before they rejected him to be their next president.

Governor Kasich is not alone in showing an indifference to injustice. Heather Bishoff, member of the Ohio House of Representatives, and Bill Seitz, member of the Ohio Senate, expressed an interest in helping. Their expressions of wanting to help was more of an illusion than actual action. Both Representative Bishoff and Senator Seitz wrote Governor Kasich regarding Keith's case. Senator Seitz's correspondence to Keith was a simple regurgitation of letter the Senator received from Kenneth O'Donnell Stanek. Representative Bishoff's response was a bit more interesting. She said she wanted to help. When she was informed of some of the new findings of the 2015 investigation, she simply gave lip service to wanting to assist. The best way to describe her responses would be to use the term polite brushoff. She claims she cannot think of anything she can do to assist, but she is interested. Apparently, she does not realize she is a member of the Ohio Legislature, who has the authority to make inquiries of state government agencies. The concept of checks and balances apparently has not taken hold in the Ohio Constitution.

Remedy

Charles "Keith" Wampler did not rape and murder Robert "David" Rowell. That is perfectly clear. The conviction was based on an investigation that lacked integrity. It failed to view all possibilities in this case. It was conducted by a police agency that was more concerned with their image than with justice. It was conducted by a police agency that lacked courtesy, professionalism, and respect. He was prosecuted by a prosecutor's office that was short on honesty and long on deception. This case is an example of the dishonest depths

AND THEN THERE WAS REASONABLE DOUBT

the Montgomery County Prosecutor's Office went to obtain a conviction. This allegation cannot be denied because look at the record of Robert Head, probably one of Ohio's most dishonest attorneys.

Charles "Keith" Wampler did not receive a fair trial before an impartial tribunal. His Constitutional rights, under several amendments, were violated. He, being one of the most vulnerable classes in society, was chewed up and spit out by a system that preys on the indigent and defenseless. He fell victim to a system that gives the illusion of fairness. In short, Charles "Keith" Wampler is in prison because he was a poor teenager who lived in a low income trailer park in Moraine, Ohio. He was at the mercy of two defense attorneys who believe they are Dayton's best but have proven to be everything but that.

As a democratic society, we have an obligation to correct injustices. We have an obligation to learn from those injustices and must strive to improve the system. It is our responsibility to force change. It is our responsibility to defend those sacred words in the Pledge of Allegiance, "With liberty and justice for all." We must remind ourselves that because a person is arrested and charged with a crime, the accused is still presumed innocent. The burden is on the state to prove guilt beyond a reasonable doubt, and it is up to the people to decide guilt. The process of deciding guilt is done in a fair and impartial arena called a trial. A trial is supposed to seek the truth. Instead, a trial often devolves into an arcane game with abstruse rules and language through which the lawyers justifies their billable hours and process the victims and the accused, the innocent and the guilty. When a judge places his vacation desires above his job of ensuring a fair and impartial trial, the judge must be held accountable. When a prosecutor suborns perjury in order to secure a conviction, not just the attorney, but the entire office must be held accountable. When a law enforcement agency fabricates reports and evidence, they too must be held accountable. For if we allow one injustice to continue, we not only place the integrity of the justice system in question, but we also allow ourselves to live at the mercy of a tyrannical government. Remember, what occurred in this case, if allowed to go uncorrected, can happen to any one of us. If that is allowed to continue, then the United States and the State of Ohio is no different than a banana republic.

The immediate remedy in this case is for the State of Ohio to admit that Keith Wampler was denied due process and immediately release him from prison or give him a new trial. A snowball has a better chance of surviving a Haitian summer than the State of Ohio doing something that makes sense. Therefore, this leaves only one alternative. Keith Wampler deserves to have a federal court issue a writ of habeas corpus. In that writ, he will be transferred to federal custody while a federal judge reviews his case. Given the improper conduct of the police and prosecution in this case, along with incompetent counsel, the federal court should issue an order demanding the State of Ohio retry Keith Wampler for the murder of David Rowell. This will force the prosecution's hand. They will either have to retry Keith on evidence that was destroyed in 1997 or drop all charges, which would result in him being released from prison. At this stage, Keith Wampler would need to consider filing, in United States District Court for the Southern District of Ohio, a sixty-eight-million-dollar civil rights against the State of Ohio, Montgomery County, City of Moraine, Robert Head, Dennis Langer, and Detective William Mullins. The suit against the government entities is clear. However, the main players in this sad injustice must also face the music and be held accountable for their actions.

Recommendations for Improvement

The case of Keith Wampler clearly demonstrates that the legal system in the State of Ohio has slipped its moorings and drifted far away from the constitutional bedrock upon which this nation was built. Many of those who wrote the Constitution were ordinary citizens and farmers—not lawyers, not professors, not politicians. They were ordinary people from their various states. The problems in the legal system have developed after more than two hundred years of total control by lawyers and professors who all have been taught to have a similar perspective on the legal system and how it should function. To improve that legal system, there needs to be more oversight by the same common sense wisdom of the people who gave us the Constitution: the people.

It is clear the legal system has some room for improvements. There needs to be more oversight by the people of the system. The *Good O' Boy* network must be dismantled and replaced with a transparent system that holds all the players accountable to the people for whom the system is supposed to benefit. Though these recommendations are geared for the State of Ohio, many of them can be applied in most other states.

1. *Nonpartisan citizen accountability review board for legal system.* One glaring issue in this case is the integrity of the attorneys. It is fascinating to see that out of the five attorneys associated with this case, three of them have been disciplined by licensing authorities. Bostick received a letter of reprimand. Stephan had his license suspended for two years, and Head lost his license but had it returned after four years. Finding out the reasons for these actions was extremely difficult and that is unacceptable in a democratic and transparent system. Therefore, a Nonpartisan

Citizen Accountability Review Board should be formed. The members would be appointed by the governor, approved by the Senate, and the board would be managed in the state supreme court. The disciplinary counsel of the state supreme court will serve as the board's legal advisor. Each member would serve one five-year term. The board would conduct a review of all adult criminal cases where the defendant is under the age of eighteen. The board will also conduct public attorney and judge disciplinary hearings. The board will have the authority so suspend or revoke a law license and, in extreme cases, refer cases to the county prosecutor for prosecution.

2. *Pay to play.* As earlier pointed out, taxpayers pay for courthouses. The same taxpayers are often denied access to any justice meted out in any of those vary courthouses because of their inability to pay enormous attorney fees. The vast majority of attorneys have forgotten they are supposed to give back to the community—at least that is the propaganda from the various bar associations. This conflict makes is painfully clear society needs to act to end this imbalance. The one way to do that is to expand the role of the public defender's office and have the legal profession finance it. One way to accomplish this is to charge each attorney, not the firm, a fee in order to practice law before a court. For example, if an attorney wants to handle cases in Franklin County Common Pleas Court, he or she would pay a $1,500-per-year fee. If he or she wishes to have access to Franklin County Municipal Court, he or she would have to pay another $1,500-per-year fee. The fees would go to finance the expansion of the public defender's office. If attorneys do not pay the fee, they do not play in court. This would not be required if attorneys

gave pro bono cases the same amount of attention as they give clients who are paying the full fee, which is required by Canon Four of the Canons of Ethics.

3. *Nonpartisan citizen parole board.* At present, the Ohio Parole Board is comprised of bureaucrats who make a career in the Ohio Department of Rehabilitation and Corrections. This is a clear conflict of interest in that the agency who is responsible for housing a prisoner should not have authority over parole decisions and releasing prisoners. Therefore, a Citizen Parole Board must be created. The board will be independent of the Ohio Department of Rehabilitation and Corrections. The board will consist of citizens appointed by the Governor and confirmed by the senate. They will serve seven year terms. They will review all parole cases and will be the agency to make recommendations to the Governor regarding clemency. This board will meet in public.

4. *Creation of state medical examiner.* In Ohio, each of the eighty-eight counties have a county coroner. In eighty-seven of the eighty-eight counties, the coroner is an elected official; the one exception is Cuyahoga County (Cleveland). Of the eighty-eight counties, only six are capable of conducting autopsies and only two are capable of conducting self-contained autopsies, which are autopsies where all the testing in conducted in one facility. To ensure that every death investigation is properly handled and the quality of the investigation is standard across the state, the Office of the State Medical Examiner should be created within the Ohio Department of Public Safety. The Office of the State Medical Examiner would operate five regional morgues with each morgue being capable of conducting all possible tests.

5. *Adoption of the Missouri Plan.* The Missouri Plan is the nonpartisan way of selecting judges. Judges are selected on merit, not because of party affiliation. Under the plan, a nonpartisan commission reviews applications for judicial vacancies. The commission sends a list of names to the governor. If within an allotted time the governor fails to make a selection for a vacancy, the commission will. After a completion of one year of service, or variation of that time, the judge faces a retention vote in the general election. If the majority of the people vote to retain the judge, he or she will keep their seat on the court. If not, then the judge must leave and the process starts anew. This process is currently being used in thirty states. This plan helps to ensure that politics stay out of the courtroom and forces judges to make decisions based on the law, not on what will get them elected. To ensure checks and balances, an Ohio modification to the Missouri Plan would have the nonpartisan commission housed in the Ohio State Supreme Court.

6. *Transparent parole hearings.* Parole board hearings must be held in public. As earlier stated, this will ensure transparency. Also, if anyone wishes to provide advice or an opinion to the parole board, they must do it in person. Twice, Keith Wampler came up for parole, and both times Robert Rowell, via telephone, told the board that Wampler should remain in prison. The decision of a person's freedom is a serious one, and those rendering an opinion should have the courage of their convictions and testify, under oath and in person, to the parole board regarding the reasons a person should or should not receive parole.

7. *No incriminating admissions.* The practice of having an inmate admit their crime before the parole board considers

parole must be, and should be, stopped. Nowhere in the Constitution of the United States does it say that if a person is convicted of a crime, they waive their rights against self-incrimination, as outlined in the Fifth Amendment. An inmate should be judged on the merits of his or her progress while in prison and the steps he or she took to self-improvement, not admit to the crime. In this case, Lori Wampler was told by Trayce Thalheimer that if Keith would confess, the board would look favorably upon his parole. For Keith Wampler, this was a chance to finally be released from prison. So in desperation, he took it. Receiving denied parole was the result. The advice that Ms. Thalheimer gave Mrs. Wampler reeks of ignorance of the Constitution of the United States and is an example of how the State of Ohio, to this day, is violating the rights afforded to Keith Wampler by the Constitution of the United States.

8. *Change retention of evidence practices.* The fact that the evidence in this case was destroyed while Keith Wampler is still in custody is absurd. Under Ohio law, the police are only required to hold the evidence for fifteen years after the case has been adjudicated. That law must be changed to requiring the police and the prosecutors to secure the evidence for as long as the inmate is in prison. The state must acknowledge there is a possibility of a wrongful conviction. If the evidence is destroyed, then it becomes almost impossible for a wrongfully convicted person to obtain justice. As long as the person is in custody, the state has an obligation to maintain the evidence and permit proper and legal reexamination of it.

9. *Expansion of disciplinary counsel.* At present, the State of Ohio has too many bar associations. Those associations

are ideal for dealing with legal issues within a certain area, but they must not have any say in discipline or licensing of attorneys. A law license must be issued by the state supreme court, and allegations of misconduct must be investigated by the state supreme court. The Office of Disciplinary Counsel in the Ohio State Supreme Court is an insult to the justice system not because of the people who work there but because of the way it is staffed and the duties they perform. Today, there is one attorney who serves as disciplinary counsel and two investigators for the Ohio State Supreme Court. The investigators spend most of their time retrieving files from dead or incapacitated attorneys and not investigating allegations of attorney misconduct. The priority of this office should be to investigate misconduct and, if adopted, report their findings to Nonpartisan Citizen Accountability Review Board.

10. *No immunity claims for public officials.* It is quite clear that Detective William Mullins, Dennis Langer, and Robert Head forced this case through the Montgomery County court system. Their arrogance, ignorance, or the combination of both caused a sixteen-year-old boy his freedom. They must be held accountable. While the various government entities must take responsibility for their actions, so must the individuals. Those wronged by public officials, who act like what we witnessed in this case, must be able to seek justice in civil court. This will go a long way to ensure that these officials will dot every i and cross every t before they deny a person their freedom. If Detective William Mullins knew he could possibly lose his savings and pension, maybe he would have thought twice before fabricating police reports.

11. *Expansion of Wrongful Conviction Project within the Ohio Public Defender's Office.* At present, correcting an error within the criminal justice system is too difficult. It practically takes an act of God. An expansion of this unit would help immensely in correcting errors. If the Wrongful Conviction Project has credible evidence that an erroneous conviction occurred, they would then present the findings before the Ohio Supreme Court, not the common pleas court in the county of origin, for an immediate decision on the course of action to be taken. This will expedite the process of freeing innocent inmates from incarceration.

12. *Reimbursement of legal fees.* At present, the government is not held accountable for bringing charges against a defendant. All the government has to say is they believed he or she did the crime and the prosecutor is protected. In a democratic society, that is not a safeguard against laziness or misconduct. To ensure that the government has to meet high standards in prosecuting a defendant, the prosecution should be made to reimburse the defendant's legal fees in cases where the defendant is found not guilty or in cases where the charges are dropped. This will ensure that the government does its homework prior to bringing charges against a citizen. One of the scary aspects of our criminal justice system is the government has the resources and they can accuse. It is up to the accused to finance their own defense. Prosecutors have used this as a way to seek punishment against the accused. The accused may not end up in prison, but they end up bankrupt. In a democratic society, if the prosecution brings charges, they better have the evidence to support them. If the prosecution ends up footing all the legal bills when they lose, then they will make sure the case is airtight before they go into court.

In Closing

The criminal justice system failed. It failed Charles "Keith" Wampler by placing him in prison for a crime that he did not commit. It failed Robert "David" Rowell by not bringing his true murderer to justice. Above all, it failed the people of the State of Ohio by committing an injustice, not by serving justice. It allowed corrupt egomaniacs to walk all over the rights of a sixteen-year-old boy. It allowed the type of trial that our founding fathers wanted to prevent when they penned the Constitution of the United States, especially the Bill of Rights. Sadly, for every day Charles "Keith" Wampler spends incarcerated for a crime he did not commit, our quality of justice diminishes.

In this case, we witnessed a criminal justice system that was managed by corruption and apathy, not compassion and the desire to seek the truth. We saw attorneys who approach the law like a business, not like a calling as the barristers centuries before them did. In this case, we have an example of how the system chewed up and spit out one of the people it is sworn to protect. Disturbingly, we saw public officials more concerned with their careers than with seeking the truth. As a result of these actions, we are all at risk.

Because the crime is heinous, do we ignore our obligation to seek the truth and simply seek a scapegoat because it gives us immediate gratification? In this case, the Moraine Police and the Montgomery County Prosecutor's Office did just that. In this case, not only did the crime shock the senses, but the unprofessional and criminal conduct of the police and prosecution did as well. Do we forgo the rules of evidence and the Constitution in order to obtain a quickie Nirvana? Does that really bring us justice? One could argue this occurred in 1982 and things have improved. Have they?

In 2016, we have a penal system that demands an inmate forgo their Fifth Amendment protection against self-incrimination in order to be considered for parole. On the surface, that looks great, but what if the inmate did not do the crime? What if the inmate spent three decades in prison for a crime he did not commit? Then, that same inmate is told if you admit to the crime, you will get released on parole. What would you do? One has to ask, what would those parole board members do if they spent thirty years in prison for a crime they did not commit? What would they say to get released? Is the parole board morally just in giving an inmate false hope? Do we as a society believe the Constitution ends at the prison door?

We have political leaders who say they care, but in reality, those words are hollow. Politicians market themselves as being compassionate like a snake oil salesman sells the latest herb tonic. Like the snake oil salesman's tonic, a politician's compassion on the surface looks great, but deep beneath the surface, it is just murky water. In this case, politician after politician expressed their desire to help. However, none has followed through. One has to ask if these same political leaders are getting their private jollies playing with people's lives. If that is the case, then shame on them and shame on us for not holding them accountable.

As a society, we must recognize that the criminal justice system has one fatal flaw, it is run by human beings and human beings make mistakes. We also must realize that some of the people working in the system are not of the highest integrity or honor. Some of the people working in the system simply view it as a way to obtain a paycheck, not a calling to seek the truth. Some of the people working in the system view their position as being a stepping stone to bigger and better things—more fame and glory. In seeking bigger and better things, these people will walk over those who are most vulnerable in society because they are easy prey. It is because of this flaw we, as a people, must demand and obtain more oversight of the criminal justice system. We must hold those who work in the criminal justice system accountable for their actions.

One can argue that Charles "Keith" Wampler was going to end up in prison anyway, so he is where he belongs. One could follow up my asking, why should we care? This argument is totally off base. One cannot predict what a young person will become, one can only speculate. Speculation is not fact. There is no doubt that Charles "Keith" Wampler showed delinquent behavior. However, does that give the criminal justice system to walk all over him just to obtain a conviction? Did the police investigate him because they had evidence of his involvement, which there was not any, or did they investigate him because he was a delinquent? Being a delinquent does not make you a murderer. It was a result of the Moraine Police incompetence, a dishonest Montgomery County prosecutor, and a lazy defense team that a scapegoat was found in this case, and a quickie Nirvana was achieved. It was because of an apathetic attitude that an innocent sixteen-year-old boy was sent to prison. It is because of these apathetic actors that we will never know what Charles "Keith" Wampler could have accomplished. Through their unethical conduct, they robbed him of the opportunity to become a productive member in society. For it was they, not the people, who played judge, jury, and executioner in this case.

Bishop Desmond Tutu once said, "If you are neutral in situations of injustice, you have chosen the side of the oppressor. If an elephant has its foot on the tail of a mouse and you say that you are neutral, the mouse will not appreciate your neutrality." For the past three decades, an elephant has been stepping on the tail of a mouse. As a society, do we remain neutral, or do we speak up and demand justice? If we choose neutrality, then who will speak up when injustice occurs to you?